REMEMBERING FOR THE FUTURE

ARMENIA, AUSCHWITZ, AND BEYOND

OTHER PARAGON HOUSE BOOKS ON
GENOCIDE AND THE HOLOCAUST

Against All Hope: Resistance in the Nazi Concentration Camps, 1938-1945
Hermann Langbein

Courage to Remember: Interviews on the Holocaust
Kinue Tokudome, Foreword by Richard L. Rubenstein

Different Voices: Women and the Holocaust
Carol Rittner and John K. Roth, eds.

Ethics After the Holocaust: Perspectives, Critiques, and Responses
John K. Roth, ed.

Genocide in Rwanda: Complicity of the Churches?
Carol Rittner, John K. Roth, and Wendy Whitworth, eds.

The Genocidal Mind: Selected Papers from the 32nd Annual Scholar's Conference on the Holocaust and the Churches
Donald B. Klein, Richard Libowitz, Marcia Sachs Littell and Sharon Steeley, eds.

Holocaust: Religious and Philosophical Implications
John K. Roth and Michael Berenbaum, eds.

Job: The Story of a Holocaust Survivor
Joseph Freeman

Narrow Escapes: A Boy's Holocaust Memories and their Legacy
Samuel Oliner

Not Your Father's AntiSemitism: Hatred of Jews in the 21st Century
Michael Berenbaum

Rape: Weapon of War and Genocide
Carol Rittner and John K. Roth

Righteous Gentiles of the Holocaust
David P. Gushee

The Road to Hell: Recollections of the Nazi Death March
Joseph Freeman

Will Genocide Ever End?
Carol Rittner, John K. Roth, and James M. Smith, eds.

REMEMBERING FOR THE FUTURE

ARMENIA, AUSCHWITZ, AND BEYOND

EDITED BY

MICHAEL BERENBAUM
RICHARD LIBOWITZ
MARCIA SACHS LITTELL

PARAGON HOUSE

First Edition 2016

Published in the United States by
Paragon House
St. Paul, Minnesota
www.ParagonHouse.com

Selected Papers from the 44th Annual Scholars' Conference on the Holocaust and the Churches
American Jewish University, Los Angeles, California, March 8-11, 2014

The Annual Scholars' Conference on the Holocaust and the Churches was founded in 1970 by Franklin H. Littell and Hubert G. Locke as an interfaith, interdisciplinary, and international organization. Throughout the decades, the Conference has been devoted to remembering, learning, and teaching the lessons of the Holocaust in tandem with educators clergy and community leaders examining the issues raised by the "Final Solution."

Library of Congress Cataloging-in-Publication Data

Names: Scholars' Conference on the Holocaust and the Churches (44th: 2014 : Los Angeles, Calif.) | Berenbaum, Michael, 1945- editor. | Libowitz, Richard, 1948- editor. | Littell, Marcia Sachs, editor.
Title: Remembering for the future : Armenia, Auschwitz, and beyond / edited by Michael Berenbaum, Richard Libowitz, Marcia Sachs Littell.
Description: First edition. | St. Paul, MN : Paragon House, 2015. | "Selected papers from the 44th annual Scholars Conference on the Holocaust and the churches, American Jewish University, Los Angeles, California, March 8-11, 2014." | Includes bibliographical references.
Identifiers: LCCN 2015038524 | ISBN 9781557789235 (paperback)
Subjects: LCSH: Genocide. | Armenian massacres, 1915-1923. | Holocaust, Jewish (1939-1945)
Classification: LCC HV6322.7 .S395 2016 | DDC 940.53/18--dc23 LC record available at http://lccn.loc.gov/2015038524

Manufactured in the United States of America
10 9 8 7 6 5 4 3 2 1

The paper used in this publication meets the minimum requirements of American National Standard for Information Sciences—Permanence of Paper for Printed Library Materials, ANSIZ39.48-1984.

Acknowledgments

This conference made possible by grants from

Claims Conference ועידת התביעות
The Conference on Jewish Material Claims Against Germany

VERBE ET LUMIÈRE
VIGILANCE

Michael Berenbaum, Professor of Jewish Studies,
American Jewish University
Executive Director, Sigi Ziering Institute
Host - 2013 Think Tank & 2014 Annual Scholars' Conference

The Zachor Society
Ann Marie Osaki & Gail H. Stanger

The Philadelphia Center on the Holocaust,
Genocide & Human Rights

***

Collegial assistance from

Richard Hovannisian, Professor Emeritus,
University of California, Los Angeles

Stockton University
President Harvey Kesselman

Consulate General of the Czech Republic (Philadelphia)
The Honorable Peter Rafaeli

***

Hubert G. Locke, ASC co-Founder
Henry Knight, ASC President
Marcia Sachs Littell, ASC Vice-President
Richard Libowitz, ASC Executive Board Member
Frances Titcombe, ASC Conference Coordinator
Sharon Steeley, ASC Executive Director

Elisabeth Meynard Maxwell z"l
March 11, 1921—August 7, 2013

In Memoriam

Dr. Elisabeth Maxwell z"l was a courageous, elegant, resilient, and tenacious woman. A Huguenot by birth, British by choice, she was born into an aristocratic French Protestant family and married Robert Maxwell, a former Member of Parliament in the United Kingdom.

"Betty," as she was known to friends, campaigned for her husband when he ran for public office, helped him establish and run Pergamon Press—a multi-billion-dollar publishing empire, bore him nine children (two of whom died in childhood), and managed a very large manor house named Headington Hill Hall, which was situated on the grounds of Pergamon Press. Elisabeth Maxwell completed her undergraduate degree and earned her doctorate at Oxford University at the age of sixty.

In researching a history of her husband's family, Elisabeth discovered that the Nazis had murdered 300 members of his immediate and extended family. This ignited her quest to learn everything possible about this horrific event, particularly why the "Lessons of the Holocaust" had not yet been internalized and acted upon in the UK and other places around the world. She engendered contempt towards her fellow Church and academic leaders whom she felt had been hiding behind the ivy tower of the University and the sanctity of the churches. As a strong advocate of education at all levels, Elisabeth endeavored to establish Holocaust remembrance and educational programs at institutions in her sphere of influence.

Our first meeting took place in Jerusalem in 1985, along with our respective spouses, to discuss Elisabeth's desire to create a Holocaust Journal through the Pergamon Press. Although Pergamon's main concentration was scientific journals, by 1986, *Holocaust and Genocide Studies: An International Journal,* was published by Pergamon Press of Oxford and New York, in association with both the United States Holocaust Memorial Council, Washington, D.C. and Yad Vashem, the Holocaust Memorial Authority, Jerusalem, Israel. Instantly, it was a hugely successful journal and now, published by Oxford University Press, remains one of the leading publications of its kind.

Elisabeth had been intrigued by our Holocaust education work in the United States since 1970, so much so that she decided to emulate the Annual Scholars' Conference on the Holocaust and the Churches—for her work in the UK. Following the Jerusalem meeting, she worked with vigor, and we were soon regular visitors to Headington Hill Hall in Oxford for conference planning meetings.

On one occasion, joined by Elisabeth Maxwell and Yehuda Bauer, the three of us were meeting with members of the Education Committee of the House of Commons advising them on the creation of a Holocaust curriculum and a mandate for the British schools. Within a year's time, the planning committee expanded and the executive group meetings grew to bi-weekly sessions.

The International Conference, "Remembering for the Future," which Elisabeth planned, organized, and, with the help of her husband, financed, was the first major conference of its kind ever held in the United Kingdom. "Remembering for the Future" took place in Oxford, England, July 10-13, 1988 and was followed by a Public Meeting at Central Hall, Westminster London on July 15, 1988. With great courage and determination, Elisabeth persuaded an entire country to begin thinking and teaching about the Holocaust.

After 1988, Elisabeth regularly attended the Annual Scholars' Conferences in the US. Several weeks before her death on August 7, 2013, Elisabeth's daughter Isabel telephoned me at her mother's bedside. Elisabeth, hardly able to speak, wanted me to know that, "The Annual Scholars' Conference has her blessing to use the title, 'Remembering for the Future,' in perpetuity." The 44th Annual Scholars' Conference on the Holocaust & the Churches, "Remembering for the Future: Armenia, Auschwitz and Beyond," was thus held at the American Jewish University in Los Angeles, California, on March 8-11, 2014, the weekend that would have coincided with Elisabeth's 93rd birthday.

Elisabeth's death was a great personal loss. She was a wise and caring personal friend, a beloved matriarch, and an invaluable mentor. For women of my generation who came of age in the early 1950s, inspirational women like Elisabeth Maxwell were rare. It was a special blessing to have her in my life.

Elisabeth dedicated the last three decades of her life to the study and pursuit of the Holocaust, a subject on which she published three books and was internationally recognized as an authority. Everything that Dr. Elisabeth Meynard Maxwell pursued was completed with integrity, conviction, grace and sincerity.

Her death makes clear witness to the passing of a unique generation for which there are no replacements. This volume is respectfully and fittingly dedicated to the memory of Elisabeth Maxwell z"l.

Marcia Sachs Littell
Merion Station, Pennsylvania
22 Elul 5775
7 August 2015

Contents

Part IV
The Aftermath

Part V
Personal Experiences and Education

Foreword

First a word of tribute: when I was a young graduate just beginning my career I attended the early conferences on the German Church Struggle and the Holocaust and remember the presentations, confrontations, debates, and dialogues that occurred among scholars who were beginning to tackle the Holocaust. There were tensions between Jews and Christians, between Christians and Christians, between Jews and Jews, between scholars of different disciplines, historians and theologians, psychologists and literary scholars. Sometime there were also tensions over individual works and even controversial topics. Hannah Arendt and the question of the banality of evil, the Judenrat and its role, the guilt of Christians and the guilt of Christianity, the guilt of American inactions, the guilt of the German Churches, the silence of the Pope and there were questions including the most basic "was the very title of the Conference misleading." Was there really such a struggle among the German Churches?

External events intruded. The 1967 War brought the issue of Christian solidarity to the fore, the urban struggles of the late 1960s intensified Black-White tensions, the emergence of the women's movement raised the question of where were the women scholars and also what about the suffering of women during the Holocaust. We did not yet speak of women perpetrators. The work had simply not been done. Emotions were raw and sometimes discussions were explosive. Thanks to its founders, the late Franklin Littell and Hubert Locke, the conference continued, the scholars got to know one another, even, over time, to trust one another—albeit not too much, not too easily—yet they did come to recognize in one another a common struggle with the Holocaust even if it led to divergent answers.

All who work in this field must be grateful to these founders for their vision, their persistence, their determination, their role model and their scholarly integrity. Franklin Littell has gone the way of all flesh, yet his presence endures in the collective enterprise he began and in the ongoing efforts of his wife Professor Marcia Sachs Littell and his students, among them Professor Richard Libowitz who continues his sacred work. Hubert

Locke could not be at this conference, but his presence was also keenly felt, the absence of his presence and the presence of his absence. My own teacher, Richard L. Rubenstein, who has passed four score and ten, was at this conference as he was in 1970 writing boldly and provocatively, insisting that we face unpleasant truths and demanding that we confront the abyss. Time has neither diminished his intellectual capacities nor tamed his unique ability to synthesize so many divergent thoughts and issues and push them in new directions. We are their students, standing on their shoulders even as we have produced a new generation of students all our own.

"By the Waters of Babylon we sat and we wept as we remembered Zion," the Psalmist proclaimed and the songwriter lamented.

The place from which we remember an event shapes how we remember the event.

Two thousand fourteen was a special year, one hundred years after the Armenian genocide, a century after World War I, and the conference was held in a different atmosphere. The shadow of antisemitism can be sensed in many of these papers, not Christian antisemitism but Moslem antisemitism with its cries of Jihad, and words of the elimination of the State of Israel and the annihilation of Jews. And "Never Again" became a hollow cry in a world that had seen several post-Holocaust genocides, where killing is ongoing in Darfur and in Syria and the threat of genocide looms large, so large that the US Military Academy at West Point is contemplating a chair in Holocaust and Genocide Studies not so much because it is committed to remembering the past but because it anticipates that the future officers it trains will confront genocide again and again during their service and wants them to understand not only the perpetrator or the rescuers, but how military power can be used to prevent and to curtail genocide, not just to alleviate the fate of its victims.

The first section of this book is properly devoted to the Armenian Genocide. Richard H. Dekmejian sheds new light on a subject that rightfully has preoccupied the Conference for a generation, namely the question of an early warning system. What can we learn from our understanding of the past that can allow us to identify conditions that lead to genocide? It is the prelude to the urgent problem that follows, if we can identify genocides in the making what can we do to prevent them.

Dekmejian is most prescient in understanding that identification and understanding are necessary but not sufficient conditions unless they are followed not only by good will and an alert conscience but by the political will to act, something sorely missing in case after case. Rubina Peroomian reminds us that the relationship between Turks and Armenians long preceded the genocide and it is necessary to understand that pre-history, including the parallels with the Jewish experience in Europe, in order to understand the events of a century ago. She also draws important contrasts between the German admission of responsibility and the Turkish denial and obfuscation. Sonia Haroutyunian has moved beyond history to literature and film as a means for understanding, comprehending and engaging the Armenian genocide. As I read her chapter I recalled an early conversation that I had with the distinguished literary scholar Lawrence Langer who said I spend much of my time reading history and my historian friends seem to feel that literature makes little or no contribution to their understanding of the Holocaust. Thanks in no small part to Langer's work such a statement can no longer be made but Haroutyunian has shown that for students of the Armenian genocide there are tools beyond history and memoir at their disposal,

This book is shaped by where we are in remembering the Holocaust and in confronting genocide. Opening papers dealt with the Armenian genocide which centenary we mark. We too listened to and now read these papers differently. When this conference was launched we were one quarter of a century after the events of the Shoah. Survivors were alive, many in the middle of their lives and their careers, the VCR had not yet been invented. The Holocaust had not yet gone mainstream. We are now far closer to the 100th anniversary of the end of the Holocaust than to this quarter century mark and everyone understands that soon—all too soon—the survivors will be gone and a generation will have to remember without those who lived through the event. We listened differently as well because the tensions between Turkey and Israel has diminished the ardor with which some wanted to repress all discussion of the Armenian question for fear of offending the Turks and threatening their alliance with Israel. I am grateful that this conference never succumbed to that temptation but remained faithful to historical truth throughout. Richard L. Rubenstein's paper forces all to confront the religious dimension of that genocide and it too reflected a world in which Moslems and Christians are in a violent struggle throughout the Middle East. It is an important continuation of the work he began with *Jihad and Genocide.* David Patterson traces the origins of Jihadism and its focus on the Jews back to the foundation of Moslem Brotherhood, which well preceded the establishment of the State of Israel and the politicization of Jewish Moslem relations. His focus on parallels between Hitler and Jihadist Jew hatred is especially poignant because as the book goes to press we are in the midst of the debate over the agreement with Iran and the echoes of threats to destroy Israel and annihilate the Jewish people are central to that debate.

In his human rights and United Nations' work Shimon Samuels confronts on a daily basis antisemitism and threats of genocide against Jews and against others. Therefore, his sense of the ethos of this era should serve as an important caution and frankly casts a shadow over our collective work. Mehnaz Afridi, a Pakistani born moderate Moslem woman who is a scholar of Islam and of the Holocaust is a poignant example of someone who occupies the uncomfortable middle. Her presence as a Moslem arouses suspicion among some Jews who feel that given her origin and her faith she cannot teach the Holocaust. Her representation of the Holocaust and her critique of Moslem antisemitism makes her distrusted by her own people. The pioneering generation of Christian scholars of the Holocaust is quite familiar with her compromised situation. By example, they can demonstrate that while a price must be paid for speaking truth to vested interests within one's own faith community and for grappling with the suspicions of others, the only solace to be found is in the quality and integrity of your scholarship.

Several chapters of this book break new ground in the scholarly area for understanding the Holocaust. Gideon Grief, whose pioneering work on the Sonderkommando, those units that worked in the vicinity of the gas chambers of Auschwitz, has deepened our understanding of the killing process and of the toll that it took on the men who were forced not only to witness the process but to engage with those who were about to be murdered and then grapple with the bodies of those who were gassed. His plea for the value of survivor eyewitness testimony is echoed by recent scholarly work by documentary historians such Yehuda Bauer and Christopher Browning who understand both the power and the problems of using such testimony. No sooner do we read Grief than Yitzhak Kerem demonstrates what can be done as he listens attentively to such testimony to explore the role of the Greek Jews who were forced to work as Sonderkommando. Kerem insists that the Holocaust was more than an Ashkenazic experience and demands the recognition of the fate of Sephardic Jewry within the Shoah. We must note not only those Sonderkommando who toiled and then who engaged in active, armed resistance but also those who chose martyrdom, to die rather than to participate in such a difficult, dare one say morally ambiguous, task at all.

Karen Franklin presented what one affluent and influential family did to save their family, showing us the determination of the Lehman family with all their wealth and power, including Governor Herbert Lehman, FDR's successor as Governor of New York, his friend and political ally to bring the extended Lehman family to the shores of the United States. Their efforts were similar to those of Carl Laemmle, the longtime head of Universal Studios, who managed to save those of his German village who were left behind. They had to overcome obstacles and to marshal their considerable resources to save a few. Even with all their power, their goodwill and wealth, the Lehmans only achieved limited but important successes. By presenting the particular story of one family her work demonstrates the hurdles that were placed even for the rich and influential, to rescue German Jews. One reads this chapter with a sense of anger and gratitude, gratitude for their efforts and anger that, even with so much power and wealth, so little could be achieved for so few.

Diane Plotkin sheds important new light on the role of medics in dealing with the aftermath of genocide. We have learned much in the past decades about the anti-ethical behavior of Nazi doctors. We knew far less about the behavior of Jewish doctors within the ghettos and within the concentration camp itself and through memoirs we have learned much about Jews helping Jews, inmates assisting inmates within the confines of concentration camps. Most have noted the important role that physicians and nurses played after the liberation and Plotkin adds to the scope of our knowledge and provides important role models for medical personnel working with Doctors without Borders and in Africa combatting the Ebola epidemic. Harriet Tamen wrote a short but important piece on the role of the French railroad in the deportation of French Jewry and its ongoing unwillingness to confront that role. As the SNCF seeks business outside of France it finds its role a source of embarrassment and political controversy but not so much so that it is willing to honestly confront its own past.

Harold Marcuse has offered as deep an understanding of Martin Niemoller's oft repeated quote. I am personally grateful to him because I remember how difficult it was to come up with an original version of the quote to use in the United States Holocaust Memorial Museum and because the quote has taken on a canonical status within Holocaust literature precision as to its correct formulation is imperative. Political sensibilities to omit all mention of the Communists may make it difficult for some to use the quote but for all an understanding of its meaning and context is an important contribution.

The place from which you remember an event shapes how it is recalled is clearly demonstrated in Joans Peterson's reconsideration of Heinrich Boll's *Billiards at Half Past Nine.* So much has happened in German literature and life since the late 1950s that her reading of Boll tells us much not only about the book in its time and its impact over time, but also of our time in the task of remembering the Holocaust and the German experience.

The final papers of this volume reflect the success that the field of Holocaust Studies has enjoyed over the past half century. A Jewish scholar teaching at a Catholic University, Harriet Sepinwall, whom I had the privilege of teaching some two decades ago, writes of the way that her University and her students have embraced the study of the Holocaust, how it has bridged "town and gown," Jews and Catholics and enabled new questions to be raised and strengthened the mission of her institution. Surely this is a tribute to her work, but undoubtedly it is testimony to the power of the Event and issues raised by that event. Ludmilla Leibman writes teaching the Holocaust in a discipline that many of us thought has little relationship to the event and shows us how a skilled and imaginative professor can reach her students and deepen their experience while presenting the Holocaust. She offers the power of her example and the testimony of her students. Sarah Valente writes of Holocaust education in Brazil, reminding European and American centric scholars of the importance of this expanding field.

We at the Sigi Ziering Institute: Exploring the Ethical and Religious Implications of the Holocaust at the American Jewish University were honored to host this conference. Bringing scholars together to discuss these issues, most especially in an ecumenical and multi-religious setting, is the very purpose of our being. We were certain that our invited guests would enjoy the hospitality we offered, not only because the facilities were comfortable but because the winter of 2014 was so harsh that the California sunshine brought smiles to our guests' faces and the freedom to enjoy the sun in short sleeves. The weather cooperated and indeed helped to shape the mood of the conference.

Judging from my experience, over the past four decades, The Scholars' Conference has been inspiring young aspiring scholars to learn and to deepen their commitment to Holocaust and genocide scholarship. It is a source of pride to the Conference that it opens its much respected forum to graduate students to make their initial scholarly presentations outside of their own graduate school. This past year was no exception and, while we have not included these presentations in this work, I suspect that these future senior scholars will look back on this experience with gratitude as they make their own contribution to the field.

Michael Berenbaum
American Jewish University
Los Angeles, California
August 17, 2015

Preface

> The Armenian genocide and the genocide of the Jews spotlight, in a shocking way, certain pathological conditions that developed in Western civilization. We are not permitted to desist from analysis of these conditions, nor may we cease to draw the lessons from such analysis...
>
> There is a question deeper than the rational, too, and that concerns the nature of history itself—and our response to the events of which we are a part. Our response to this question defines us as human persons.... History is not the dead hand of the past weighing down the present.... In the dialogue with the past, we encounter sources of character formation as powerful as our participation in contemporary events, as gripping as our hope of things to come....
>
> A museum puts the question of memory—of our identity in the continuum of history—to us. The sensibilities of the survivors and their descendants must be respected, but also the zeal of the scholars to analyze "Why?" and "How can genocide be prevented?" On the one hand a posture of preciousness in the inner circle must be muted: "Only a Jew [or Armenian] can understand."
>
> Just as certainly, on the other hand, those carrying on research must avoid the Eiskalt indifference to the human measure that marked the style of the perpetrators of the crime itself. The scientist must carry himself in awareness that he is laying profane hands on sacred material—that his kind of remembering is an activity which carries its own perils."
>
> *—Excerpts from an address by Franklin H. Littell in Yerevan, Armenia, at the 80th Anniversary Conference of the Armenian Genocide, April 21,1995*

When Franklin Littell and Hubert Locke convened the first meeting of what would become the Annual Scholars' Conference on the Holocaust and the Churches in 1970, they were aware that the events to be discussed by the group gathered at Wayne State University represented neither the first genocidal act in human history nor even the first in the 20th century. So vast was the topic of the *Shoah*, however, so complicated the inter-twining of politics, economics, psychology, theology, et al, that the focus remained on the events of 1933-45 and their aftermath for many years.

The first significant attempt at a more inclusive study of genocide came at a conference held in Israel in 1982, organized by Israel W. Charny, Shammai Davidson and Elie Wiesel and co-sponsored by the Armenian Patriarchate. Called "The First International Conference on the Holocaust and Genocide," the assembled scholars and myriad representatives of victim groups—most notably Jews and Armenians – did not escape notice by a Turkish government that had continually denied the Armenian Genocide of 1915. That government threatened to close the routes by which Iranian Jews were fleeing the regime of the Ayatollahs, if Israeli governmental facilities were made available to the Conference. Despite the threats, the Conference continued. The Armenian experience, having occurred a generation prior to the *Shoah*, offered a unique occasion to study the effects of monumental tragedy upon the survivors and their descendants, reaching to the third and fourth generations. Never before had the opportunity for comparative study of genocides presented itself: not to establish a scale of victimization or suffering, but to learn from the multiplicity of experiences. Despite the bold beginning, little was done to advance collective studies for many years.

As the Centenary observance of the Armenian Genocide approached, the leadership of the Annual Scholars' Conference extended an invitation to representatives of the Armenian community—scholars and laypeople alike—to participate in the 2014 Conference. Hosted in Los Angeles by the American Jewish University, the venue was within a major Armenian-American population center and major research sites on the Armenian Genocide. The Conference was a great success, as scholars met in both formal and informal settings, learning from one another and forming professional and personal connections. The papers presented herein testify to the breadth of research shared during those several days in southern California and illustrate the cooperative efforts that have begun, opening the way to new perspectives for understanding the unknowable, in the effort to walk from great darkness to the light.

Richard L. Libowitz
Temple University
Philadelphia, Pennsylvania
August 7, 2015

Part I

The Armenian Experience: 100 Years Later

Chapter 1

Pioneers of Risk Assessment: The Armenian Genocide, the Holocaust, and Early Warning Systems

Richard Dekmejian

The decade between the Iranian Revolution and the Soviet demise was marked by over a dozen wars and insurgencies that claimed thousands of lives reaching genocidal proportions.[1] Pol Pot's Cambodian Genocide had already occurred (1975-79) and crisis conditions, extending from Afghanistan and the Middle East to Africa and the Asian subcontinent, pointed to an era of protracted conflict and bloodshed.

In view of the worsening human condition, the newly chosen UN Secretary General Boutros Boutros-Ghali called for an "early warning system" in November 1992, in order to identify new threats to peace and take preventive measures.[2] Although UN's Humanitarian Early Warning System (HEWS) had a short life, similar efforts were made by the Organization of Security and Cooperation in Europe (OSCE), and the International Crisis Group, followed by Vice-President Al Gore's project in academic forecasting by specialists;[3] however, these efforts unfortunately failed to foresee the Rwandan Genocide of April 1994. Meanwhile, a plethora of emerging genocide scholars in the 1980s and 1990s had begun to develop more systematic and effective modalities of early warning systems.[4]

Unfortunately, there were no warning systems in operation to predict two early genocides of the 20th century—the Armenian Genocide and the Jewish Holocaust. Instead of computerized risk assessment centers, there were pioneering risk analysts consisting of "thinker-activists," endowed with causal reasoning, precognition and leadership skills, who detected the "signs" of oncoming cataclysms and took steps to resist by proactive and preventive actions by issuing warnings through the press, speeches, diplomatic channels, lobbying, grassroots mobilization, resort to international law, and covert action. The best known thinker-activist was Raphael Lemkin as reflected in his multidisciplinary mastery of the history of human behavior, dedication to justice, professional life, public activism, and publications.

This study will use Lemkin's risk assessment approach to evaluate the roles of two cohorts of thinker-activists—the prognosticators of the Armenian Genocide, and a decade later, the Jewish Holocaust. A comparative analysis will assess the efforts of the two cohorts—their precognitive effectiveness, preventive campaigns through political and social activism and their impact on the work of post-Holocaust scholars in developing more effective early warning systems for prognosticating and preventing future genocidal events.

Lemkin: Armenian-Jewish Genocidal Linkage

As a Jewish child growing up during wartime, near sites of massacres and pogroms of Jews in Poland and Russia, Lemkin developed an abiding interest in histories of mass atrocities since ancient times. At age fifteen, he learned of Ottoman Turkey's campaign to slaughter its Armenian citizens that prompted him to promulgate an international criminal law designed to deter governments from committing mass murder.[5] Thus, Lemkin was destined to become a "bridge" between two of the Twentieth century's human cataclysms. Reaching manhood during the eight-year duration of the Armenian Genocide (1915-1923), Lemkin eventually foresaw, with horror, the replication of the same genocidal dynamic in Europe targeting his kinsmen, along with other victims of the Third Reich.

Lemkin's writings on Armenian issues are truly revealing, showing a deep interest in the subject as reflected by prodigious research and insightful analysis. According to international lawyer and professor Michael J. Bazyler, Lemkin's works indicate his conviction that the Armenians' mass victimization in Ottoman Turkey was an archetype of what he came to define as genocide.[6] In a similar vein, the editor of Lemkin's papers, Professor Steven L. Jacobs asserts:

> the Armenian Genocide *did* occupy a central place in his thinking, along with the Holocaust against his own Jewish people and the genocidal barbarity practiced against so many others . . . For one who saw a direct causal linkage between what was done to the Armenians by the Turks, with the full knowledge of their German allies, and what was done to the Jews by the Nazis and their allies, Adolph Hitler's rhetorical question in August 1939, on the eve of World War II, 'Who now remembers the extermination of the Armenians?'—was answered affirmatively by one whose own moral courage and integrity led him to translate words into challenges and the devastation of others into preventative actions.[7]

In his book-length manuscript on the Armenian massacres, Lemkin presents a striking comparative analysis of the Armenian and Jewish cases of genocide:

> A strong parallel may be drawn between the extermination of the Armenians by the Turks and the extermination of the Jews by the Germans. The position of the Armenians in the Ottoman Empire closely approximated that of the Jews in Germany. The Armenians were the industrious citizens of the Empire, with a talent for handicraft and intellectual pursuits. They had the same gift for commerce as the Jews, and in Asiatic Turkey it was the Armenian who was the skilled workman and the man of business. Every town in Anatolia had its prosperous Armenian quarter, the centre of local skill, intellectual life and trade, as well as of the town's commercial relations with Constantinople and Europe.[8]

Prognosticators of the Armenian Genocide

In contrast to the Holocaust, the 1915 Armenian Genocide was the culmination of successive genocidal carnages and pogroms dating back to the 1850s. Thus, attempts at precognition of Armenian mass killings had begun in the decades leading to the 1894-96 Hamidean Massacres, defined by Kaiser Wilhelm II's government as *Armeniermord* (Armenocide), which claimed up to 300,000 lives, without opposition from Germany.[9]

Prognosticators of the Hamidean Massacres and the 1915 Genocide included European officials, scholars, authors, political leaders and a cleric. On September 7, 1880, the six Great Powers sent the Ottoman government a Collective Note expressing displeasure at Turkish tactics of refusing to implement the Armenian reforms and linking these issues to Art. 61 of the Berlin Treaty of 1878, which was binding on Turkey. This implied their premonition that failure to execute the reforms "would in all probability lead to the destruction of the Christian [i.e. Armenian] population of vast districts."[10] This clear prediction fourteen years before the Hamidean Massacres, was preceded by a warning from an Armenian teacher and linguist, Dikran Amirjanian of Van. As Armenians were celebrating the promulgation of the Constitution by Sultan Abdulhamit in 1876, Amirjanian called it a "a deceptive gimmick" and forecast "the extermination of the Armenians of the Ottoman Empire."[11] He was partly right, as eighteen years later, up to 300,000 died in the 1894-96 Hamidean Massacres. Soon after these killings, the Sultan declared that "The Armenian Question was closed," prompting Harvard historian William Langer to see Hamid's act as a step forward in the genocidal process: "It was perfectly obvious that the Sultan was determined to end the Armenian question by exterminating the Armenians."[12]

The precedent of the Hamidean Massacres prompted prognosticators to be more vigilant and apprehensive by pointing to the high risks of a greater human cataclysm. A case in point was the British ethnographer Sir William Ramsay who travelled around Turkey for 30 years and wrote two books on what he witnessed. Based on the portents of the Hamidean carnage, in 1897 Ramsay stated: "The Armenians will in all probability be exterminated except the remnants that escape to other lands."[13] In 1898, *The New York Herald* sent a team to investigate and report on the Hamidean atrocities. The team included author George Hepworth, who made a prognostication anticipating the 1915 Armenian Genocide, fully two decades before its occurrence:

> During my travels in Armenia I have been more and more deeply convinced that the future of the Armenians is extremely clouded. It may be that the hand of the Turk will be held back through fear of Europe but I am sure that the object of the Turk is extermination, and that he

> will pursue that end if the opportunity offers. He has already come very near to its accomplishment . . . [14]

Thus, the Hamidean Massacres served as a "testing ground"—destined to be the prototype of the *Medz Yeghern*—The 'Great Genocide' of 1915-1923.[15]

The 1908 Young Turk Revolution against the Sultan brought a brief return to constitutional rule amid celebrations of freedom—*Hurriyet*—which was ended abruptly by the 1909 Adana massacre claiming 30,000 Armenian lives. This unexpected atrocity triggered a new wave of prognostications. Dr. Rupen Chilingirian—pen name Sevag—a Swiss educated doctor and brilliant poet and essayist, issued repeated warnings in speeches and writings—e.g., a lengthy poem, *The Last Armenians* and the *Red Book* on the Adana killings. In April 1915, Sevag was taken to Chankiri with other Armenian leaders and brutally murdered.[16]

In February 1914, Rostom (Stepan Zorian), a leader of the Dashnaktsutiun (Armenian Revolutionary Federation) wrote to Simon Vratsian in Boston, urging Armenians in the United States to provide greater financial support to Armenian schools in Turkey to turn their homeland into paradise. However, he remained skeptical whether the Turks would allow such advancement, and was equally skeptical of the European powers and Russia serving as protectors of the Armenians. Rostom noted prophetically that the ongoing reform negotiations with the Great Powers in Constantinople seemed no more than a game, and expressed his grave concerns that these games of reform would lead to a new round of persecutions and massacres.[17] In another letter, Rosdom expressed his premonition that 1914 would be a critical year.[18]

Grigoris Balakian, distinguished Bishop of the Armenian Church educated in Germany, was shocked on his return in 1914 by the contagion of psychopathology sweeping Constantinople and the provinces. In his writings, the Bishop speaks on being caught between knowing something awful is going to happen to the Armenians, and his astonished disbelief regarding what happened to him in April 1915 when he was arrested and imprisoned in Chankiri along with other Armenian leaders awaiting execution. Before prison, the Bishop had quickly summoned his brother-in-law from the Eastern provinces to Constantinople in Fall

1914, saving him and his family from death. Meanwhile, the Bishop's repeated warnings to the church leadership and the Patriarchate fell on deaf ears as thousands of Armenian priests were massacred in the provinces, including those recently sent from Constantinople. Eventually, he was released from prison and survived to continue his ministry in France.[19]

Prognosticators of the Holocaust

Precognition of the Holocaust was a more difficult task when compared to the Armenian Genocide for several reasons:

1. Armenians had suffered persistent persecution and several genocidal episodes during the Nineteenth Century leading to the Hamidian Massacres of 1894-96 and the Adana Massacre of 1909. Thus, the threat of oncoming persecutions and pogroms were felt by many who had emigrated to the United States, Europe and other countries. In contrast, the Jewish community of Germany under the KaiserReich and earlier, had not experienced large scale persecutions and targeted killings, like the Jewish pogroms and suffering in Czarist Russia's Pale of Settlement.

2. Jews were better integrated into German society than Armenians in the Ottoman Empire, who had sought physical security and human rights by repeated appeals to the European powers. As such, Armenians were seen by the Sultan and Young Turk leaders as an existential threat for seeking European-sponsored autonomy and even independence. It was ironic that Armenian soldiers dutifully fighting in Ottoman armies in World War I were disarmed and killed by Turkish commanders, while Jewish soldiers were serving in the Kaiser's armies as German patriots. The positive stance of the KaiserReich toward Jews extended to the Jewish inhabitants of Ottoman territories who feared death as part of the ongoing genocidal campaigns targeting Armenians, Assyrians, Greeks, and Arab Christians and some Muslims. Indeed, there were clear indications and attempts of Turkish persecution and killings of Zionist Jews, especially in Palestine,

> but no mass atrocities occurred due to German pressure on their Turkish allies to refrain from harming Jewish settlers in Palestine.[20]

The Genocidal Transition

Germany's tolerance toward Jews during World War I was mostly a consequence of geopolitical, ideological, and economic factors. To understand the dynamics of the quick transition to Nazism, several converging ideological, historical and social-psychological developments need consideration. These began with the quest for Pan-German unity led by Prussia in response to the Napoleonic conquests. The crucial transition from German humanistic liberalism to German nationalism connecting the 18th and 19th centuries was reflected in the writings of Kant, Fichte and Hegel. The rational internationalism of Kant was replaced by Hegel's vision of the German Reich where "the state is the divine will."[21] The accelerated march to nation-statehood with jump-start industrialization and imperial conquests was successfully led by Otto von Bismarck—"The Iron Man," ending in victory in the Franco-Prussian War.

While the Jewish community flourished in this period economically, intellectually, and culturally, it had to pay a price as a religious minority surrounded by growing Germanic nationalist fervor. One option for well-educated Jewish families was conversion to Lutheranism as done by the Mendelsohns and Marxes. Yet, near the century's end, German anti-semitism had reached a zenith with the *völkisch* books of Wilhelm Marr (1873), Paul de Lagarde (1878), Houston Stewart Chamberlain (1899) and other racist publications such as the bestselling *The Protocols of the Elders of Zion*, blaming Jews for all of the world's evils.[22]

Germany's disastrous World War I defeat, followed by the great depression, triggered a mass transformation of the German psyche as a prelude to Nazi rule in 1933. The emerging psychopathological milieu set the stage for Raphael Lemkin and a plethora of Jewish thinker-activists to engage in precognitive risk analysis of oncoming genocidal situations facing Jewish communities in Europe, Palestine and the Soviet Union.[23]

One of the earliest predictors of the Holocaust was Eca de Queiroz, a famous novelist of Portugal, who in 1882 saw growing threats after the

Franco-Prussian 1870-71 war: "increasingly anti-Semitic fury . . . we are going to see real persecution of Jews."[24] In 1911, Max Nordau warned The World Zionist Congress: "The same righteous governments are preparing to complete annihilation of 6 million people."[25] In 1932, German writer and anti-war activist Arnold Zweig "told Zionist leader Menahem M. Ussishkin during a visit to Jerusalem, when the ascendance of Hitler seemed imminent . . . that this would lead to the total destruction of German Jewry."[26] The aftermath of Hitler's takeover in 1933 evoked more warnings from Jewish leaders such as Stephen Wise, Hillel Kook and Ira Hirschmann as desperation began to set in among American Jewry.[27]

With the intensification of Nazi persecutions, there was escalating fear among diaspora leaders and warnings expressed by Chaim Weizmann in November 1936 and Dr. Franz Borkenau who wrote in April 1939, that "no less than seven million Jews are bottled up in an area where most of them are no longer wanted" and predicted that "There is little doubt that within a few years the fate of the Jews in eastern Europe will resemble that of Armenians in Turkey."[28] Equally ominous was Revisionist Zionist Ze`ev Jabotinsky's speech in Poland on Oct. 24, 1938, warning Jews that "a catastrophe is coming closer." "Let anyone of you save himself as long as there is time, and time there is very little." He went on to emphasize the need to evacuate Jews to Palestine.[29] With the War's onset, World Jewish Congress President Nahum Goldmann and other leaders began to cry out about the Nazi threat to "six million Jewish victims"—in retrospect, a tragically accurate premonition.[30]

A Comparative Overview

An overview of the two cohorts of pioneering prognosticators reveals that tragically their predictions came true in the genocidal outcomes of the Armenian and Jewish cases. Similarly, their predictions of timing until genocides' onset corresponded to what transpired in reality. As thinker-activists, clearly they were competent in reading the "signs" of their pre-genocidal environments and went public with warnings and preventive efforts.

It was somewhat easier to predict the Armenian massacres because the predictors had learned the long history of atrocities Armenians had suffered under Ottoman rule. In the Jewish case, the Reich's psychopathological transition until the start of mass killings was relatively brief—prompted by the rise of Nazi power in the early 1930s, which shortened the time period for predictors to a decade.

Did the predictions save lives? While difficult to estimate, thousands of potential victims escaped both genocides whenever possible. For many thousands, the warnings fell on deaf ears, even coming from a family member like Raphael Lemkin who lost forty-nine of his relatives.[31]

Despite their capabilities of discernment, precognition, and leadership, the cohorts of thinker-activists failed in preventing or disrupting the genocidal process because both Ottoman Turkey and Nazi Germany possessed unchallenged military power to continue executing their respective genocidal imperatives under the protective umbrellas of the world wars being fought.

Early Warning Systems?

Clearly, the prediction of the two Twentieth Century genocides proved to be far easier than their prevention—a painful reality that remains true in today's technologically advanced, globalized and interdependent world system under UN's unsteady structure of international law.

In the half-century since Lemkin's contributions to the causal dynamics and anatomy of genocides throughout history and Boutros Ghali's 1992 UN early warning initiative, major advances have come to strengthen the prognosticative power of genocide scholars and policymakers. Among the pioneering contributors to the literature on genocide risk analysis and early warning systems are: Barbara Harff, Ted Robert Gurr, James Davies, Helen Fein, J. Joseph Hewitt, Israel W. Charny, Franklin H. Littell, Gregory Stanton, Adeel Ahmed, Elizabeth Voulieris Kassinis, James Glass,[32] and others who emphasize the psychological, sociological, ideological and leadership determinants of genocidal triggers.[33] Using a combination of these early warning systems, a risk analyst can easily identify up to fifteen high-risk pre-genocidal situations in specific Middle Eastern, African and Asian countries that require external intervention and long-term deployment of military forces to achieve peace. The political will for collective action is an imperative necessity but difficult to implement, given divisive conflicts within the UN Security Council and growing interstate and sectarian enmities destabilizing the international system.

Notes for Chapter 1

1. These crises included Afghanistan, Lebanon, Syria, Israel, Sri Lanka, Kashmir, Sudan, Argentina, Chile, and Somalia.

2. Boutros Boutros-Ghali, *An Agenda for Peace: Preventive Diplomacy, Peacemaking, and Peacekeeping.* (New York: United Nations, 1992), par. 26.

3. Barbara Harff, "How to Use Global Risk Assessments to Anticipate and Prevent Genocide," Paper prepared for *Poloitorbis*, special issue on "Today's Conversations about Genocide Prevention," January 2010.

4. Ibid.

5. William Korey, *Midstream*, June-July 1989, pp. 45-48. Box 1, Folder 2.

6. See Michael J. Bazyler in "Foreward," *Raphael Lemkin's Dossier on the Armenian Genocide,* by Vartkes Yeghiayan, (Glendale, CA: Center for Armenian Remembrance, 2008) p. xxviii.

7. Steven L. Jacobs, "Raphael Lemkin and the Armenian Genocide" in *Looking Backward, Moving Forward,* edited by Richard G. Hovannisian (Transaction Publishers, 2003), p. 133.

8. *Dossier*, p. 80

9. Vahakn N. Dadrian, *The History of the Armenian Genocide* (Berghahn Books: Providence, RI, 1995) pp. 92, 97.

10. Dadrian, *History*, pp. 175-176.

11. Dadrian, *The Warrant for Genocide*, (Transaction Publishers, New Brunswick: NJ, 1999) p. 28.

12. William L. Langer, *The Diplomacy of Imperialism 1890-1902*, Vol. 1 (New York, 1935) p. 203.

13. Dadrian, *History*, p. 175; For details on Sir William Ramsay's writings on the tragic situation of Armenians in Ottoman Turkey, see Jirair Tutunjian, "Did You Know?" *The California Courier,* November 7, 2013, p.11.

14. Dadrian, *History*, p. 175.

15. In order to avoid antagonizing Turkey, President Obama has regularly used a common Armenian term—*Medz Yeghern*—instead of the word "Genocide" in his yearly April 24th Armenian Genocide commemorative declarations.

16. Grigoris Balakian, *Armenian Golgotha:A Memoir of the Armenian Genocide, 1915-1918*, translated by Peter Balakian with Aris Sevag, (Alfred A. Knopf: New York. 2009) p. 442.

17. Rostom to Simon Vratsian, Feb. 12, 1914, in *Rosdom: Namakani* [Rostom: Collection of Letters] Press Hamazkain p. 611-612.

18. Ibid., see Rostom to Simon Vratsian, Apr. 2, 1914, pp. 613-614.

19. Grigoris Balakian, *Armenian Golgotha*, Preface xxiv.

20 Dadrian, *German Responsibility in the Armenian Genocide*, (Cambridge: MA, Bluecrane Books, 1996) p. 255.

21. George H. Sabine, *A History of Political Theory* (Holt, Rinehart and Winston; Third Edition, 1961) pp. 659, 896-900.

22. Norman Cohn, *Warrant for Genocide: The Myth of the Jewish World-Conspiracy and the Protocols of the Elder of Zion*, (New York: Harper & Row, 1966), pp. 15–40.

23. Samantha Power, *"A Problem From Hell," America and the Age of Genocide* (HarperCollins, New York: NY, 2003) pp. 23, 26-30, 35, 38-40.

24. *National Vanguard*, October 24, 2010.

25. Ben Hecht, *Perdfidy*, 1961.

26. Jacob Katz, "Was the Holocaust Predictable," *Commentary Magazine*, May 1, 1975.

27. David Morrison, *Heroes, Antiheroes and the* Holocaust, (Gefen Publishing House, Jerusalem, 1999) pp. 111-132, 218-221.

28. John Cooper, *Raphael Lemkin and the Struggle for the Genocide Convention*, (Palgrave, New York: NY, 2008) pp. 29-30.

29. *Jewish Post*, Oct. 25, 1938.

30. *The Palm Beach Post*, June 25, 1940.

31. *Lemkin on Genocide*, Written by Raphael Lemkin; Edited & Introduced by Steven Leonard Jacobs (Lexington Books: Lanham, MD, 2012) p. viii.

32. Barbara Harff, "How to Use Risk Assessment and Early Warning in the Prevention and De-Escalation of Genocide and other Mass Atrocities," *Global Responsibility to Protect 1* (2009), pp. 506-531; Ted Robert Gurr and Barbara Harff, "Early Warning Systems," in Kevin M. Cahill (ed.), *Emergency Relief Operations* (New York: Fordham University Press, 2003) pp. 3-31; Barbara Harff and Ted Robert Gurr, "Toward Empirical Theory of Genocides and Politicides: Identification and Measurement of Cases since 1945," *International Studies Quarterly* 32/3 (1988) pp. 359-371; Barbara Harff, "No Lessons Learned from the Holocaust? Assessing Risks of Genocide and Political Mass Murder since 1955," *American Political Science Review*, vol. 97, no. 1 (2003) pp. 57-73; Franklin H. Littell, "Essay: Early Warning," *Holocaust*

& Genocide Studies, Vol. 3, No. 4 (1988) pp. 483-490; Steven Leonard Jacobs, "Franklin H. Littell's and Israel W. Charney's Early Warning Systems," *Journal of Ecumenical Studies*, 46:4, (Fall 2011) pp. 599-608; Helen Fein, *Genocide: A Sociological Perspective* (London and Newbury Park, CA: Sage, 1993).

33. Ervin Staub, *Overcoming Evil*, (London: UK,Oxford University Press, 2011); Robert Melson, *Revolution and Genocide: On the Origins of the Armenian Genocide and the Holocaust*, (Chicago: University of Chicago Press, 1996); Manus I. Midlarsky, *The Killing Trap: Genocide in the Twentieth Century*, (Cambridge: UK, Cambridge University Press, 2005); R. Hrair Dekmejian, *Spectrum of Terror*, (Washington D.C., CQ Press, 2007); David A. Hamburg, M.D., *Preventing Genocide: Practical Steps Toward Early Detection and Effective Action*, (Boulder: CO, Paradigm Publishers, 2008); Steven K. Baum, *The Psychology of Genocide: Perpetrators, Bystanders, and Rescuers* (Cambridge: Cambridge University Press, 2008); Leo Kuper, *The Prevention of Genocide,* (New Haven, CT: Yale University Press, 1985).

Chapter 2

The Symbiotic Relationship between Turks and Armenians: A Macabre Outcome Obstructing Healing and Reconciliation

Rubina Peroomian

The Armenian-Turkish relationship spans the long period since the eleventh-century incursions of Seljuk, Mongol, and other Turko-Mongol tribes toward the west, the final encroachment of the Armenian plateau, and the eventual establishment of the Ottoman rule over Armenia.[1] The basic principles for this relationship, established at the outset with the initial contact on the battlefield and the terror spread within the civil society, were those of the conqueror and the conquered and consequently the ruler and the ruled. They also developed through time through governmental policies on minorities, especially during the Ottoman era, down to the societal perceptions and behavior. The outcome was a sort of a *modus vivendi* between these two people quite dissimilar in ethnicity, religion, culture, tradition, and history.

During centuries of coexistence, intermingling through marriage and conversion to the religion of the ruler majority was inevitable. Beginning with the Seljuk invasions, the kidnapping of thousands of Armenian women to keep as wives or concubines or to sell in the slave markets was a usual practice. So was the capturing of Armenian youth to serve in military forces. These captives were all forced to convert to Islam. Voluntary conversions for social, economic, and/or social gain were also abundant. In fact Muslim Armenian men reached high positions in ruling circles and in the army, and Muslim Armenian women mothered heirs of the thrones. In the process of this long coexistence, besides ethnic co-mingling, Muslim rulers of Turkic origin adopted many traits from Armenian culture and lifestyle.[2]

After going through a series of devastating incursions and submerging into a dark age in terms of political and cultural life, Armenia and Armenians were incorporated into the huge Ottoman Empire. During this period, as Dickran Kouymjian attests, "[D]espite devastating invasions, accompanied by pillaging and enslavement, despite taxes on a level never before imposed, despite the recurring famines, occasional plagues, locusts .... Armenians tried to maintain Armenian life as they understood it ....At times the struggle must have seemed unsurmountable, the nation condemned." [3]

In addition to the official policy of absolute subjugation, the unbridled Turkish and Kurdish assaults on Armenian rural communities, confiscation of a large part of the harvest and personal belongings, and most dreadfully the kidnapping of young women, had created an atmosphere of fear among Armenians and a state of social death. While *Devshirme*, the gathering of Christian youth, and Armenians among them, was many times beneficial for the youth who did not remember their origin, it was another brutal practice to spread terror and break the Christian, in this case the Armenian, family. The gathered male children were Islamized and given the best education to serve in high ranking positions in the system.[4]

Armenian culture and civilization suffered significant setbacks, and Armenians, the brave mountaineers of the Armenian highlands, with a long history of struggle for national freedom, were turned into subservient slaves, under constant harassment and persecution. Turkish-Armenian relationship was more like that of a lord and a serf.

In this overall relationship, it was only natural for Armenians to see the Turks and the Kurds, who at that time were not considered a separate ethnic group but only mountain Turks, as frightful evil-doers. Likewise, Turks perceived Armenians as infidels, unbelievers or *giavours*, slaves of the Muslims, *rayas*, and *fallahs*.

To avoid simplification of the equation in this relationship, the gradual rise of the Armenian traders, the *khojas* in the rural areas, beginning mid-15th century, and later the *chelebies*, the industrialists in the urban areas giving way to *amiras*, the financial and industrial magnates of the 19th century in the Ottoman Empire should also be taken into consideration. They were wealthy, influential, and supported Armenian religious and cultural undertakings. Their role in this equation, based on their prominence in the empire's economy, added a feeling of jealousy on the part of the Turkish officials and the society at large. This jealousy was often translated into hate and malevolence as an added ingredient in the Turkish-Armenian relationship. In this long symbiotic period before WWI, stereotyping and name-calling were thus expected phenomena.

In the Muslim-dominated Ottoman Empire, Armenians were segregated, like Greeks and Jews, as a religious-ethnic community with the legal status of a *millet*, second class citizens, subjected to discriminatory laws and taxation. They had to wear distinctive signs or clothing to indicate their being non-Muslims. They were not allowed to bear arms or to ride a horse. Apparently, Armenians were the most obedient *millet* and made less trouble for the Ottoman sultans, so over time they were viewed as good and honest people and were called *millet-i-sadika* (the loyal *millet*).

The Armenian-Turkish *modus vivendi* lost its livable balance in the late 18th and 19th centuries with, on the one hand, the economic, political, and social decay of the Empire, which meant more pressure on Armenians to collect additional taxes and more frequent assaults in rural areas for financial gains. On the other hand, on the Armenian side, liberal ideas infiltrating from Europe had brought about a cultural and political revival which resulted in attempts to call on the Sublime Porte and demand reforms and amelioration of the Armenian plight with some also resorting to armed self-defense against their assailants.

As a result of this development, the Turkish iron fist pressed more heavily and the Turkish-Armenian relationship was studded with sporadic massacres, forced Islamization of groups of Armenians, and persecution of Armenian revolutionaries, including incarceration in filthy prisons, torture and hangings. Armenian popular culture of the period—songs, sayings, and anecdotes—are manifestations of a complex collective psyche structured by fear, hatred, helplessness, frustration, and even vengefulness.

The period immediately preceding the Young Turk Revolution,[5] beginning from April 1908, was one of yearning and anticipation for both Armenian and Turkish intellectuals. Promises of equality, freedom, brotherhood, and justice could efface the centuries of acrimony and the bitter memory of maltreatment to bring about a peaceful coexistence among the two peoples who were destined (or, rather, condemned) to live side-by-side, even intermingled with each other. There was hope of a better future in the air.

In a letter dated October 16, 1908, written to her husband in Paris, Zabel Essayan (1878-1942),[6] a prominent female writer and an eyewitness to the events in Constantinople, optimistically stated: "The two nations have now begun to understand each other's mentality, and they had time to penetrate each other's inner feelings. Now no administration can set one against the other."[7] But there does not seem an absolute trust to exist vis-à-vis the leadership, as to how the implementation of the great change would go, and how the masses would perceive the ideology of the Revolution. Further down in that same letter, she writes, "This race has something incorrigible ....We have daily proof of this."

In any event, the artificially aroused honeymoon between the oppressors and the oppressed in the Empire was short-lived. The massacre of Armenians in Cilicia, only a few months after the revolution, was a shocking manifestation of the continuing policy of Turkification or rather Ottomanization as the ideology of the time suggested. In April, 1909, concurrent with the counter-revolution movement in Constantinople, the same anti-revolutionary, reactionary elements instigated the Muslim masses to attack Armenian quarters in Adana. Pillage and murder followed in this city with a significant Armenian population. Armenians were being punished for their outspoken support of the Revolution and claiming equality and justice they did not deserve. Soon the massacres spread to other Armenian towns and villages in Cilicia. It is believed that the Turkish army regiment ordered to stop the carnage was deliberately late to arrive. It is also believed that these soldiers entering in Adana actually participated in the attacks.[8]

As a member of the second delegation sent by the Armenian Patriarchate of Constantinople, Esayan visited the disaster stricken area to assess the loss and provide means of assistance. In a letter to her husband, dated June 18, 1909 from Mersin, she writes, "Cilicia is destroyed.... The Armenian people have fallen victim to a premeditated plan.... The conspiracy of the present government is evident.... For centuries our hard working people have nourished our enemy. Today, they receive their reward.... Even cannibals are better than these monsters; at least they eat each other to satiate their hunger."[9] Her addressee is not this and that Turk, the criminal, the culprit, or the conspirator, but the entire nation, the Turkish race (if there is such a thing after so much mingling of Turkic tribes with the locals). In an effort to explain the Turkish behavioral pattern, in that same letter, she compares the "national characteristics" of the two peoples and concludes that one is civilized, builds, and creates; the other nurtures bloody aspirations and destroys.

In *Averaknerun mej* (Amid the Ruins), a collection of stories depicting her devastating encounter with the agonizing situation, Esayan views the victimizers through the eyes of Armenian orphans left behind after the carnage, and these eyes reflect unspeakable horror, the slaughter of their parents they have witnessed. They see the Turk as a cold-blooded murderer whose eyes burn with evil passion to destroy and kill.[10] To their victims' last prayers these killers responded laughing, "You don't have a God. Just as your Christ died by torture, so will each one of you die by torture."[11]

In this detailed eyewitness account, she portrays the hatred that Turks hold against Armenians, and shows that even Turkish women are not immune to this destructive sentiment. She describes a Turkish woman crushing the head of an Armenian child as he knelt over his mother's dead body. Another Turkish woman loaded wounded Armenians onto a carriage as if to save their lives only to push them into the river.[12] The thrill of bloodshed and plunder intoxicated them so much so that they forgot the friendship and the salt and bread they shared for long years with their Armenian neighbors.

Suren Partevian (1876-1921),[13] a member of the first delegation to visit Cilicia, has a similar take on the 1909 Cilician massacres. His hopes are shattered. He believes that "the Armenian-Turkish brotherhood is being strangled, murdered, and buried in the ashes and blood in Cilicia," and doubts if Armenians could ever have a future in the new society ruled by the Ittihad (Young Turk) party.[14] In one of the essays in his collection of eyewitness accounts, he quotes a wounded and dying Armenian priest, "If my God is also the God of these unbelievers, these ferocious beasts, I don't believe in God...I don't believe in God."[15]

So, even before the massacres and deportations of the war years,

Armenian trust in Turkish goodwill was shattered. A wound was slashed open that would not heal. As Partevian put it, "There is something broken, something sunken in our souls; there is a ravage of faith, a pain of frustration that will remain unhealed."[16]

The Turkish-Armenian relationship was increasingly deteriorating. Worsening the situation and adding to the whetted sentiments was the government initiated anti-Armenian or rather anti-Christian propaganda just before and during the war years, the November 21, 1914 calling of Jihad, a holy war against Christians with undercurrent emphasis on Armenians. Turks were being instigated to see Armenians as vermin, microbes, infidel *giavours* or *kafirs*, enemies of Islam unworthy of living; in other words, deserving to be killed. Degradation and dehumanization of the victim facilitated their extermination, and the perpetrators were instinctively aware of that.

Hatred for Armenians had been transmitted from generation to generation, manipulated from time to time according to governmental policies and ground sharper if necessary. The testimonial stories of Hagop Oshagan (1883-1948)[17] are manifestations of this phenomenon. "A fifteen year old hero [Turkish of course] had nailed the head of a slaughtered man [Armenian of course] to the end of a long wooden stick. The eyes were gouged out, and the eyebrows were plucked. The stick on his shoulder and a rifle on his chest, he walked up and down the streets of the Armenian village to experience the pleasure of the terror he spread among women and children around him."[18] The year was 1915.

This is not only an appalling childish game, but also an act of religious gratification. God's name is ultimately sanctified through the shedding of the blood of the infidel, burning and looting their belongings, while praying to that same God to give strength to their arms and peace to their conscience to continue their holy work. The old religious leader of the Turkish village, dressed in white, the embodiment of God himself, gives the first example to start the carnage. His victim is the priest of the Armenian village down below. The God of Islam observes the carnage and accepts the sacrifices the Turkish villagers offer to him. The slaughter of the entire Armenian village is completed, and "the old man's soul found a rare satisfaction that only a sacrifice of such a grand scale could offer. His conscience was stilled and cleared with that sacred offering."[19]

Sultan Abdul Hamid's political message corroborated what the holy Jihad was propagating. He too had proclaimed, "Whoever oppresses the Christians is a true son of the Turkish homeland."[20]

The Turkish-Armenian relationship had reached rock-bottom. With a sarcastic tone, Oshagan cites the biblical analogy of wolves and lambs grazing together. By presenting this metaphor for the Turkish Armenian relationship, he derides the naïveté of the world to believe that such things are ever possible. Like Essayan, Oshagan too examines racial attributes as well as cultural, religious, and traditional factors that shape the victimizer's behavior. "From the vizier to the peasant shepherd, they all calmly and peacefully accepted the decree of the annihilation. That was an invitation to their centuries old instincts, and a pleasant one."[21]

Comparing his own artistic literature to those of others entertaining the theme of Turkish-Armenian relationship, he argues that he has given the executioner a face and a character, "In the Armenian novels," he notes, "the Turk is a cliché scarecrow, the ogre of the legend. Oshagan has not retouched the picture, of course, but he has retained the original."[22] He analyzes the Turkish character, the genetic elements arousing the drive to loot and kill, the religious determinants conditioning patterns of behavior, and all of this at work in the making of the criminal. The conclusion: "There exist not only criminal people but also criminal races."[23]

Throughout the almost 3000 pages of *Mnatsortats* (Remnants), Oshagan uses the words Turk, Turkish, and Turkishness as qualifiers and adjectives synonymous with corruption, criminality, hatred, pitilessness. "Turkish translates into Turkishness without explanation," he writes. "The Turk is the animal outlined by our historians of a thousand years ago, but they gave no explanation either. He kills for want of being able to do something else." Nothing has changed since the first hostile encounter and subjugation of Armenians by the Turkic hordes, the barbarians raiding from Central Asia centuries before WWI. "It was not the outbreak of war [WWI] that made the Turks so much Turk. Before or after the war, it has been the same. The soldier, the volunteer, the layman, the clergy, with an inexplicable smile on their face, would twist the tortured half-dead Armenian prisoner's head and shamelessly ask, 'is your wife pretty?'...."[24]

Then Oshagan describes two unspeakable, outrageous scenes of the Turk killing or raping, "The deep, inexplicable ugliness of all this," he concludes, "I stress these, because the world confuses the massacres with the passion of violence."[25] Oshagan describes a Turkish wet-nurse who had found an unusual way to express her hatred for Armenians. In a Turkish orphanage, where Armenian orphans, remnants of the Genocide were being brought up as Turks, she wetted her nipple in poison when nursing an Armenian baby. She was poisoned herself.[26]

Despite all the strategic planning and preparations, the leaders of the CUP were not able to achieve the total annihilation of the Armenian population in the Ottoman Empire. Indeed, whereas the prior stages of the genocide of Armenians, as delineated by Gregory Stanton—Classification, Symbolization, Dehumanization, Organization, Polarization, Preparation—had been effectively implemented throughout the years, the stage of Extermination was not entirely successful.[27] There remained a mass of survivors some of whom found refuge in different countries of the world, forming new Diasporan communities or joining the existing ones. Others continued living in Turkey, either Islamized (genuinely or pretending), some thoroughly absorbed in the Turkish society, or within small communities mainly in Istanbul, segregated, under constant fear and pressure, discriminated and persecuted, with no voice to tell their wrenching stories, or speak-up against personal and collective ongoing injustices.

The post-WWI Turkish governments and the Turkish society, thus, faced three fronts of unavoidable encounter and relationship with Armenians in the Diaspora, within their own country, and finally, as a new development, in the Republic of Armenia.

The most problematic of these relationships is the one in their own backyard. The Turk who had been given assurance that there would be no Armenians left after the final solution, viewed these Armenian survivors as unjustified "leftovers of the sword," a new moniker added to the old ones. They deserved to die, and if they still existed in Turkey, these *gavours* and *gavouroghlu gavours* were "rejects of the sword" (ký́lý́c artý́ðý́). This was the basis of the Turkish perception of Armenians in post-WWI Turkey.

The generations born to the Armenian survivors in the Diaspora, on the other hand, learned from their parents to fear the Turks, even in some cases hate them for what they had done to their family and their homeland. It is a known and unchallenged reality that the new Armenian Diaspora is the outcome of the Genocide. The history of the contemporary Armenian Diaspora begins with Genocide. Naturally and consequently, the Genocide, with the whole array of complex influences—psychological, physical, social, economic, and geopolitical—becomes the core of the Diasporan Armenian's identity. It is thus undeniable that the Turkish-Armenian relationship has a heavy bearing on both the Turkish and Armenian identity.

The symbiotic relationship between the descendants of the Armenian survivors and Turkish perpetrators continues. But the basis of this symbiosis has shifted drastically. It is built not on the necessity of coexistence as before, but on the way Turks and Armenians perceive themselves in relation to the other, based on past experience and the perception of the past experience, the Genocide and the memory of the Genocide on both sides. The relationship continues as symbiotic because of the crucial role it plays in the shaping of both identities.

Whereas the Armenian perception of the other—the Turk, the perpetrator of the calamity—is based on the survivors' narratives and the transgenerational transmission of the psychological effects of the traumatic experience of the past—fear of the Turk, hatred, and a feeling of revenge, which by the way triggered the "terrorist" acts in the 70s and 80s[28]—the Turkish perception of Armenians, to use James Wertsch's terminology, is "textually mediated," that is, it is shaped by the official Turkish state narrative.

For the majority of new generation Diasporan Armenians, Turkey, Turk, and Turkish have negative connotations. They have learned from their grandparents that there is no such thing as a good Turk. In the case of the generations of Turks growing up after the 70s and 80s, the absolute silence on the existence of an Armenian issue was replaced by the rationalization of the event, by using new terminology, "relocation" or "demographic engineering," and the reversal of the blame by showing the Armenians as the villain, the traitor, the secessionist, and the collaborator with the enemy to destroy Turkey. This is according to an educational policy to follow strictly the official narrative which, after a period of total silence about the existence of an Armenian issue, shifted direction.

The denial of the Armenian Genocide, as the 8th and last stage of the act of genocide, is intensified and corroborated with rationalization, trivialization, the blaming of the victims themselves, and euphemistic explanations such as "relocation," *tehchir*, or "demographic engineering," for the murder and deportations that occurred. Denial of the Armenian Genocide manifests in all the 12 forms suggested by Israel Charny for any genocide to occur in the world.[29] The denial of the Armenian Genocide is at the core of the Turkish identity.

Turkish governments have followed an unchanging policy of instigating in different ways the Muslim society against Christians. A most recent example is "Fatih 1453," an entirely anti-Christian film about the conquest of Constantinople and the fall of the Christian empire, as well as the film "Seri Gelin" before that. A few years ago, the Ministry of National Education of Turkey organized a writing contest among high school students. The topic was who could best rebut Armenian lies about events during WWI.

The annual report of the US Commission on religious freedom lists Turkey among countries with the least tolerance towards religious minorities. The increasing number of killings of Catholic and Protestant priests is a result of the formally disseminated and harbored anti-Christian ideas. Such manifestations of the prevailing attitude are many. The recent killings and harassment of elderly Armenian women is one, and the ongoing TV interviews and shows about Armenians killing innocent Turks during the war years and Turks suffering as much as Armenians did is another. Turkey is preparing with much vigor for the centennial of the 1915 genocide with completely reversed discourse, a contra-genocide narrative.

With its control stretched over Turkish organizations outside Turkey, the Turkish government ensures the continuation of anti-Armenian sentiments. This effort stems from the fear that Turks traveling abroad for business, education, or emigration may come face to face with the truth and no longer ascribe to the official narrative and prescribed behavior. One example is the utterly distorted position paper disseminated in April 2013 by the ATAA (Assembly of Turkish-American Associations) describing the "revolt of Van" and "the slaughter of innocent Turkish population" as justification for the arrest and imprisonment of Armenian notables in Constantinople in 1915. So too was the letter-writing campaign by the same Assembly. Turkish-Americans were encouraged to send a form letter to US President Barack Obama, asking him not to use the word genocide in his annual April 24 proclamation, reminding him that it was actually Armenians who killed the Turks, 523,000 of them between the years 1910-1922.

Unfortunately, there are racist Turks and racist groups, organizations, and individuals who are susceptible to embracing the prescribed and propagated anti-Armenian sentiments. There are also Armenians with psychological hang-ups or strong political determinations never ready to accept rapprochement with Turkey and the Turks. And this stance has also spread in the Republic of Armenia whose population was considered by Turkey as softer Armenians with whom it was easier to deal.

As long as this grim symbiosis exists between Turks and Armenians, artificial interventions, directly supported or advocated by foreign entities in the form of opulently financed meetings, joint events, etc., will remain as scratches on the surface with no effect on the disposition of the masses. The continued Turkish denial and inflammatory statements by government officials fuels the conflict. Is healing ever possible after a catastrophe of that magnitude?

Hope is a virtue and despair is a vice. So, I want to end this presentation on an optimistic note.

Human biology tells us that the human species operates on a primitive, reptilian brain, in which violence is a dominant behavioral pattern. It is only culture that can counteract and suppress that part of the human brain. Turkey has taken big strides in terms of culture and civilization. There is hope that this change predominant in intellectual levels will affect both the lower echelon of the society, the mass of Turkish population, as well as the political exigencies of the ruling circle. Then, it is plausible that both sides may engage in the process of healing with genuine resolve to remedy the historical scar inflicted on the souls of both Armenians and Turks.

Notes for Chapter 2

1. Because of these invasions that were coupled with looting, murder, and destruction, during this period, Armenia came out devastated. The ruling class of *Nakharars* (nobles or lords) vanished except for pockets of mountainous and hard-to-reach areas. The settlements of the newcomers, mostly nomadic, in the Armenian plateau and exodus of groups of Armenians fleeing the horrors of the invaders changed the demography of the region. Armenians were a majority hardly anywhere in the predominantly Armenian populated Armenia. Gradually, Asia Minor from east to west with Armenian and Greek Christian population had become Turkish and Muslim.

2. For a brief survey of the situation in Armenia, Armenian life during the Seljuk and Mongol eras, the 14th century invasions of the Timurids, as well as the emergence of Crypto-Christianity among those who were converted to Islam but secretly practiced Christianity, see Robert Bedrosian, "Armenia during the Seljuk and Mongol Period," pp. 241-71, in *The Armenian People from Ancient to Modern Times*, volume I, Richard G. Hovannisian, editor (New York: St. Martin's Press, 1997).

3. See Dickran Kouymjian, "Armenia from the Fall of Cilician kingdom (1375) to the Forced Emigration under Shah Abbas (1604)" in *The Armenian People from Ancient to Modern Times*, volume II, Richard G. Hovannisian, editor (New York: St. Martin's Press, 1997), p. 22.

4. Examples of famous men of Armenian origin, gathered through the *Devshirme* as young children and brought up as Muslims, are architect Sinan, mid18th century, and Grand Vizier Khalil of Kayseri, early 17th century. See ibid., p. 47.

5. For a brief discussion of the Revolution by the Young Turks (the Ittihad ve Terrakki Party) that reached Constantinople on July 23, 1908, see Christopher J. Walker, *Armenia, The Survival of a Nation* (New York: St. Martin's Press, 1980), pp. 181-82.

6. For a detailed analysis of Zabel Esayan's response to the massacres of Cilician Armenians, see Rubina Peroomian, *Literary Responses to Catastrophe, A Comparison of the Armenian and Jewish Experiences* (Atlanta, Georgia: Scholars Press, 1993), pp. 89-116.

7. Zapel Esayan, *Namakner* (Letters), ed. Arpik Avetisian (Yerevan: Yerevan University Press, 1977), pp. 76-77.

8. See Christopher J. Walker, *Armenia, The Survival of a Nation*, pp. 182-88.

9. Esayan, *Letters*, pp. 93-94

10. Zapel Esayan, *Averaknerun mej* (Amid the ruins), multiple editions since 1909 (Beirut: Ervan Press, 1957), p. 40.

11. Ibid., p. 169.

12. Ibid., pp. 126-27.

13. For a detailed analysis of Suren Partevian's response to the massacres of Cilician Armenians, see Peroomian, *Literary Responses to Catastrophe,* pp. 117-150.

14. Suren Partevian, *Kilikian arhavirke* (The Cilician catastrophe) (Constantinople: Neshan Papikian Bookstore, 1909), p. 34.

15. Ibid., p. 169.

16. Ibid., p. 200.

17. For a detailed analysis of Hagop Oshagan's response to the Armenian Genocide, see Peroomian, *Literary Responses to Catastrophe,* pp. 173-215.

18. Hagop Oshagan, *Kayseragan haghtergutiun* (Imperial song of triumph), ed. Boghos Snapian (Beirut: Altapress, 1983), p. 27. This collection of five stories about the massacres of 1915 was first published in *Chakatamart* Armenian periodical in 1920 in Constantinople.

19. Ibid., p. 31.

20. Hagop Oshagan, *Mnatsordats* (Remnants), volume II (Cairo: Husaber Press, 1933), p. 192.

21. Hagop Oshagan, *Hamapatker arevmtahay grakanutian* (Panorama of Western Armenian literature), volume 9, (Antilias, Lebanon: The Cilician Catholicosate Press, 1980), p. 278.

22. Hagop Oshagan, *Hamapatker arevmtahay grakanutian* (Panorama of Western Armenian literature), volume10, Oshagan about himself (Antilias, Lebanon: The Cilician Catholicosate Press, 1982), pp. 8-9.

23. Oshagan, *Panorama*, volume 9, p. 279.

24. *Remnants*, volume II, p. 381.

25. Ibid.

26. Ibid., p. 417.

27. "The 8 stages of Genocide," Classification, Symbolization, Dehumanization, Organization, Polarization, Preparation, Extermination, Denial, originally presented as a briefing paper at the US State Department in 1996, by Gregory H. Stanton, President, Genocide Watch. Stanton has since expanded the stages into ten to read, Classification, Symbolization, Discrimination, Dehumanization, Organization, Polarization, Preparation, Persecution, Extermination, Denial. See http://genocidewatch.org/genocide/tenstagesofgenocide.html

28. Frustrated and angered by the continuous Turkish denial of the Armenian Genocide, disappointed by the world's silence, and seeing the predicament of diasporan Armenians on the verge of total assimilation and extinction, some groups of young Armenians unleashed a series of attacks on Turkish diplomats and institutions. These acts of assassination and destruction aimed to revenge the murder of their forefathers

from the indifferent and denying descendants of the murderers and to draw world attention to the Armenian Question, urging the recognition of the Armenian Genocide. These acts gave rise to various interpretations in the world news services. Some considered them as acts of Armenian freedom fighters demanding justice. Others labeled them as terrorism. The Turkish government, on the other hand, uses these incidents to teach the world about yet another show of Armenian brutality and treachery against the Turks.

29. Israel Charny, "Templates for Gross Denial of a Known Genocide: A Manual," in *The Encyclopedia of Genocide*, volume 1, page 168. The twelve ways to deny a genocide are the following, 1. Question and minimize the statistics. 2. Attack the motivations of the truth-tellers. 3. Claim that the deaths were inadvertent. 4. Emphasize the strangeness of the victims. 5. Rationalize the deaths as the result of tribal conflict. 6. Blame "out of control" forces for committing the killings. 7. Avoid antagonizing the genocidists, who might walk out of "the peace process." 8. Justify denial in favor of current economic interests. 9. Claim that the victims are receiving good treatment. 10. Claim that what is going on doesn't fit the definition of genocide. 11. Blame the victims. 12. Say that peace and reconciliation are more important than blaming people for genocide.

CHAPTER 3

Translation and Representation of the Armenian Genocide in Literature and Film

SONA HAROUTYUNIAN[1]

This chapter represents a portion of my work in progress concentrating on Italian Armenian writer Antonia Arslan's genocide narrative "Skylark Farm." I shall first focus on the literary genre as an instrument, which brings greater attention to the historical phenomenon of the Armenian Genocide. With the projection of some exclusive documents we'll have a unique chance to "visit the backstage" of the novel and I'd like to thank my dear friend Antonia Arslan for leaving at my disposal her family relics: some photos and documents for my research. Then we will discuss the dramatized version of "Skylark Farm" by the Italian directors the Taviani brothers and finally we will explore and problematize the power of translation related to the Genocide narrative.

The aim of the paper will be to analyze the different effects that each medium (literature-translation-cinema) may have on the experience of its readers and audience: what that medium is trying to cultivate, the limitations of each and how each of them in different ways brings greater attention to the historical phenomenon of the Armenian Genocide.

One of the consequences of the Armenian Genocide was the scattering of those who survived into a global Diaspora. Traumatized, impoverished, forced exiles and immigrants in a new land, they struggled to live.

---

1. My special thanks go to the Knights of Vartan Fund for Armenian Studies, co-administered by the National Association for Armenian Studies and Research (NAASR), to the Armenian Communities Department of Gulbenkian Foundation and to the Society for Armenian Studies for providing me with partial travel grants which enabled me to participate in this important conference.

Part of their survival strategy was to write what they had experienced and witnessed. The immigrants, despite all the trauma and difficulties, decided to put pen to paper to document that which the world needed to better know. These important survivor memoirs emerged, often in isolation, in small print runs, and sometimes as unpublished manuscripts. They emerged in a variety of locales and conditions that characterized the global Diaspora. These Diaspora fragments spread Armenian culture and seeds across differing landscapes. In so doing, the Armenian identity evolved, becoming more diverse and complex and contributing to an emerging multiculturalism in the 20th and 21st centuries.

The survivor memoirs provided and continue to provide an invaluable research tool not only for scholars but also for Genocide fiction writers who take insights from those stories and, under thousands of literary flavors, offer the reader the historical dimension of the Armenian Genocide . One of these works is the Italian-Armenian novelist Antonia Arslan's Genocide novel *La Masseria de/le allodole* [Skylark Farm] (Arslan, 2004).

Skylark Farm belongs to a genre that mixes autobiography and biography, history and fiction, documentary and memory. First of all Arslan introduces her grandfather Yerwant, 53, an important physician living in his adopted Italian hometown of Padua in the months before WWI.

> ... his mother, Iskuhi, the little princess, died at nineteen giving birth to him. My great-grandfather then remarried an "evil stepmother," who bore him many other children; my grandfather couldn't stand her, and so, at the age of thirteen, he requested and was granted permission to leave the little city and go to Venice, to study at Moorat-Raphael, the boarding school for Armenian children. (Arslan, 2006, p. 17)

Yerwant never returned home. Now, after 40 years, he hopes to reunite with his brother Sempad, a successful pharmacist, who continued living in his little city in Anatolia.

> In 1915, Yerwant enters his fiftieth year, and he is satisfied and alone... "I am now a citizen of Italy; the Ottomans can't touch me any more," he thinks. (Arslan, 2006, p. 45)

But WWI ignites, and the ruling Young Turk party closes the border and when, on May 24, 1915, Italy enters the war, Yerwant's dream vanishes. He will never see again his family as they will be exterminated almost entirely by the Young Turks.

From that moment on for Yerwant the far Fatherland remained forever closed in a cloud and when his children got older Yerwant would even change their name. Antonia Arslan talks about a contradiction in the behavior of her grandfather: at first he did not want to deny his ancestry, giving his children four Armenian names each: Yetward Erwand Armenak Vardan and Khayel Anton Aram Maryam, but later tried to erase their origin:

> And in 1924, he will petition the Italian government to allow him to legally remove from his surname that embarrassing three-letter suffix, –*ian,* that exposes so plainly his Armenian origin. (Arslan, 2006, p. 160)

Here we as readers witness familiar historical narratives-perhaps we share similar ones, perhaps we have read first-hand accounts in books. But, what happens when a historical event penetrates into literature? First of all, the literary genre becomes a powerful medium that calls major attention from the masses on the historical phenomenon. By reconstructing her family history, Arslan is merging both historical research and imagination from a collective memory; she also becomes the protector of her familial memory and historical archive.

Taking a clue from Bella Brodzki's idea that "Culture's necessarily overarching orientation toward the future only obtains by sharing its past," (Brodzki, 2007, p. 113) I conducted an experiment on collective memory and testimony in an assignment I gave to my students at California State University, Fresno, in which they were called to write the story of their ancestors' survival. Most of them said to me, "I know something about my great grandparents, but I'm missing a lot of details. What should I do?" This is exactly what I was hoping for, and advised them to fill in the gaps with their imagination while taking advantage of asking their parents and grandparents. As evidenced by Brodzki "Thinking both psychoanalytically and historically also means that while we harbor the dream of plentitude, we always begin with a gap." (Brodzki, 2007, p. I 13)

In order to fulfill the assignment, some of them contacted relatives living in other countries to inquire about their grandparents and, as we shared as a class, we heard some amazing stories.[2] This assignment contributed in raising their personal awareness of their ancestors' voyages towards refuge.

Antonia Arslan has done the same in filling in the gaps of an unknown past. The geography, the places and the itineraries that she describes in her novel reveal not only significant moments of family history but also its inclusion in a determinate social space and national history. This is important because it gives the *historical* part to "historical fiction."

In yet another class assignment, based on the concept of Rushdie's "translated man," students together wrote the names of their ancestors' native cities and villages, as well as the places through which they passed on their long journeys of emigration before reaching the United States.[3] We also included in the map the languages they had learnt along the way. This initial exercise helped the students in order to visualize, re-realize and appreciate both their ancestors' geographical passages and their (the students) indelible connection to them. Further, the act of writing it on the board—taking the pen in hand—implicated them as the bearers and maintainers of their ancestral memories. I have always been obsessively diligent throughout my academic carrier to erase the board after any given lesson. However, what was created on the board that day was an interwoven tapestry of names, places, times and languages that neither my students nor I even dared to erase. The memory seemed at once too fresh and validated yet again. So, we decided to leave it so. I took a picture before the next instructor could "erase our ancestors," preserving this image at least through another medium, if not the word, the image.

In the same way, Antonia Arslan's undertaking the mission of retelling the story continues the voyage of her ancestors. So, through the

2. Some of these stories are already published in the newspaper *Hye Shal':/100111(Fresno2013* 35/1 ,2).

3. In his book of essays *Imaginary Homelands* Salman Rushdie asserts, "Having been borne across the world, we are translated men. It is normally supposed that something always gets lost in translation; I cling, obstinately to the notion that something can also be gained" (Rushdie, 1992, p. 17).

pen of Antonia Arslan, the Armenian Genocide is carried beyond its historical limits, slipping from the desks of historians and entering the minds and imaginations of ordinary people. Of course, when an historical event becomes literature it is enriched with new shades and colors. New heroes are born, given names, and assigned identities. Families are created belonging to one nationality or to the other that are placed in this or that social class. Here comes into play the literary fiction. And she weaves the plot. Through a love story, a common conversation in the home, or between neighbors, and through a description of a relationship between individuals of two different nationalities (such as the Armenian and Turkish) or minorities (Armenians and Greeks), Arslan introduces the historical dimension to the story.

A sentence from the prologue that was also put on the book cover reads:

> My aunt always used to say: When I've finally had it with you, when you got too mean, I'm leaving. I'll go stay with Arussiag in Beirut, with Uncle Zareh in Aleppo, with Philip and Mildred in Boston, with my sister Nevart in Fresno, with Ani in NY, or even with Cousin Michel in Copacabana—him last, though, because he married an Assyrian. (Arslan, 2006, p. 5)

With this sentence, the author introduces the complex phenomenon of the Armenian Diaspora created by the Armenian Genocide. When a non-Armenian reader, completely ignorant of not only the essence but also the existence of the Armenian Genocide, buys the book for its literary value, reading the above- mentioned sentence may lead to a question; How can a single person, Antonia's aunt, have so many relatives around the world? The answer will come after reading the book.

The Genocide narrative *Skylark Farm* has been translated into 15 languages; the translations have been executed according to the standard ways when a publisher decides to commission a book's translation. However, the book's Hungarian edition bears a strange phenomenon that strikes one at first as quite odd; it was published in Romania instead of Hungary. When I found this out, I was eager to discover the reason for it. Here is the explanation from the releaser: "As you perhaps know," she said, "Hungary still does not recognize the Armenian Genocide. The publishers I contacted simply did not respond to my proposal—to publish the Hungarian version of Skylark farm."

While I was in Budapest for a conference, I met the releaser and asked her about the impact and the translation's contribution on raising awareness in Hungary. She replied:

> The majority of the people I gave the book as a present and they shared it with their friends said that by reading it for the first time, they were able to understand what the Armenian Genocide meant. They usually had knowledge about the Jewish Holocaust, but not about the Armenian one—at least, the younger generation did not know anything about it. The mother of a friend of mine was revolted, and cried, "why are people in Hungary not informed about all of this, and why is this not included in the history classes at the school?"

Now, some of my personal thoughts about the Genocide novel as an Armenian experience and as the Armenian translator of Antonia Arslan's Genocide narratives.

In 2004, when I read the *Skylark Farm* in one sitting, I could not imagine that three years later I would have the honor of being the Armenian translator of this best-seller. I was too involved emotionally in the story. I was feeling a kind of duty to make the story available to Armenians. I was often skipping lunch; I was so immersed in the book and its characters that I was almost ashamed to take a break to eat, while they were there, walking along the dusty roads of Anatolia, hungry and exhausted, destroyed by deportation. It seemed that they were beckoning me to tell their story because they desperately wanted to be heard. When I arrived at the episode that recounts the horrific massacre at the Farm I was completely blocked as it was too hard to switch myself off emotionally and think about the *word order* of the sentence or make a choice of *adjectives* when the plot was describing the murder of the little boys in front of their mother. After a while, emotionally drained, I decided to skip those passages and return to them once I completed the book.

I finally managed to keep my promise, finishing the book before the screening of the film, which took place July 10, 2007, at the opening of the Golden Apricot Film Festival in Yerevan. (Arslan, 2007)

In the translation I have maintained the foreign expressions in Turkish, French, and English used by the author in the Italian text, because it was worth reviving in Armenian those expressive nuances, especially taking into account that these terms not only characterized precisely the cultural environment of that generation during the Genocide, but also were a part of the characters' everyday lives. So I completely preserved foreign words in transliteration, inserting notes to facilitate the comprehension and reading.

Film adaptation.

Every book has its birth story and analogously every film has its birth story. When the Italian film directors and screenwriters, the Taviani Brothers, proposed Antonia Arslan to dramatize *Skylark Farm,* there was also a strong interest from Hollywood in acquiring the movie rights. But Arslan was aware that in the past the several attempts to produce a Hollywood film on the Armenian Genocide were blocked. She knew that prominent directors and actors throughout the decades have attempted to produce the film based on Franz Werfel's novel *Forty Days of Musa Dagh,* but they had no success.[4] Hence, she agreed to the Taviani Brothers' suggestion.

The Taviani Brothers announced right in the beginning that the film would have been freely inspired from *Skylark Farm,* i.e. the plot would have been relatively the same but the directors had the right to change something or make additions and in fact they editorialized, accessorized the film, and inserted fictional material in the movie like love episodes, etc. This is quite normal because, even if it originates from a novel, the filmmaker translates to film his perception/translation of the fiction. Naturally there is always the matter of fidelity of the film to the novel, generally expressed as a function of adequacy and acceptability, whereby the former is more or less what we mean by equivalence, and the latter is more or less what we mean by believability to the audience. Many readers watch movies based on books they have read and come out disdainful,

4. According to *Variety* magazine, *The Forty Days of Musa Dagh* has become "the most on-again and off-again motion picture production in Hollywood history." (Torosyan, 2012)

because so many parts of the story are cut out. As readers, we search for mistakes and sometimes disregard whether the movie was nicely directed, produced, etc. I think we should never compare them, but rather consider each genre separately.

When a book is translated into a movie some questions arise. One of the first questions is to ask about the genre (documentary, drama, historical narrative, etc.) that the filmmaker has chosen since each film genre will create a different kind of viewing experience for an audience. The film's genre is drama, based on a historical novel, so the goal is to awaken curiosity, interest, even engagement in an historical event; the limitations and strengths of the film adaptation are evident in the selection of passages from the novel, the cinematic treatment of those passages, the omission of passages, etc. This reflection leads into the relationship of the source (novel) and the target (film) and opens up such questions as what other source modeling material is evident in the film? In fact, the Tavianis not only cut episodes from the novel but also added events. There is an episode in the film which recalls a passage from another Genocide narrative by Alice Tachdjian, "Stones on the Heart," published in Italy. In the book there is a scene of two women forced to dispose of a child by suffocating it back to back (Tachdjian, 2003).

The film is a Spanish co-production and the Spanish actress Paz Vega is a central character in the movie. Even the Spanish translation of the movie *Skylark Farm* is entitled *El Destina di Nunik* as she interprets Nunik's role.[5] In fact when the film had just come out, some Armenians were concerned that the filmmaker had inserted a double love story of Nunik for two Turkish officers (interpreted by two handsome actors, the Italian Alessandro Preziosi, and the German actor Moritz Bleibtreu). In her novel Arslan has one love story.

> A change I dislike in the film is Nunik's second romance with a Turkish soldier, one who is helping lead a caravan of Armenian women to their death in Syria, *wrote one of my students at California State University Fresno in his final paper.* I feel like Nunik must have a very deep case

5. This role is *A=niv* in the book and unlike the film is not a central character in the volume.

> of Stockholm Syndrome, as she seems to only fall in love with Turkish soldiers. Besides catering to fans of romance movies I can't understand why this change was made. It almost seems to pander to a Turkish audience by showing a sympathetic Turkish participant in the Genocide, who we're meant to feel sorry for because he doesn't really want to be there. Was he added to make any Turk watching feel less guilty? Obviously, the Turkish audience for this movie would be small if not nonexistent, so the addition of this character is puzzling. The two characters are both serving the same purpose as a sympathetic perpetrator and love interest, so it would make a lot more sense to merge them together, from a storytelling perspective. As it is, the second Turkish soldier is redundant at best and raises a lot of unfortunate implications.

From my perspective, the film works especially well for the audience with little or no knowledge about the Armenian Genocide. By contrast, Armenians, more aware of the Genocide, can have more mixed sensations, either of gratitude towards the filmmakers or critically judging the accuracy, as we saw above. A completely unaware person, however, begins to learn about the historical phenomenon of the Armenian Genocide.

The filmmakers managed to have an excellent cast with Paz Vega, Moritz Bleibtreu, Alessandro Preziosi, Angela Molina, Arsine Khanjian, Mohammed Bakri, Tcheky Karyo, Andre Dussollier, Laura Efrikian, etc. The Tavianis testified in one of their interviews that the actors were not only involved professionally but also emotionally. According to the directors, after watching the whole film for the first time, the Turkish-born Greek Jewish actor Tcheky Karyo had burst into tears and when he got quiet he said that he had not only watched the tragedy that they had interpreted, but he had also seen his Jewish uncle and grandfather. So in the imagination of the actor Karyo the Armenian Genocide and the Jewish Holocaust suddenly had crossed.

When we ask about the effect of a film, we are dealing with the rhetorical and artistic purposes of the film, i.e. we are probing into the film's *skopos* or purpose with regard to audience. A novel would have similar artistic and rhetorical purposes, but executed along different lines since the experience of reading a novel is stretched out over several hours if not days while the experience of viewing a film is usually contained in under two hours. This is a very important point, as movies usually reach a larger audience, and sometimes viewing a massacre with your own eyes might prove more powerful than reading about it. The grammar, syntax, and vocabulary of film create meaning in their own right but also invite the audience to make meaning out of the viewing experience. Film has the potential to be an excellent tool to raise awareness about a historical event in less than two hours to an audience of hundreds of thousands.

When, in 2006, the Taviani brothers were shooting the film, their desire was to see their movie circulating in the schools. Today their goal is fulfilled as the film is shown in many Italian schools mainly among the students of the 8th grade year when they learn about World War I and students in the last year of high school.

The directors' intention was to raise awareness about the Armenian Genocide and show the world the need to stop such crimes against humanity from reoccurring.

Conclusion

In her novel, by reconstructing her family history, Arslan is merging both historical research and the imagination from a collective memory. Historical research and imagination that have both been brought together by a *collective* memory are very important even independently, and the merger of them all is quite fascinating, especially with regards to the *collective.* And the consequence of the novel is a sort of catharsis for Antonia and her family as she becomes both receptacle and protector. Here we can also call into question the very genre of art and literature, depending on the author's intention. For example, "art for art's sake" or art for a social cause, or testimony for catharsis. Literature and testimony are different, and then there is the literature of testimony, which is another genre all together. Why is the "literature of testimony" an actual genre? And further, even if it is not exactly Arslan's testimony but a re-telling of a re-telling, Arslan's text is a literature of testimony.

Finally, in *Skylark Farm,* through the research of original documents and acts of post-memory, the author unites her present to the lost world of her family, and in this way strengthens her roots and anchors her identity.

Antonia Arslan's Genocide narrative with its 36 editions in Italy alone, where the Armenian community has only 2,000 members, has sold over 500, 000 copies to an Italian readership for the most part previously unaware of the Armenian Genocide.

However, it is through the power of translation into fifteen languages that *Skylark Farm* has surpassed the borders of Italy taking the knowledge of the Armenian Genocide throughout the globe and thereby contributing to its "afterlife"—to use the word of Walter Benjamin (1999)—as well as its cinematic rendering to a global audience.

Bibliography

Arslan, A. (2004). *La masseria delle allodole.* Milano: Rizzoli.

Benjamin, W. (1999). The Task of Translator: An introduction to the translation of Brodzki, B. (2007). *Can These Bones Live? Translation, Survival, and Cultural Memory* . Stanford: Mieke Bal and Hent de Vries.

Rushdie, S. (1992). *Imaginary Homelands: Essays and Criticism 1981-1991.* New York: Penguin Books.

Tachdjian, A. (2003). *Pietre sul cuore.* Milano: Sperling & Kupfer Editori S.p.A.
Torosyan, L. (2012, October 5). *New Documentary on 'The Forty Days of Musa Dagh' and Hollywood.* Retrieved from Armenian Weekly: http://www .armenianweeklv. com/20 I 2/ I 0/05/ new-documentary-on-the-forty-da v s-of musa-dagh-and-holly\\ ood/

Part II

Past or Future?

CHAPTER 4

The Armenian Genocide as Jihad

RICHARD RUBENSTEIN

There is a 1919 silent film about the Armenian genocide, "Ravished Armenia," originally produced in Hollywood using Turkish documentary footage. It was based on a book by a survivor, Aurora Mardiganian, who also starred in the production. The film originally consisted of nine reels, most of which have been lost. Recently, a twenty-minute clip was found that contains brief scenes of many of the incidents that took place during the genocide. [1]

Although low-definition, there is one terrible scene toward the end of the clip that is especially difficult to watch. Seldom, if ever, have I viewed a film scene that matches this one in sadistic obscenity. It is a crucifixion scene, but unlike Christian images of Christ on the cross that express symbolically the triumph of eternal life over evanescent human pain, this film's crucifixion scene carried a very different symbolic meaning. There are eight crosses in a row to which are nailed eight naked, young Armenian women. After the film offers a panoramic view of all of the crosses and their victims, it focuses on a single sufferer. Nailed to the cross, she is helplessly alive. One could tell by her eyes and facial movements that her cognitive functions were unimpaired as she *awaited the painful doom of her crucifixion.*

In this writer's opinion, that scene symbolically expressed much that the Turks wanted to convey about their behavior towards both the Armenians and their religion. In 1915, there were no pocket-sized cell phones with high-definition video capabilities. Motion picture cameras were heavy instruments and the terrible scenes of the deportations, confiscations, sadistic brutality, rapine, outright murder of helpless Armenians, and the crucifixion of the Armenian maidens could not have been filmed without the involvement and consent of Turkish authorities.

The perpetrators took the most sacred symbol of Christendom and turned it into a blasphemous obscenity, symbolically proclaiming absolute Muslim dominance. Nevertheless, something else was involved: women are the child bearers. Their wombs carry the next generation. No words were necessary. The message was clear: "We express our utter contempt for you and your religion. We intend to destroy your future. You have no human rights. We can do with you whatever we wish."

Nevertheless, shortly after the film was released, Turks apparently had second thoughts about what could be made available publically. Since then, for almost a century, Turkish governments have vehemently rejected the charge that Turks committed *genocide* against the Armenians. The most Turks have been willing to acknowledge is that *both* the Turks and Armenians inflicted war time harm on each other, thereby arguing for moral equivalence between Turkish genocidal violence and rare instances of Armenian defensive action. Admitting that there were massacres, Turkish authorities have insisted that the number of Armenians killed has nevertheless been greatly exaggerated.[2] Moreover, in spite of the publication of a host of well-documented eye-witness reports and testimonies, Turkish governments have used their diplomatic influence to prevent governments, such as the United States, the United Kingdom, Israel, and others, from taking any action that would validate the Armenian claim that a nearly successful attempt to exterminate the Armenians of the Ottoman empire took place during the first World War.[3]

Admittedly, the subject is complex, but I concur with the overwhelming weight of scholarly opinion that affirms that genocide did take place. Yet while concurring with the judgment of groups such as the International Association of Genocide Scholars, my interest lies elsewhere: *In view of the fact that post-war German governments have acknowledged the role of National Socialist Germany in planning and implementing the extermination of Europe's Jews, why have successive Turkish governments refused to tread a similar path with regard to the Armenian victims?*

Briefly stated, while steadfastly denying that genocide took place, Turkish governments have also implied that, no matter how terrible Turkish behavior may have been, no crime was committed and the actions taken against the Armenians were fully justified. This is not the view that the Turkish government has publicly expressed. Nevertheless, no other view appears able to explain the consistent behavior of the Turkish governments for almost a century.

In order to understand why, we must turn to the realm of religion in addition to politics and military affairs. This suggestion is in accord with the first words in Vahakn N. Dadrian's magisterial study of the Armenian genocides. Dadrian begins: "As a first step toward a full analysis of the nationality conflicts [in the Ottoman Empire], it is necessary to examine Islam as a major determinant in the genesis and escalation of these conflicts."[4]

As is well known, the Ottoman Empire was governed as a theocratic state at the apex of which stood the Sultan, both the supreme head of state and, for Sunni Muslims, the Caliph and, as such, the successor to the Prophet and supreme protector of Islam.

Moreover, Islam was an indispensable part of Turkish personal and national identity, even for those members of the Turkish elite who were unaware of the extent to which they were influenced by their own religious inheritance. According to Turkish historian, Taner Akcam, "...the Turks, as a ruling stratum (even though they themselves were not conscious of their Turkishness) , and under the influence of Islamic thought, identified themselves with Islam and felt themselves superior to the empire's other religious groups. The idea of the "ruling nation" (*Millet-i Hakime*) dominated the thinking of the Ottoman-Turkish ruling elite." [5]

According to Dadrian, the Young Turks or Ittihad, the Committee of Union and Progress, that gained power in 1908 and consolidated that power in 1913, were not "followers of the tenets of Islam." Dadrian adds, "While the Ittihad continued to run the State largely as a theocracy, its leaders were personally atheists and agnostics."[6]

Nevertheless, although the ruling elite had a very elevated opinion of themselves and their empire in comparison with neighbors whom they had once dominated, the actual situation of the Empire throughout the nineteenth century was one of decline and defeat at the hands of European Christian powers and their own Christian subject people. One can argue that the process of decline began with the Ottoman defeat at Vienna in 1683. It accelerated in the nineteenth century when Greece (1820), Serbia (1867), and Romania (1878) gained their independence. In addition, Turkey lost Libya to Italy in the Italo-Turkish War of 1911-12 and was defeated in the Albanian Revolt of 1912. The European borders of the Ottoman Empire shrank and those of their formerly Christian subjects expanded. There was a painful dissonance between the Young Turk image of themselves as leaders of the "ruling nation" and what was happening to their nation.

Another series of humiliations came from the Capitulations, a series of treaties or contracts between European powers, especially France, and the Ottoman Empire in which the Empire limited its jurisdiction over those Christians domiciled in the Empire who were the subjects of Christian rulers. In general, traders and later other foreigners were exempt from local prosecution, taxation, conscription, and the searching of their homes. Initially, such treaties were not seen as humiliations although they did constitute a limitation on Ottoman sovereignty but by the beginning of the twentieth century they were seen as such. After World War I, they were finally abolished.

According to Taner Akcam, an important Turkish scholar who teaches at Clark University, the second half of the nineteenth century witnessed a new problem for the Ottoman Empire: There was a very large in-migration of Muslim refugees from territories recently lost by the Ottoman state. There were also expulsions and the Muslim immigrants had nowhere else to go. While the Ottoman state was shrinking, the number of Muslim immigrants had become a serious demographic problem. The problem peaked in the 1912-13 Balkan wars, not long before the genocide was initiated in 1915.

Akcam adds that until then, the Ottoman government solved its immigration problem on an ad hoc basis but, in keeping with the modernizing and rationalizing bias of the Committee of Union and Progress, they decided to solve the problem systematically as part of a plan for the "homogenization" of Anatolia.[7] In effect, plans for homogenization meant that Christians would either be expelled in a population exchange program, such as took place between Turkey and Greece, largely after the war, or the unwanted population would be exterminated, as happened with the Armenians.

Unlike most Armenian scholars, Akcam had access to Turkish archives and found that before World War I, the Committee of Union and Progress had already formulated a detailed, rational plan "to free [themselves] of non-Turkish elements" in the Aegean region. When the war came, they were fully prepared to implement their project of "ethno-religious homogenization" of Anatolia.

At this point, I would suggest a word of caution. Suny and other scholars have argued that the predominant motive for the murderous homogenization project was nationalism and there is no doubt that radical nationalism played a part. Nevertheless, I would argue that the most important motivation for the monumental "ethnic cleansing" projects was religious and specifically a consequence of the unchanging nature of certain aspects of Islam.

Although the official religion of the Ottoman Empire was Islam, over the centuries the empire had conquered a number of non-Muslim nations. This resulted in a double problem: The empire was thinly spread and many of the subjugated nations had skills that the conquering Muslims needed but did not possess. The problem was solved by a system of structural inequality that has persisted wherever Islam has been dominant.

According to Dadrian, the fundamental common law principle governing the relations between Muslim and non-Muslim subjects was a quasi-legal contract, the *Akdi Zimmet* (contract with the ruling nationality), in which the sovereign guaranteed non-Muslim subjects the safety of "their persons, their civil and religious liberties, and, conditionally, their property in exchange for the payment of poll and land taxes, and acquiescence to a set of social and legal disabilities"[8]

In reality, the *Akdi Zimmet* was in spirit and substance the *dhimma,* the Muslim pact of submission that terminated the state of war with Christians, Jews, and Zoroastrians and stipulated the conditions under which the subjugated "peoples of the book" were permitted domicile in Islamic lands.[9] *Strictly speaking, Islamic tradition envisages no such thing as enduring peace between faithful Muslims and infidels.* There can be a truce when combat appears unlikely to succeed or when it serves Muslim convenience. There could also be conditional toleration in a multi-national, multi-religious empire based on an hierarchical gradation of status, such as the Ottoman in which the distinctions of rulers and ruled, Muslims and non-Muslim, were strictly maintained.[10] This arrangement worked well until the nineteenth century when intervention by European powers,

England, France, and Russia, that had provided a system of extraterritorial rights for their citizens living and trading in the Ottoman Empire, became a source of Turkish resentment.

There had also been an hierarchical gradation of status in Christian Europe, but under the influence of the Enlightenment and the French Revolution, there was a definite move toward equality of legal, if not social, status in the countries of western Europe and the United States in which law was not thought of as unchanging in character or divine in origin.

This does not mean that there were no forces for change in Islamic law. There were, but the agency of change was interpretation by recognized scholarly authorities who maintained the fiction of an unchanging law while change was effected through casuistry and interpretation. There was, incidentally, a comparable phenomenon in traditional rabbinic law.

There was, however, one area in which interpretation could change nothing, the legally enforced social, religious, and political inferiority of non-Muslims to Muslims. Nor did this change when the modernizing Young Turks, the Committee of Union and Progress, took power in 1908. Although some Christians were under the mistaken impression that the Young Turks favored an Ottoman polity based upon equality of status, they were quickly disabused of the notion. The Young Turks were as committed, as were their predecessors, to the idea of Muslims as the ruling nation and non-Muslims as, at best, tolerated infidels. In reality, the defeats suffered by the Ottoman Empire made them, if anything, more committed to the idea, so much so that they were willing to commit mass murder for it.

The idea of Muslims as the ruling nation is best understood by two related concepts, dhimmitude and dhimmi. According to Bat Ye'or, who has done much to acquaint western readers with the terms:

> Dhimmitude designates the civilizations of peoples conquered by jihad over the past thirteen centuries and subjected to shari'a law. A "dhimmi" is a non-Muslim belonging to the civilization of dhimmitude. Having surrendered to the armies of jihad, the dhimmi loses his territorial rights and his sovereignty, but in exchange he is protected by a contract (dhimma) against jihad—the obligatory and irrevocable war against

the infidels. This protection provides some relative security, conditioned upon a series of demeaning restrictions and discrimination."[11]

The Christians of the Ottoman Empire were all descendants of conquered peoples and were, as such, dhimmis. It made no difference that, in many cases, their ancestors had settled the land long before Muslim conquest. The Muslims were the conquerors and the Christians were the conquered peoples and were treated as such.

There was only one way a conquered person or community could achieve, at least theoretically, full equality with his or her overlords: conversion to Islam which made a person a member of the Muslim *umma* or nation. Not only did equal status depend on religion, so too did subordinate status. Put differently, personal and political status were religiously legitimated.

As Peter Balakian and other scholars have shown, the Christian population of the Ottoman Empire was both wealthier and better educated than the Muslim population. This is not an uncommon phenomenon where there is a system of structured inequality. Apart from land-owning and control of the peasantry, the personal characteristics valued by a dominant group are those that facilitate dominance, such as bureaucratic skills and military leadership. Money making skills that require advanced schooling, such as large-scale trading, finance, and commerce are looked down upon.

In the Ottoman Empire, Christians took advantage of the schools and colleges, largely established by American Protestant missionaries, or they sought training at European universities. As a result, they acquired the skills necessary for wealth, but they also became the objects of envy, resentment, and hostility.

During the nineteenth-century, Armenians tended to rise above the Turks economically. The more affluent sent their sons abroad to receive their education in a rapidly modernizing Europe. As Christians, they had links to Europe that were not available to the Muslim majority. Diaspora Armenians sent home remittances and brought back new machines and technology to their families in the empire. When the sale of Muslim lands to non-Muslims was permitted by the reforms of 1856, Armenians had the resources to buy up large landholdings, especially after 1870.[12]

This resulted in a reversal of status in a world newly oriented toward industry and commerce. Resentment was bitter and fed upon itself, so that Sultan Abdul Hamid II's efforts to undo the emancipatory reforms received widespread Muslim support.

A related source of Turkish resentment stemmed from the fact that the Armenians were a "market dominant minority."[13] As noted above, discriminated minorities, barred from service in the military or the state bureaucracy and subject to other forms of social and vocational discrimination, tend to rely on education and training for their economic survival and well-being to a much greater extent than do indigenous majorities. Such minorities are also likely to be concentrated in urban centers and to specialize in urban trades and crafts, finance, and the professions. Their capital consists in what is in their heads and is easily transportable. Often subject to expulsion, they formed diaspora networks that were intrinsically advantageous in both finance and commerce. This had been the case with the European Jews before World War II, the Chinese in Southeast Asia, the Lebanese in West Africa, and the Armenians in the Ottoman Empire.

During the first half of the nineteenth century, reformist sultans, such as Mahmud II (1789-1839) and Abdülmecid (1823-1861), as well as prominent European-educated Turkish bureaucrats, recognized that traditional religious and military institutions could no longer meet the needs of the modern empire. Among the changes introduced were universal conscription, and educational and institutional reforms. The measures were known as the Tanzimat reforms, the objective of which was the creation of a common Ottoman identity in the empire for Muslims and non-Muslims alike. The policy was initiated with the Imperial Rescript of the Rose Chamber of 1839 that stipulated that the different peoples within the empire were declared equal before the law. The reforms guaranteed the life, honor, and property of all Ottoman subjects, regardless of race or religion. In 1856, a second, expanded edict of reform asserted the equality of all Ottoman subjects, Muslim and non-Muslim.[14]

The era of reform came to an end shortly after the accession of Sultan Abdul Hamid II (1842-1918). The response, especially from the Armenians, was not long in coming. In the 1880s, Armenian exiles in Europe, influenced by western ideas about national self-determination and the "people" as the source of political legitimacy, began to campaign for national autonomy. The Armenians did not initially seek full political independence, but nationalism provided a powerful legitimation for separation from the multinational Ottoman Empire. As such, it was profoundly subversive of the imperial order. Armenian rebels in the Caucasus organized raids into Ottoman territory. While the vast majority of Armenians sought amelioration of their situation within the empire, by 1890, an Armenian Revolutionary Federation was established in Tiflis (Tbilisi, the capital of Georgia) that demanded Armenian freedom "with gun in hand."[15] In 1891, the Sultan responded by raising a force of Kurdish Muslim irregulars and sanctioning their predatory attacks on Armenians.[16] Within a year, the Kurds had formed cavalry units totaling 15,000 men. Assured of legal immunity, the Kurds attacked and spread terror among Armenians in the capital and the hinterland. In 1893 Armenian revolutionaries posted placards in many towns and cities calling on Muslims to rise up against the Sultan's oppression. Since, as noted, the Sultan was also the Caliph, combining the traditional functions of political and religious leadership, the Armenian challenge was seen by traditionalists as a radical breach of the *dhimma.*

Actual massacres first broke out in the summer of 1894 in Sasun in southern Armenia. Turkish authorities used Armenian resistance to a system of double taxation and officially sanctioned Kurdish violence and sexual abuse of Armenian women as a pretext for indiscriminate rape and slaughter.[17] News of the outrages quickly spread to Europe and Britain, France and Russia demanded a commission of inquiry. These same powers also sought to persuade the Ottoman government to adopt reforms in those provinces where most of the Armenians were domiciled. The Sultan made an empty show of accepting some reforms, although he had no intention of implementing them. In September, 1895, Armenians demonstrated in Constantinople in order to pressure the Sultan and the European powers to implement the reforms. The police and radical Muslim elements in the capital city responded with ten days of massacre and terror. About the same time, an unprovoked, premeditated massacre began in the city of Trebizond on the Black Sea (Adalian). The massacres then spread through almost every town with a significant number of Armenian inhabitants. There was nothing spontaneous about the massacres. They were in fact military operations that began and ended daily with the call of a bugle.[18]

The worst massacre occurred in the city of Urfa, known to the ancient world as Edessa, where Armenians constituted about a third of the population. In December 1895, after a two-month siege of the Armenian quarter, Armenian leaders gathered in their cathedral and requested official Turkish protection. The Turkish commander agreed but then surrounded the Cathedral of Urfa, after which Turkish troops and the mob rampaged through the Armenian quarter burning, looting, and killing all adult males. Two thousand five hundred Armenians were burned alive in the cathedral. Dadrian comments that *wherever possible the killing was done in such a way as to emphasize the religious nature of the deed.*[19] Lord Kinross describes the manner in which the slaughter was assimilated to a sacrificial ritual: "When a large group of young Armenians were brought before a sheikh, he had them thrown down on their backs and held by their hands and feet. Then, in the words of an observer, he recited verses of the Koran and "*cut their throats after the Mecca rite of sacrificing sheep.*"[20]

The mosques were places of incitement; the Christian churches served as slaughterhouses. Murderous mobs were urged on by their imams. The worst butchery often followed Friday services. Dadrian also comments on the importance of local religious authorities in the implementation of the massacres. The sultan in distant Constantinople could issue orders for the massacres, often framed in covert language, but the interpretation, planning, and implementation of such orders required the leadership of local authority figures. *Because of the empire's theocratic nature, local religious leaders* used their authority to assure the mob that the massacres were in accordance with the *Seriat* (*shari'a*).[21] With very few exceptions, the *muftis* [jurisconsults who dispensed formal legal opinions], *kadis* [magistrates and guardians of law and order], *ulemas* [Muslim theologians] *and mullahs* played a crucial role in conferring religious legitimacy.

The reactions of both the Muslim and non-Muslim populations were recorded by Cevet Papa, an astute observer and a high Ottoman official:

In accordance with this *ferman* [edict] Muslim and non-Muslim subjects were to be made equal in all rights. This had a very adverse effect on the Muslims. Previously, one of the four points adopted as the basis for peace agreements had been that certain privileges were accorded to

Christians on condition that these did not infringe on the sovereign authority of the government. Now the question of (specific) privileges lost its significance; in the whole range of government, the non-Muslims were forthwith to be deemed the equals of the Muslims. Many Muslims began to grumble: 'Today we have lost our sacred national rights, won by the blood of our fathers and forefathers. At a time when the Islamic *millet* was the ruling *millet,* it was deprived of this sacred right. This is a day of weeping and mourning for the people of Islam."

> As for the non-Muslims, this day, when they left the status of *raya* [*dhimmi*] and gained equality with the ruling *millet,* was a day of rejoicing. But the patriarchs and other spiritual chiefs were displeased, because their appointments were incorporated in the *ferman*. Another point was that whereas in former times, in the Ottoman state, the communities were ranked, with the Muslims first, then the Greeks, then the Armenians, then the Jews, now all of them were put on the same level. Some Greeks objected to this, saying: "The government has put us together with the Jews. We were content with the supremacy of Islam."
>
> As a result of all this, just as the weather was overcast when the *ferman* was read in the audience chamber, so the faces of most of those present were grim. Only on the faces of a few of our Frenchified gentry dressed in the garb of Islam could expressions of joy be seen. Some notorious characters of this type were seen and heard to say: 'If the non-Muslims are spread among the Muslims, neighborhoods will become mixed, the price of our properties will rise, and civilized amenities will expand.' On this account they expressed satisfaction.[22]

Even before Abdul Hamid II abolished the reforms, their likely negative consequences were already understood in 1856 by Grand Vizier, Mustafa Reşid Pasha (1800-1858), a brilliant diplomat. In a memorandum addressed to the sultan in the wake of the reforms of that year, Reşid foresaw the possibility of a "great slaughter" as a result of the efforts to establish the civic equality of all Ottoman subjects through legal enactment.[23]

Reşid's views were prescient. Muslim traditionalists regarded the emancipation of Jews and Christians as profoundly offensive. Before emancipation, payment of the *jizya*, the poll tax imposed upon all male *dhimmis,* symbolized their subjection, inferior status, and suspension of *jihad.* By voiding *dhimmi* disabilities, traditionalists believed the *dhimma* had been rendered null and void. In their eyes, *dhimmi* emancipation did not mean an end to civic disabilities but the *restoration of the state of war against the dhimmis.* Under the circumstances, the traditionalists believed that, at least in theory, the *umma*, the Muslim community, could commit any outrage against them.[24] Moreover, these actions were regarded "not only as justified but also as mandatory and even as praiseworthy"[25]

Peter Balakian has described one of the most agonizing disabilities imposed upon the Armenians because of their *dhimmi* status:

> Another burden solely for the Armenians was the *kishlak,* or winter-quartering obligation, which enabled Kurds and Turks to quarter themselves, their families, and their cattle in Armenian homes during the long winter months. The fact that the Kurdish way of life was nomadic and rough and the Armenian dwellings did not allow for much privacy made the intrusion unbearable, and knowing that the unarmed Armenians had neither physical nor legal recourse, a well-armed Kurd or Turk could not only steal his host's possessions but could rape or kidnap the women and girls of the household with impunity."[26]

In the 1880s, Armenian exiles in Europe, influenced by western ideas about national self-determination and the "people" as the source of political legitimacy, began to campaign for national autonomy. The Armenians did not initially seek full political independence, but nationalism provided a powerful legitimation for separation from the multinational Ottoman Empire. As such, it was profoundly subversive of the imperial order. Armenian rebels in the Caucasus also organized raids into Ottoman territory. The vast majority of Armenians sought amelioration of their situation within the empire, but, by 1890, an Armenian Revolutionary Federation was established in Tiflis (Tbilisi, the capital of Georgia) and demanded Armenian freedom "with gun in hand"[27] In 1891, the Sultan responded by raising a force of Kurdish Muslim irregulars and sanctioning their predatory attacks on Armenians.[28] Within a year, the Kurds had formed cavalry units totaling 15,000 men. Assured of legal immunity, the Kurds attacked and spread terror among Armenians in the capital and the hinterland. In 1893 Armenian revolutionaries posted placards in many towns and cities calling on Muslims to rise up against the Sultan's oppression. Since, as noted, the Sultan was also the Caliph, combining the traditional functions of political and religious leadership, the Armenian action was seen by traditionalists as a radical breach of the *dhimma.*

The massacres of 1894-1896 constituted an unprecedented level of violence on the part of the Ottoman Empire against one of its subject peoples. In spite of pressure from the Great Powers, Abdul Hamid II was clearly determined to frustrate Armenian hopes of reform. He also sought to crush any Armenian attempt to organize politically. Estimates of the number of dead range from 100,000 to 300,000. Tens of thousands emigrated; thousands were forcibly converted to Islam. Moreover, the Sultan understood that he could deal with his subjects with utter impunity because the Great Powers were more interested in good relations with his empire than the fate of a minority subject-people. From the sultan's point of view, the Armenians got what they deserved. *By seeking to overcome their religiously-defined subordinate status and seeking the help of foreign rulers, they had broken their contract of submission and had placed themselves in a state of war with his realm in which no violence, expropriation, or indignity was out of bounds as we see in the crucifixion of the eight Armenian maidens.*

Abdul Hamid's massacres can be characterized as pre-genocidal. The slaughter had irretrievably marginalized and dehumanized the Armenians. The massacres thus prepared the way for the full-scale genocide and ethnic homogenization perpetrated by the modernizing twentieth-century regime of the Committee of Union and Progress, the Young Turks.

Nevertheless, the political agenda of the Young Turks was different from the sultan's. They were a Turkish reform party that responded to the weakness of the Ottoman Empire as manifested in Austria-Hungary's annexation of Bosnia-Herzegovina in 1908, Italy's seizure of Libya and the island of Rhodes in 1912, the independence of Albania in 1912, and the Ottoman defeat in the First Balkan War of 1912-1913 that led to the loss of much of the Ottoman territory in Europe. Moreover, as noted, in the empire itself, Muslims had been losing ground to *dhimmi* minorities, the Greeks, Jews, and Armenians, who dominated the world of commerce and the professions. The Young Turks were modernizing, rationalizing "progressives" who understood, as did the Japanese elites at the time of the Meiji Reformation of 1866-1869, that, absent modernization, the independence and territorial integrity of their respective empires would be at risk.

In 1908, the Young Turks effectively overthrew Abdul Hamid II's traditionalist regime. In their initial enthusiasm, many Armenians made an understandable but deadly miscalculation. They assumed that the overthrow of an inefficient and corrupt traditional regime by one that was less corrupt and more rational augured well for their own community. The Young Turks had given public assurances of equal treatment of the empire's non-Muslim minorities, but the logic of their modernizing revolution made ethnic homogenization rather than diversity the almost inevitable political outcome.

The first generation of Turkish revolutionaries were divided on the issue of working with the Armenians, as was evident at the First Congress of the Ottoman Opposition that met in Paris in February, 1902. Some of the more liberal Young Turks thought that an alliance with the Armenians would get a favorable response from the Europeans. Armenian activists declared that cooperation with the Turkish revolutionaries was conditional on the implementation of reforms in the six Anatolian *vilayets* (provinces) with significant Armenian populations to be guaranteed by the European powers. The conditions were acceptable to the majority attending the Congress but were vehemently rejected by the nationalist minority. The latter regarded European support as wholly at odds with their fundamental objective, the creation of a strong, independent Ottoman realm in which the traditional status hierarchy would remain more or less intact. The views of the minority ultimately carried greater weight as they represented the dominant tendency among most Young Turk organizations and newspapers.[29]

According to Ronald Grigor Suny and other scholars, in the first decade of the twentieth century there was a shift by the Young Turks from what he characterizes as an "Ottomanist orientation" that emphasized the equality of the *millets* in a multinational society to a more Turkish nationalist position that stressed the predominance of the ethnic Turks over the subordinate communities that were regarded as "the protected flock of the Sultan," Armenian, Catholic, Jewish, and Orthodox.[30] Until World War I, loyalty to the empire remained part of Young Turk rhetoric, but it was increasingly supplanted by nationalist ideology. The shift placed the Armenian political leaders in a difficult position. Their community was to be found on both sides of the Ottoman-Russian border. In addition, the Armenians were split into two factions, largely along socio-economic lines. The Dashnak, members of the Armenian Revolutionary Federation *(Hai Heghapokhakan Dashnaksutiun*), represented the Armenian petty bourgeoisie of Anatolia; the patriarchate represented the wealthy commercial class of the capital and other larger cities.[31] The Dashnak ultimately sought autonomy if not complete Armenian independence. The patriarchate and its allies sought a restoration of their traditional privileges as *dhimmis* in the *millet* system that was threatened by the centralizing tendencies of government.

When the war began, the Dashnak urged Armenians to volunteer in the Ottoman army. In Tsarist Russia, the Dashnak urged Armenians to enlist in the Tsarist army. As a result, both the Tsarist and the Ottoman governments suspected the Armenians of disloyalty. The situation was aggravated by the dangers confronting the Ottoman Empire in 1914 and 1915. In November, 1914, over the objections of field commanders, Turkish forces led by Enver Pasha, Minister of War and one of the ruling Young Turk triumvirate, attempted to regain land in the Caucasus lost to the Russians in 1878. Enver's effort ended catastrophically at Sarikamis, a Turkish town in the Caucasus. In the west, Djemal Pasha led an attack in February 1915 on the Suez Canal that also ended in defeat. In March 1915, in response to a Russian request for aid, Allied naval forces under Admiral Sir John de Robeck, Commander of the Aegean Squadron, made preparations to force a passage through the Dardanelles Strait. The evacuation of Constantinople began and the state archives and the empire's gold reserves were sent away. Most observers anticipated the empire's collapse. However, on March 18, 1915, as a result of an unsuspected Turkish minefield in the Strait, five Allied warships were destroyed. The Allied attempt to force the Strait ended in disaster. [32]

When the Young Turks contemplated evacuating from

Constantinople to the Anatolian heartland, they could not ignore the issue of security. Anatolia's population was mixed. In addition to Turks, it was inhabited by Greeks, Armenians, and Kurds whose loyalty was suspect in Turkish eyes. Some Greek civilians were deported from the coastal areas, but those deportations were not genocidal in intent. In the first months of 1915, the Young Turks responded to the defeat at Sarikamis by blaming the Armenians whom they accused of sympathizing with the Russians.[33] The Ottoman authorities disarmed and demobilized Armenian soldiers who were then forced into labor brigades and compelled to dig their own graves before being shot.[34]

Rumors of the slaughter spread in the Armenian villages.[35] On April 20, 1915, the Armenians of Van rose up in self-defense when Djevdet Bey, the recently appointed governor of Van and Enver Pasha's brother-in-law, demanded that the Armenian leadership hand over four thousand men for the Ottoman army's labor battalions. With no illusions concerning the fate of the men if they complied, the leadership refused, an action depicted by the Turks as a revolutionary uprising.[36] The Armenians held out in Van until May 14, 1915, when the city was captured by the Russians with the aid of some Armenian guerrillas who proclaimed Van the capital of an independent Armenian republic. When the Turks recaptured the city in July, they were infuriated by what they regarded as Armenian treason and launched a massacre, butchering the men, and robbing, raping, and leaving the women to die. Dr. Clarence B. Ussher, an American medical missionary in Van, reported that 55,000 Armenians were killed there in May.[37] On April 24, 1915 the Ministry of the Interior ordered the arrest of Armenian parliamentary deputies, former ministers, and some intellectuals. Thousands were arrested, including 2,345 in the capital, most of whom were subsequently executed.[38]

On May 27, 1915, a new emergency law was promulgated, the Temporary Law of Deportation. The law authorized military leaders to order the deportation of population groups on suspicion of espionage, treason, and military necessity. With this sweeping authorization and without explicitly naming the Armenians, the Turkish government arrogated to itself the genocidal deportation of its Armenian population. Shortly thereafter, Djevdet Bey, Van's governor, gave an order to "exterminate all Armenian males of 12 years and older" in that border region.[39]

Actual genocide had begun in April, 1915, with the rounding up and deportation of Armenian men in one population center after another. The men were usually imprisoned for several days, after which they were marched out of town and massacred. Later women, children and older men were also deported. The women were often raped and mutilated before being killed. Thousands of the female deportees were given the choice of conversion to Islam or death. Having lost their men and completely at the mercy of hostile Turks and Kurds, many of the women converted. We return to that subject below.

In June, 1915, the government began to use the railroads to expedite deportation and extermination. Freight cars were employed to transport thousands to remote areas where they were left to starve to death while being assaulted by the ravages of nature and human malice. Many were murdered outright. The Armenian deportees were among the first men and women in the twentieth century to learn that *human rights are inseparable from political status*. Having been deprived by the Ottoman government of all political status, save that of outlaw, there was no abuse that could not with impunity be inflicted upon them.

The extermination project was thoroughly modern in spirit and implementation from its initial planning stages to its execution.[40] Mass extermination was advocated in the planning sessions as the appropriate "scientific" response to the universal struggle of the races for survival.[41] Like other modernizing elites of the period, the largely European-trained Young Turks interpreted the relations between races and nations in Social Darwinist terms. Above all, the Young Turks had a reliable, centralized bureaucratic network. Taalat Bey, one of the ruling triumvirs and Minister of the Interior, did not entrust the assignment to old-fashioned provincial bureaucrats but sent Young Turk bureaucrats to act as his personal representatives and, when necessary, to punish governors and local governors who, out of compassion or greed, failed to carry out orders. There was a special organization with responsibility for organizing the massacres. At the local level, much of the actual killing was carried out by death squads who were given the name of "Butcher Battalions."[42]

Taalat Bey spelled out the objectives of his government in a telegram to the Police Office in Aleppo, Syria, dated September 15, 1915:

> It has been reported that by order of the Committee [of Union and Progress] the Government has *determined completely to exterminate the Armenians living in Turkey*. Those who refuse to obey this order cannot be regarded as friends of the Government. Regardless of the women, children or invalids, and however deplorable the methods of destruction may seem, an end is to be put to their existence [i.e., the Armenians] without paying any heed to feeling or conscience." (emphasis added). Taalat, Minister of the Interior[43]

The Young Turks characterized their aggression as "deportations," and insisted that they were acting in the interests of national security. However, it was quickly apparent that the number of victims far exceeded the nineteenth-century massacres. In 1915 deportation had acquired a new and sinister meaning. It had become an instrument of extermination in which no fewer than one million Armenians perished.[44]

Many volumes have been written about the Armenian genocide. One of the earliest was also one of the most comprehensive, the report assembled by Viscount James Bryce in 1916 in partnership with Historian Arnold Toynbee and presented to Sir Edward Grey, the British Foreign Secretary. The authors concluded their report with an observation concerning the slaughter: "It was a deliberate, systematic attempt to eradicate the Armenian population throughout the Ottoman Empire and it has certainly met with a very large measure of success."[45]

To this day, Turkish authorities have denied that genocide ever took place, and insist that their actions were necessary defensive measures against a disloyal and rebellious minority.[46] That claim has been refuted by the vast majority of responsible scholars. Nevertheless, the Turkish government has used every threat in its diplomatic arsenal to prevent friendly governments from officially taking issue with its denial of genocide.

As noted above, there is little reason to doubt that Abdul Hamid's massacres were in large measure religiously motivated. The sultan-caliph was responsible for mass murder on an unprecedented scale but extermination of the entire community was beyond his capacities. Not so, the Young Turks. Within months after Turkey's entrance into the Great War, the decision to exterminate the Armenians had been taken. When the deed was done, the justifications the Young Turks offered were largely political and economic.

When I first wrote about the Armenian genocide of 1915, I stressed the modernity of the enterprise and its economic, political and military motives.[47] I did not consider the possibility that the perpetrators' motives might have included a very important religious component. Today, I would argue that religion was an indispensable component in the motivation for genocide. It was certainly an indispensable element in defining the otherness of non-Muslims in the Ottoman Empire. I would further argue that the crimes perpetrated against the Armenians were regarded by the Turks as legitimate defensive methods of dealing with *dhimmis* who had violated the conditions of the *dhimma,* and, hence, were outlaws for whom everything, including life, property, freedom, and family, was forfeit. I would also argue that the persistent Turkish genocide denial—so different from the German way of dealing with their genocide—has been due, at least in part, to the Turkish belief that they did no wrong in exterminating the Armenians, a belief that rests ultimately on the traditions of *jihad* and the *dhimma.*

In the massacres of 1894-1896, Turkish authorities were quite open about religious legitimations. In 1914, religion was once again an important component in the conduct of Turkish authorities, this time in the way the war was initiated and its purposes defined. On November 2, 1914, the Ottoman Empire declared war on the Entente powers, Britain, France, Russia, and their allies. On November 13, the Ottoman Sultan, in his capacity, as Caliph, issued an appeal for *jihad.* The next day Mustafa Hayri Bey, the Sheikh-ul-Islam, and as such the chief Sunni religious authority in the Ottoman world, issued a formal (and inflammatory) declaration of *jihad* "against infidels and enemies of Islam." *Jihad* pamphlets in Arabic were also distributed in mosques throughout the Muslim world that offered a detailed plan of operations for the assassination and extermination of all "unbelievers" except those of German nationality, the empire's wartime ally.[48] Killing squads and their leaders were "motivated by both the ideology of *jihad* and pan-Turkism influenced by European nationalism."[49] While the practical influence of the *jihad* on the masses was limited, "it later facilitated the government's program of genocide against the Armenians."[50] It is also worth noting that although the Sheikh-ul-Islam was customarily appointed by the Sultan, Hayri Bey was appointed by the Committee of Union and Progress, the Young Turks who were to instigate the genocide.

According to historian Ara Sarafian, in addition to the killings and general massacres, a large number of Armenians were "'abducted,' 'carried off,' or 'converted to Islam'"[51] Sarafian argues that "the fate of this latter class of Armenians was part of the same genocidal calculus as those who were murdered." It is estimated that in 1915-1916 between 100,000 and 200,000 Armenians, most of whom were women and children, escaped death by converting to Islam. The absorption of these converts into the Muslim community had the same objective as outright genocide, the elimination of the Christian Armenian community as a demographic presence in the Ottoman Empire. In addition to killing a very large number of Armenians through forced marches and starvation, the deportations served to weaken and terrify women and children who had lost their male protectors before or during the deportations. According to Sarafian, "...young women and children were rendered prime candidates for absorption into Muslim households after they were isolated from their families and terrorized during the forced marches and execution of their elders."[52]

Sarafian contends, with considerable justice, that the authorities were implementing a "single policy of destruction" in both the outright murder of adult males and in the absorption of Armenian women and children into the Muslim community. The same Ottoman bureaucrats who controlled the deportations were also in charge of the conversion program. In the initial stages of the assault on the Armenians, there were "voluntary" conversions. Some individuals were selected by individual Muslims for absorption into their households. In addition, government agencies distributed Armenians to Muslim families. Children in government-sponsored orphanages were converted and directly absorbed into the Muslim community.

Events in Trebizond are illustrative of how the program functioned. Between July 1 and July 18, 1915, five deportation convoys left Trebizond. Oscar Heizer, the American Consul, reported that most of the deportees were killed by their guards shortly after leaving.[53] Approximately 3,000 children, girls up to 15 years old and boys no older than ten, were placed in a number of houses designated by the Turks as "orphanages." Another 300 were housed in the American missionary school which was turned into an orphanage. Both orphanages were subsequently closed down by an official sent from Constantinople to supervise the extermination of the Armenians. Some children were drowned by the Turks; others were distributed to Muslim households where, according to Heizer, they were assimilated as Muslims within weeks.[54] Elsewhere, U.S. Consul Leslie Davis reported on the passage of thousands of deportees through Harpoot, which was situated on a principal route to the deserts of Syria. Davis wrote that hardly any men had survived among the deportees. Subject to constant beatings, with little or no food or water, the victims were rapidly dying. The gendarmes guarding the Armenians refused to permit them to leave the convoy or to receive aid from American missionaries. They did, however, permit Turks to visit the convoys with doctors to select "the prettiest girls" for their own purposes. Davis further reported that the Turks were not only seeking to exterminate the Armenians; they were also seeking to absorb a large number as Muslims. Sarafian concludes that there was a mass transfer of Armenians into Muslim households in 1915. By destroying the Armenian social structure in the early stages of the genocide through the murder of young men, heads of families, and community leaders, the Turks were able to garner "the ideal candidates for absorption" into Muslim households and the general Muslim population.[55]

As cruel as this program was, it was fundamentally different from the Nazi Final Solution. Suny has observed that, "To a considerable degree, religious differences were transmuted by both the Armenians and the Turks into racial and national differences, far more indelible and immutable than religion."[56] Nevertheless, Suny's qualifier, "To a considerable degree," is important. For the Nazis, the racial divide between the so-called Aryans and Non-Aryans was absolute and unbridgeable. In the National Socialist universe, there was no room for an absorption program for Non-Aryans, save for a miniscule number of "Honorary Aryans." Some Poles and others with the appropriate physical characteristics could be absorbed, but not the Jews. By contrast, even in genocide, religion made a difference in the Ottoman Empire. Conversion could and did save some Armenians even as it destroyed their community. Moreover, as noted, both the extermination and the conversion process were fully consistent with Islamic tradition in the eyes of the Turks.

Nor were the Armenians the only Christian minority eliminated by the Turks, albeit by somewhat gentler means. In January, 1923, after Greece's failed invasion of Turkey's Anatolian mainland and Turkey's repudiation of the 1920 Treaty of Sèvres, at Turkey's insistence both countries agreed to an "exchange" of populations. Between 1923 and 1930, 1.25 million "Greeks" were "repatriated" from Turkey to Greece; a smaller number of "Turks" departed from Greece to Turkey. However, as Bernard Lewis points out, the exchanges did not imply acceptance of the European principle of nationality in which Greeks and Turks, "unwilling or unable to live as national minorities among aliens," elected to return to their homeland and live among their own people. In reality, the great majority of Anatolia's "Greeks" spoke little or no Greek. They spoke Turkish among themselves although they wrote in the Greek script. Similarly, many of the "Turks" in Greece and Crete spoke Greek among themselves and knew little or no Turkish. The expulsions were actually based on religion. Turkish-speaking Christians faithful to the Greek Orthodox Church were expelled to Greece, a "homeland" they had never known, while Greek-speaking Muslims were expelled to Turkey.[57] The Armenian genocide, the absorption-conversion program, and what was, in effect, the expulsion of Turkey's "Greeks" all shared a common objective, the elimination of a significant Christian demographic presence from Turkey. The methods varied, but all three can be seen as religiously-motivated state-sponsored programs of population elimination.

Finally, I take note of an authoritative report based entirely on Arab sources entitled "Contemporary Islamist Ideology Authorizing Genocidal Murder" by Yigal Carmon in which he demonstrates that today's radical Islamists regard genocide as a legitimate weapon against those whom they regard as enemies of Islam.[58] Holding that Islam is now under attack, they see unremitting *jihad* as both defensive in character and *the single most important Muslim religious obligation*. It is obligatory for Muslims without restriction or limitation. No weapons or types of warfare are to be excluded. Without exception, all infidels are to be fought and, barring conversion, are to be exterminated. I must, however, stress that these are the views of the most radical elements within contemporary Islam. We do not know the extent to which the extremists can persuade or compel the Islamic mainstream to share their views.

Notes

1. http://en.wikisource.org/wiki/A_Letter_from_The_International_Association_of_Genocide_Scholars.

2. See, "Inflated Figures of Armenian Genocide & Credibility,"

3. See the text of an 'open letter from the members of the International Association of Genocide Scholars to Prime Minister Tayyip Erdogan of Turkey, dated June 7, 2005, calling on him "to acknowledge the responsibility of a previous [Turkish] government for the genocide of the Armenian people, as the German government and people have done in the case of the Holocaust." The text is available at: http://en.wikisource.org/wiki/A_Letter_from_The_International_Association_of_Genocide_Scholars

4. Vahakn N. Dadrian, *The History of the Armenian Genocide: Ethnic Conflict from the Balkans to Anatolia to the Caucasus* (Providence: Berghahn Books, 1995), p. 3.

5. Taner Akcam, *The Genocide of the Arrmenians and the Silence of the Turks,* p. 49

http://www.wbarrow.co.uk/rememberarmenia/pdfs_in_chapters/04_armenia2_turk_affirms.pdf.

6. Dadrian, *The History of the Armenian Genocide,* 5.

7. Akcam, *op. cit.,* Kindle location 1239.

8. Dadrian, *The History of the Armenian Genocide,* 4.

9. Bat Ye'or, *Islam and Dhimmitude: Where Civilizations Collide* (Madison, NJ, Fairleigh Dickinson University Press, 2002) 37-38.

10. Suny, "Religion, Ethnicity," 30-31.

11. Bat Ye'or, *Europe, Globalization, and the Coming of the Universal Caliphate* (Rowman & Littlefield, Kindle Edition), p.1.

12. Suny, "Religion, Ethnicity," 39.

13. For an exploration of the phenomenon of market-dominant minorities, see Amy Chua, *World on Fire: How Exporting Free Market Democracy Breeds Ethnic Hatred and Global Instability.* (New York, NY: Doubleday, 2003)

14. On the *Tanzimat* Reforms, see Dadrian, *The History of the Armenian Genocide,* 25-27, 32-33.

15. Lord Kinross (John Balfour, 3rd Baron Kinross), *The Ottoman Centuries: The Rise and Fall of the Turkish Empire.* (New York, NY: William Morrow, 1977), 556-557.

16. Dadrian, *The History of the Armenian Genocide*, 45-47.

17. On the origins of the Sasun massacres, see Balakian, *The Burning Tigris,* 54-56 and Dadrian, *The History of the Armenian Genocide*, 114-116.

18. Kinross, *The Ottoman Centuries,* 559.

19. Dadrian, *The History of the Armenian Genocide*, 147.

20. text

21. Dadrian, *The History of the Armenian Genocide,* 149.

22. Benjamin Braude and Bernard Lewis, *Christians and Jews in the Ottoman Empire: The Functioning of a Plural Society* (New York: Holmes and Meier Publishers, 1982), 30.

23. J. C. Hurewitz, *Diplomacy in the Near and Middle East, A Documentary Record: 1535-1914* (Princeton: Princeton University Press, 1956), Vol. 1, 154;

24. See "Infidel Status in the Ottoman Empire" in Balakian, *The Burning Tigris,* 40-43.

25. Bat Ye'or, *The Dhimmi: Jews and Christians under Islam* (Rutherford, NJ: Fairleigh Dickinson University Press, 1985), 101.

26. Balakian, *The Burning Tigris,* 41-42.

27. Kinross, *The Ottoman Centuries*, 556-557.

28. Dadrian, *The History of the Armenian Genocide*, 45-47.

29. Suny, "Religion, Ethnicity," 46-47.

30. Suny, "Religion, Ethnicity," 47.

31. Braude and Lewis, *Christians and Jews,* 418.

32. David Fromkin, *A Peace to End All Peace: The Fall of the Ottoman Empire and the Creation of the Modern Middle East* (New York: Henry Holt, 1989), 152-153.

33. Balakian, *The Burning Tigris,* 178.

34. Balakian, *The Burning Tigris,* 178.

35. Suny, "Religion, Ethnicity," 52.

36. Balakian, *The Burning Tigris,* 179.

37. Henry Morgenthau, *Ambassador Morgenthau's Story* (New York: Doubleday, Page, 1919), 299. For an American eye-witness's account of the events in Van in 1915, see Grace Higley Knapp, "The American Mission in Van" in Viscount Bryce, *The Treatment of Armenians in the Ottoman Empire 1915-1916: Documents Presented to Secretary of State for Foreign Affairs by Viscount Bryce*, 2nd ed. (Beirut: G. Doniguian & Sons, 1972), 21-47.

38. Dadrian, *The History of the Armenian Genocide,* 221.

39. Mark Mazower, "The G Word," *London Review of Books*, 8 February 2001, Vol. 23, No.3, <http://www.lrb.co.uk/v23/n03/mazo01_.html>.

40. Dadrian, "The Secret Young-Turk Ittihadist Conference and the Decision for the World War I Genocide of the Armenians," *Holocaust and Genocide Studies,* Vol. 7, No. 2, Fall 1993, 173-201 and Michael J. Arlen, *Passage to Ararat* (New York: Farrar Strauss and Giroux: 1975), 343-344.

41. Taner Akçam, "The Genocide of the Armenians and the Silence of the Turks," <http://www.omroep.nl/human/tv/muur/artikel2.htm>.

42. Bryce, *The Treatment of Armenians,* 84. This information was also presented by Professor R. Hrair Dekmejian of the University of Southern California at the Seminar in Commemoration of the 65th Anniversary of the Armenian Genocide, St. Vartan's Cathedral, New York, N. Y., 25 April 1980.

43. The telegram is quoted in Manuel Sarkisianz, *A Modern History of Transcaucasian Armenia* (Privately printed by the author, Nagpur, India: Udyama Commercial Press, 1975 [Distributed by E. J. Brill, Leiden]), 196.

44. According to Mazower, "Deportation—a traditional instrument of imperial rule—had little to do with it: the old-fashioned version [of deportations], which valued subject populations for economic reasons, aimed to relocate rather than destroy them." Mazower, "The G Word," *London Review of Books.*

45. Bryce, *The Treatment of Armenians,* 648.

46. For an early example of the Turkish justification of the slaughter, see the interview granted by Halil Bey, The Turkish Foreign Minister, to the Associated Press representative at Vienna, 25 Oct. 1915. Halil attempted to throw the blame for the massacres of Armenian men, women, and children upon the Armenians themselves, asserting that they had risen in revolt when the Russians invaded the country. "Turkish Foreign Minister's Defense of the Armenian Massacres," *Current History*, December 1915. <http://www.cilicia.com/armo10c-nyt191612.html>.

47. Richard L. Rubenstein, *The Cunning of History* (New York: Harper and Row, 1975), 11-12 and *The Age of Triage: Fear and Hope in an Overcrowded World* (Boston: Beacon Press, 1983), 12-19.

48. Henry Morgenthau, *Ambassador Morgenthau's Story* (Garden City, NY: Doubleday, 1919), 162-163. See also Balakian, *The Burning Tigris,* 169-170.

49. Balakian, *The Burning Tigris,* 183.

50. Richard Kloian, ed., *The Armenian Genocide: News Accounts from the American Press: 1915-1922* (Richmond, CA: Anto Publishing, 1988), XIII.

51. Ara Sarafian, "The Absorption of Armenian Women and Children into Muslim Households as a Structural Component of the Armenian Genocide" in Bartov and Mack, *In God's Name*, 210.

52. Sarafian, "The Absorption."

53. Oscar Heizer, "Report on the treatment of Trebizond" to Ambassador Henry Morgenthau, 15 July 1915, forwarded to the Secretary of State, 20 July 1915, <www.armeniangenocide.org/us-7-20-15-text.html>.

54. Sarafian, "The Absorption," 212-213.

55. Sarafian, "The Absorption," 217.

56. Suny, "Religion, Ethnicity," 50.

57. Bernard Lewis, *Islam and the West* (New York: Oxford University Press, 1993), 132-143.

58. Yigal Carmon, "Contemporary Islamist Ideology Authorizing Genocidal Murder," MEMRI (Middle East Research Institute), 27 Jan. 2004, Special Report No. 25, http://memri.org/bin/articles.cgi?Page=archives&Area=st&ID=SR2504#_edu2.

CHAPTER 5

From Hitler to Jihadist Jew Hatred: Influences and Parallels

DAVID PATTERSON

True to the Jew hatred that was at the core of his identity, as he prepared for his suicide, Adolf Hitler's dying plea to humanity was to continue to "resist mercilessly the poisoner of all nations, international Jewry."[1] Those who have most fervently and systematically heeded that call in the post-Holocaust era are the Islamic Jihadists. To be sure, the association between National Socialism and Islamic Jihadism goes back to the inception of modern Jihadism's seminal organization in March 1928, when Hasan al-Banna founded the Muslim Brotherhood, the group that would spawn most of the major Jihadist movements of our own time. A professed admirer of the Führer,[2] al-Banna indicated that he had learned a great deal from the Nazis about the importance of propaganda,[3] particularly as a means not of persuasion but of inciting what Hitler called "wrathful hatred" of the Jews.[4] The Jihadist leader of the Brotherhood "gave careful thought to all the details of a far-flung propaganda campaign,"[5] and in 1935 he assembled the Brotherhood's first propaganda committee.[6] Slogans extolling the Nazis were part of an effective propaganda campaign that he launched throughout the region during the Palestinian Arab Revolt of 1936–1939, which was instigated by Haj Amin al-Husseini, the Mufti of Jerusalem.[7] Indeed, as early as 1929 Hasan's brother, Abd al-Rahman al-Banna, had met with al-Husseini to establish an official connection between the Brotherhood and the Mufti, who in turn connected the Brotherhood and the Nazis. Indeed, al-Husseini proved to be pivotal in the linkage between Nazism and Islamic Jihadism. We shall have much more to say about the Mufti below. For now, let us begin with the Brotherhood.

The Rise of Modern Jihadism: The Muslim Brotherhood

Matthias Küntzel notes that by November 1945, when the Second World War had come to an end, "the core of anti-Semitism had begun to shift from Germany to the Arab world. On the anniversary of the Balfour Declaration, demonstrators rampaged the Jewish quarters of Cairo. They plundered houses and shops, attacked non-Muslims, devastated the synagogues and then set them on fire."[8] Therefore, writes Küntzel, "the Muslim Brothers were inspired not by the Nasserism of the 1960s, but by the European Fascism of the 1930s. Their pre-1951 campaigns were not anti-colonialist, but anti-Jewish. The anti-Jewish passages in the Koran were fused with the anti-Semitic methods of the struggle of the Third Reich and hatred of the Jews acted out as jihad."[9] The Brotherhood became a hybrid of Nazism and Islam to form Islamic Jihadism, making the ultimate extermination of the Jews not just a political or territorial aim but a fundamental, defining element of their worldview: one cannot be part of the Brotherhood, just as one cannot be a Nazi, without espousing the extermination of the Jews.

Similar to the Nazis, a key component of the Brotherhood's ideology is the *Führerprinzip*, or "leadership principle," as Richard Mitchell, the author of a seminal work on the Muslim Brotherhood, has pointed out.[10] Küntzel explains: "Tightly organized around the leadership principle," the Brotherhood "demanded the dissolution of all parties and the abolition of parliamentary democracy in favor of an 'organic' state based on *sharia* law."[11] Küntzel has further demonstrated that "the history of the Muslim Brothers shows that revolutionary anti-Semitism is no mere supplementary feature of modern jihadism; it is its core."[12] In this statement the term *modern* is crucial: what makes modern Jihadism "modern" is its exterminationist ideological stance toward the Jews. Echoing the cry of "*Ein Volk, ein Reich, ein Führer*," the Brotherhood's goal is to reestablish a worldwide Caliphate ruled by Sharia, with one people, under one leader. Here the *Volk* consists of the umma, that is, the Muslims of the world; the *Reich* is the Caliphate, within which Sharia rules over every aspect of life; and the leader is none other than the *al-Murshid* or the "Supreme Guide" of the Muslim Brotherhood. Like the Führer whom he venerated, the Supreme Guide al-Banna was known to have possessed three distinctive qualities: personal charm, eloquence as a speaker, and a good command of his native tongue,[13] talents he used to incite a murderous hatred of the Jews.

Between 1936 and 1938, during the Arab Revolt, the Brotherhood's membership grew from eight hundred to two thousand.[14] "This conflict in Palestine gave Hasan al-Banna an unexpected opportunity for action and expansion," Christina Phelps Harris observes. "His loyalty helped earn him the warm commendation of the powerful Mufti of Jerusalem, Hajj Amin al-Husseini,"[15] who relied heavily on Nazi funding to finance the uprising he instigated. It is also worth noting that in 1937 Ruhullah Khomeini hooked up with the Brotherhood and studied the writings of Hasan al-Banna, planting the seed of the Brotherhood's evil in the thinking of the future Ayatollah of Islamic Jihadist Iran. By that time the Nazis had begun their broadcasts from Zeesen in Farsi and, according to Küntzel's research, Khomeini was an avid listener.[16]

In April and May 1938 the Brotherhood led violent demonstrations against Egyptian Jewish communities. Nazi journalist Giselher Wirsing applauded the attacks and the "return to the religious traditions of Islam" in Egypt,[17] a tradition that included Jew hatred. In 1939, bombs were placed in a Cairo synagogue and in Jewish homes, making it clear that the Islamic Jihadists targeted not just the "Zionists" but Jews everywhere. In October 1938, a month before the infamous, nation-wide pogrom of *Kristallnacht* in Germany, the Brotherhood organized the Parliamentary Conference for Arab and Muslim Countries in Cairo. At that conference they distributed Arabic translations of *Mein Kampf* and the *Protocols of the Elders of Zion*. That same year al-Husseini began the systematic elimination of his enemies, particularly in the Nashashibi clan, which was sympathetic toward the Peel Commission's proposals to find a two-state solution to the tension between Arabs and Jews; the murder of the Nashashibis was largely incited by the Muslim Brotherhood, who "called on the Palestinians to kill the Nashashibis in the name of God and who mobilized the masses in support of the Mufti against Jews."[18] Here too we see the Brotherhood's calculated involvement in promoting the agenda of Haj Amin al-Husseini.

Once the war broke out in Europe, the Brotherhood became even more supportive of the Nazis' aims, not only in Europe but also in the

Middle East. In 1940 al-Banna arranged a meeting between Anwar Sadat and General Aziz al-Misri, both of whom were among the Nazis' most ardent supporters in Egypt. In 1941 Sadat joined the Brotherhood's military organization; in 1943 Nasser and his cohorts followed suit. Sadat was soon arrested by the British for his activities as a Nazi spy. By 1943, the Brotherhood's "Secret Apparatus" (*al-Jihaz al-Sirri*), whose functions were similar to those of the Nazi Gestapo, was operational. Like the Nazis, they considered the communists "to be one of their principal enemies"; also like the Nazis, they identified the communists with the Jews.[19] Finally, like the Nazis, they viewed the Jew not as "the other" but as evil incarnate, whatever form that evil might assume: the capitalist, the communist, the racist, the colonialist, the violator of human rights, the war criminal, the perpetrator of apartheid, and so on to this day. When on 20 June 1946 King Farouk granted asylum to al-Husseini, now wanted as a Nazi war criminal, al-Banna applauded the decision, declaring that "in Berlin he [al-Husseini] had been purely and simply carrying out jihad [just as the Nazis had done]. Thus, the Muslim Brothers cleared the way for the second career of the Mufti, whose pro-Nazi past they considered a source of pride."[20] More than a source of pride, the former Mufti was a source of inspiration for his devotion to the Nazis' extermination of the Jews. In al-Husseini, then, we have another important key to the influences and parallels between the National Socialist and the Islamic Jihadists.

Haj Amin al-Husseini: The Jihadist Nazi

On 8 May 1921 British Mandate Governor Herbert Samuel appointed Haj Amin al-Husseini Grand Mufti of Jerusalem (a grandiose title invented by Samuel). One of al-Husseini's first acts as Grand Mufti was to declare a jihad against the British and the Jews.[21] Two months after Hitler's appointment as Chancellor of Germany on 30 January 1933 al-Husseini had his first meeting with German General Consul Heinrich Wolff in Jerusalem. On 31 March 1933 Wolff sent a telegram to Berlin: "Today the Mufti gave me assurances that Muslims both within and outside of Palestine send greetings to the new regime in Germany and that they hope to see the spread of fascism and anti-democratic leadership in other lands. The current Jewish influence on the economy and politics is harmful everywhere and must be fought."[22] Bernard Lewis observes that the Mufti's "immediate aim was to halt and terminate the Jewish settlement of Palestine. Beyond that, however, he aimed at a much vaster purpose, conceived not so much in pan-Arab as in pan-Islamic terms, for a holy war of Islam in alliance with Germany against world Jewry, to accomplish the final solution of the Jewish problem everywhere."[23] The Mufti's early overtures to the Nazis soon paid off.

We have already noted the Nazi backing of the Arab Revolt of 1936—1939 instigated by al-Husseini. The uprising, notes Küntzel, "took place against the background of the swastika: Arab leaflets and signs on walls were prominently marked with this Nazi symbol; youth organizations... paraded as 'Nazi-scouts,' and Arab children greeted each other with the Nazi salute. Those who had to pass through the rebellious quarters of Palestine attached a flag bearing the swastika to their vehicles so as to insure protection against assaults by the Mufti's volunteers."[24] This intimate bond between National Socialism and Islamic Jihadism was firmly rooted in their mutual hatred of the Jews. The Nazi-Jihadist bond of Jew hatred ran so deep that on 18 June 1936 Vicco von Bülow-Schwante of the German Foreign Ministry informed the German Embassy in Cairo that "the Nuremberg race laws are aimed only at the Jews."[25] By 1937 al-Husseini had organized a movement inspired by the Hitler Youth called *Al-Jihad Almuquaddas* (The Holy Jihad). On 21 July 1937, he visited the German Consul in Jerusalem Hans Döhle in order to express his support for the Nazis' cause and to reinforce the Nazis' involvement in his own cause. On 2 October of that same year, he met with Adolf Eichmann and Herbert Hagen; Chuck Morse relates that "Eichmann wrote glowingly of 'the national and racial conscience' that he observed while amongst the Arabs. He reported that 'Nazi flags fly in Palestine and they adorn their houses with Swastikas and portraits of Hitler.'"[26] Days later, on 13 October, al-Husseini fled from Palestine to Lebanon, wanted for inciting insurrection against the British Mandate government.

Soon after the outbreak of the war, on 13 October 1939, al-Husseini set up his base of operations in Baghdad. In a letter to Hitler, dated 20 January 1940, the Mufti "gave his assurance that the Arabs had deep sympathy for the Axis states and were ready to rise against the common enemy" and "contribute... to 'the well-deserved defeat of the Anglo-Jewish coalition."[27] On 21 June 1940 he sent a letter to the German minister to Turkey Franz von Papen, in which he assured Von Papen that the Palestinian Muslims were prepared to take an active role to spread the fight against "international Jewry" to other Arab lands.[28] A little more than six months later the Nazis stated their own assurances: in a memorandum dated 5 February 1941 the Wehrmacht High Command "stressed the 'favourable position' of Germany in relation to the Arabs" and that Germany could promise "everything they [the Arabs] wanted on 'the solution of the Jewish question in Palestine.'"[29] In keeping with this general design aimed at the eventual extermination of the Jews, on 3 April 1941 al-Husseini orchestrated an Iraqi government takeover, with Nazi support and financing, led by Rashid Ali al-Gaylani; he took advantage of the turmoil to incite the slaughter of 600 Jews in Baghdad; 911 houses were destroyed and 586 businesses ransacked.[30] Yunis es-Sewabi, who had worked on an Arabic translation of *Mein Kampf*, played a major role in the coup.[31] When the British suppressed the coup in May, al-Husseini blamed the Jews for the failed Iraqi Nazi takeover. On 9 May, in a broadcast over Iraqi and Axis radios, he issued another *fatwa* announcing a jihad against Britain and the Jews.[32]

On 22 July 1941, al-Husseini fled to Teheran. From there he charted his course to Berlin. After his initial meeting with the Führer on 28 November 1941, the Mufti recorded in his diary Hitler's avowal of the war against the Jews and his insistence that the Nazis and the Arabs are engaged in the same struggle, namely, to exterminate the Jews.[33] According to the war crimes testimony of Adolf Eichmann's deputy, Dieter Wisliceny, from 26 July 1946, soon after meeting with Hitler al-Husseini met with Eichmann, whereupon he "was informed of the plan concerning the 'Final Solution of the Jewish Question in Europe.'"[34] Said Wisliceny, "The Mufti repeatedly suggested to the various authorities with whom he was maintaining contact, above all to Hitler, Ribbentrop and Himmler, the extermination of European Jewry. He considered this as a comfortable solution of the Palestine problem."[35] Further, David Dalin and John Rothman have shown that "of the major Nazi leaders, Heinrich Himmler was the one with whom al-Husseini collaborated most actively and consistently.... One of the common goals shared by al-Husseini and Himmler, who was the architect of the Nazis' 'Final Solution,' was the extermination of the Jews."[36] According to Joseph Schechtman, al-Husseini was very close to other murderers who had a direct involvement in the slaughter of the Jews: he visited Auschwitz and Majdanek and knew Auschwitz commandant Rudolf Hoess, Mauthausen commandant Franz Ziereis, Theresienstadt commandant Siegfried Seidl, and Belsen commandant Josef Kramer, the "Beast of Belsen."[37]

As a Nazi, al-Husseini was involved in radio propaganda, espionage in the Middle East, and the establishment of the Arab Legions and the Arab Brigade, Muslim military units that fought for the Nazis. He had at his disposal six stations for radio broadcasts, from which he urged Muslims everywhere to kill Jews everywhere. On 11 December 1942 he summoned all the Arab people, calling them to "martyrdom" as allies with Germany in the war against the English and the Jews. "The spilled blood of martyrs," he cried, echoing the Jihadist dictum, "is the water of life." And: "We Arabs should clearly join the Axis powers and their allies in common struggle [i.e. jihad] against the common enemy [i.e. the Jews]." And: If England and her allies should win the war, "Israel would rule the whole world"; if the Nazis should win, "the Jewish danger" would be defeated.[38]

In addition to being a man of hateful words, al-Husseini was a man of murderous deeds. As early as January 1941 he had gone to Bosnia to convince Muslim leaders that a Muslim SS division would bring honor and glory to the followers of Islam. Dalin and Rothman estimate that as many as 100,000 Muslims were recruited by al-Husseini and fought for the Nazis.[39] Each battalion had its Imam and each regiment its Mullah. The Mufti set up a Mullah school for them in Dresden and personally saw to their training. The largest of the Mufti's Muslim killing units was the 13th Handschar Division of 21,065 men. They began recruiting for the Waffen SS Mountain Division Handschar in February 1943, with Imams selected by Husseini for ideological indoctrination. In a speech to the SS on 11 January 1944, "Himmler argued that the bond between Nazism and Islam was built on enduring common values as well as shared enemies in the war. He also presented Hitler as a gift sent from God—and Allah."[40] The commander of the Handschar, Karl-Gustav Sauberzweig, "reported that the Muslim recruits gladly adopted Nazi doctrine and even that 'the Muslims, SS men in the Division, and the civilians are beginning to see in our Führer the mission of a second prophet,' that is, one following Mohammed." The Division went into action in February 1944.[41]

When the war came to an end, Yugoslavia officially placed al-Husseini on its list of war criminals, accusing him of organizing SS Muslim killing units in the Balkans. Al-Husseini's status as a fugitive, Schechtman points out, "and his association with the Axis had enhanced rather than shattered his halo" in the Muslim world.[42] When he turned up in Egypt on 20 June 1946, as already noted, the Muslim Brotherhood gave him a hero's welcome. Within a week of his arrival in Cairo he met with Hasan al-Banna and the man who would become the Brotherhood's most prominent ideologue, Sayyid Qutb. "Husseini," observes Jeffrey Herf, "was continuing *the same* struggle that Hitler and Germany—and Husseini himself—had been waging during the war."[43] In 1946 the Mufti embraced Yasser Arafat, whose mother was the daughter of al-Husseini's first cousin, as his protégé and brought in a former Nazi officer to teach Arafat "the fine points of guerilla warfare.[44] To be sure, Chuck Morse presents a convincing argument that "al-Husseini was himself most likely the true founder of the al-Fatah,... Arafat's terror cell,... the nucleus of the PLO."[45] And so we see how intricate is the web linking the Nazis to the Jihadism of the Muslim Brotherhood and its offspring.

In 1948 the Mufti played an active role in the Arabs' attempts to destroy the Jewish State. In May he "called for Arabs throughout the Islamic Middle East to wage a holy war against the newly established Jewish State. The goal of this jihad, he emphasized, was the extermination of the Jews,"[46] thus affirming what had always been and continues to be the aim of the Nazi-influenced Jihadist movement. Pulitzer Prize-winning journalist Edgar Ansel Mowrer said of al-Husseini, "As a murderer, this man ranks with the great killers of history.... In the evil of his intentions, Haj Amin equaled Hitler."[47] Indeed, affirming his intimate ideological bond with al-Husseini, Hitler regarded him as "the decisive voice in Arab affairs as the most authoritative spokesman for, and as *the* leader of, the Arabs."[48] The Muslim Arabs, however, particularly those of a Jihadist ilk, were ripe for the relation. This affinity can be found in a musical refrain that ran throughout the Arab Muslim world during the reign of the Third Reich: "*Bala Misou, bala Mister, bissama Allah, oria alard Hitler* (No more monsieur, No more Mister, in heaven Allah, on earth Hitler)."[49] Just as the Christian hatred of the Jews had prepared the ground for the Nazis' exterminationist anti-Semitism, so had an Islamic inclination toward Jew hatred paved the way toward the Jihadists' exterminationist Jew hatred.

The Evolution of the Nazi-Jihadist Bond

We have seen that the Nazi influence in the Arab Muslim world took root from the onset of the Third Reich; Nazi anti-Semitism, however, took Jihadist Jew hatred to unprecedented levels. Deeming the Jew as inherently, essentially, and unredeemably evil, the Jihadists placed the Jew in a metaphysical category, which in turn removed the Jews from the traditional option to save themselves by converting to Islam. The most influential of all the Jihadists, Muslim Brother Sayyid Qutb, insisted that Jews are "*by nature* determined to fight Allah's Truth"[50] and are therefore are "the blackest devil and source of the worst anti-Islamic machinations."[51] A shared ideology, then, cemented the Arab-Nazi collaboration. In May 1937, to illustrate this point, "on the occasion of the observance of Mohammed's birth, German and Italian flags were displayed [in Palestine] as well as portraits of Hitler and Mussolini."[52] In other words, to be anti-Zionist was to be pro-Nazi. Confirming that Jew hatred constituted the common link between the Germans and the Muslims, on 9 January 1938 the Arab newspaper *Al-Jamia al-Islamiyya* printed, "Many Arabs consider that Germany is a friend of the Arabs. This friendship is perhaps the result of the German hatred of the Jews."[53] Later that year, on 16 October, the New York *Times* ran an article by Harold Callender, who related that "the Nazi press this week gave vent to an outburst of sympathy for the Arabs in Palestine who were reported to be forming a 'free corps' on the Sudeten German model, in order to 'fight against Judaism.'"[54] Here we see the shift from friendship to influence: not only were the Muslims imitating the Germans, but they were also learning from them.

To be sure, as Bernard Lewis has shown, the Arab overtures to the Germans between 1933 and 1945 were just as frequent and just as fervent as any attempts on the part of the Germans to win over the Arabs.[55]

Even earlier, in 1932, the Syrian Social Nationalist Party was formed, modeled after the National Socialist Party. Its leader, Antun Saadeh, called himself the Führer of the Syrian nation; their flag displayed a swastika on a black-and-white background.[56] When Hitler was appointed Chancellor of Germany on 30 January 1933, he received his first congratulatory telegrams from the Arab Muslims. Throughout the 1930s, Küntzel reports, "students from Arab countries received German scholarships, firms took on Arab apprentices, and Arab party leaders were invited to the Nuremberg party rallies and military chiefs to Wehrmacht manoeuvres. An 'Arab Club' was established in Berlin as the centre for Palestine-related agitation and Arabic-language broadcasting."[57] In the fall of 1938, the French newspaper *Marianne* reported that British troops in Nablus were greeted with shouts of "Heil, Hitler!" At the time journalist John Gunther wrote, "The greatest contemporary Arab hero is probably Hitler."[58] In a report dated 8 May 1941 Shirdar Telkaz of the British Colonial Office wrote, "There are Arab Nazi organizations which operate from Damascus, Aleppo and Beirut. The Nadi El Arabi is the most dangerous Nazi propaganda machine. Its members are a group of fanatical Arabs turned Nazis at German universities."[59] And so, when "the Germans intensified their Arabic propaganda campaign" that same year,[60] they had an eagerly receptive audience.

These seeds planted during the reign of the Third Reich sprouted and grew during the postwar years. "In 1969," for example, "the PLO recruited two former Nazi instructors, Erich Altern, a leader of the Gestapo's Jewish affairs section, and Willy Berner, who was an SS officer in the Mauthausen extermination camp. Another former Nazi, Johann Schuller, was found supplying arms to Fatah. Belgian Jean Tireault, secretary of the neo-Nazi organization La Nation Européenne, also went on the Fatah payroll. Another Belgian neo-Nazi, Karl van der Put, recruited volunteers for the PLO."[61] Expressing not only the admiration but also the assimilation of Hitler's ideology, Dr. Yahya al-Rakhawi published an article on 19 July 1982 in the Egyptian newspaper *Al-Ahrar*; in it he invokes "that great man Hitler, may God have mercy on him, who was the wisest of those who confronted this problem... and who out of compassion for humanity, tried to exterminate every Jew." Al-Rakhawi goes on to argue that Ruhullah Khomeini is best suited to carry on the war against the Jews, declaring, "Defeat in this battle, failure to 'excise the Jewish cancer on the body of humanity,' could lead to the destruction of humanity itself."[62] Thus the Arab intellectuals—and not just the "poverty-stricken" Muslim masses—adopted the Führer's ideological line on the "nature" of the Jew. Much more than an issue of race, it is an issue of essence, which can be neither altered nor redeemed.

In another article espousing Hitler's views, this time in *Al-Ahram*, published on 27 September 1982, Dr. Lutfi Abd al-Azim wrote, "The first thing we have to make clear is that no distinction must be made between the Jew and the Israeli.... The Jew is a Jew, through millennia... in spurning all moral values, devouring the living and drinking his blood for the sake of a few coins."[63] The one reservation that the Arab Muslim world seems to have about Hitler was expressed by Egyptian scholar Ahmad Ragab, who on 18 April 2001 wrote, "Our thanks go to the late Hitler, who wrought, in advance, the vengeance of the Palestinians upon the most despicable villains on the face of the earth. However, we rebuke Hitler for the fact that the vengeance was insufficient."[64] And on 29 April 2002 Egyptian journalist Fatma Abdullah Mahmoud declared in *Al-Akhbar*, "I, personally, complain to Hitler..., 'If only you had done it, brother, if only it had really happened, so that the world could sigh in relief without their evil and sin.'"[65] As one can see from these examples, the expression of the Jihadists' exterminationist Jew hatred is not confined to their diatribes from the pulpit or to the bravado of their covenants, but has been woven into the fabric of Muslim popular culture.

The Jihadist anti-Semites have also learned very well Hitler's lesson that "something of the most insolent lie will always remain and stick,"[66] accusing the Jews of everything from the age-old Blood Libel to secretly plotting to take over the world. At a UN seminar on religious tolerance Saudi representative Dr. Maruf al-Dawalibi averred, "If a Jew does not drink every year the blood of a non-Jewish man, then he will be damned for all eternity."[67] Syria's Defense Minister Mustafa Tlas wrote a book, *The Matza of Zion*, in which he asserts the truth of the age-old Christian claim that Jews murder children to obtain blood for Passover matzo.[68] Jews "are accused of infecting girls with AIDS and syphilis and sending them to Egypt to spread these diseases. They are also accused of supplying Egyptian women with hyper-aphrodisiac chewing gum which drives them into a frenzy of sexual desire," as well as "deliberately spreading cancer among the Egyptians and other Arabs by devising and disseminating carcinogenic cucumbers and shampoos; of promoting drug-taking and devil-worship, and organizing a campaign to legalize homosexuality in order to undermine Egyptian society."[69] In other words, Jews are behind every evil that threatens society. "In Islamist eyes," as in the eyes of the Nazis, Küntzel states, "not only is everything Jewish evil, all evil is Jewish."[70] That is why the Jews *must* be hated and ultimately exterminated.

The Jew hatred that shapes Jihadist anti-Semitism is not confined to the media or to popular culture; it also emerges in the halls of Islamic academia and flows from the printing presses of academic publishers. In *The People of Israel in the Quran and Sunna*, a study based on his Ph.D. dissertation, Grand Sheikh of Al-Azhar University Muhammad Sayed Tantawi maintains that the Jews were behind the French and Russian revolutions and both world wars, they control the world's media and the world's economy, they endeavor to destroy morality, and they set up brothels throughout the world. He echoes Hitler's claim in *Mein Kampf* that "in resisting the Jews, I am doing the work of the Lord," and he praises the *Protocols of the Elders of Zion* as a profound exposure and irrefutable evidence of the world Jewish conspiracy.[71] Similarly, political and economic expert, Dr. Amira al-Sinwani, published an article in the 26 October 2001 edition of the Egyptian newspaper *Al-Akhbar,* affirming the authenticity of *The Protocols*.[72] "The same ideas," Küntzel points out, appear "in Muhammad Qutb's *Muslims and Globalization*, which appeared in 2000."[73] Muhammad Qutb was the brother of Sayyid Qutb and the teacher of Osama bin Laden at King Abd al-Aziz University in Jeddah from 1974 to 1978. Learning from a man who in turn learned from the Nazis, bin Laden espoused the view that the Jew is a threat to all humanity and the corrupter of everything decent. The "Jewish enemy," he declared in a letter to Saudi mufti Bin Baz, dated 29 December 1994, "is not an enemy in his own original country fighting in its defense until he gains a peace agreement, but an attacking enemy and a corrupter of religion and the world."[74] The extermination of the Jews, therefore, is a moral and religious necessity.

The insistence upon a secret world Jewish conspiracy to assume control of all humanity continues to be not only part of Muslim popular belief but central to Jihadist doctrine. Article Twenty-Two of the Hamas Charter, or "The Charter of Allah" (with the implication that Hamas *is* Allah), is a good example. The Jews, it states, "were behind the French Revolution, the Communist revolution and most of the revolutions we heard and hear about, here and there. With their money they formed secret societies, such as Freemasons, Rotary Clubs, the Lions and others in different parts of the world for the purpose of sabotaging societies and achieving Zionist interests. With their money they were able to control imperialistic countries and instigate them to colonize many countries in order to enable them to exploit their resources and spread corruption there."[75] The proof text for this allegation is *The Protocols of the Elders of Zion*. Here we begin to realize the ramifications of Hitler's description of the Jew as an "invisible wirepuller."[76] Casting the Jew in metaphysical categories, the Jihadists render the Jew as invisible—and as threatening—as the devil. Rendering the Jew invisible, they transform the Jew into a ubiquitous threat; the effort to eradicate the evil must be equally ubiquitous. Finally, given the invisibility of the evil, one cannot be certain of its defeat until the Jihadists have become the rulers of all humanity, which is, indeed, their stated aim, just as it was the stated aim of the Nazis.[77] Like the Nazi war against the Jews, then, the Jihadist war against the Jews is far more than a war against the "Zionist entity." Transcending political contingencies or issues of scapegoating or xenophobia, it is a metaphysical war.

In 1921 Nazi ideologue Alfred Rosenberg published his diatribe *Der staatsfeindliche Zionismus* (Zionism: enemy of the state), in which he argued that Zionism is a Jewish strategy for world domination.[78] Even prior to the formation of the Nazi Party, says Hitler, during his years in Vienna (1907—1913) he discovered the "national character of the Jews"—that is, the true evil of Jewish world domination—"in the Zionists."[79] As though writing the script for the Islamic Jihadists, he asserts, "While the Zionists try to make the rest of the world believe that the national consciousness of the Jew finds its satisfaction in the creation of a Palestinian state, the Jews again slyly dupe the dumb *Goyim*. It doesn't even enter their heads to build up a Jewish state in Palestine for the purpose of living there; all they want is a central organization for their international world swindle."[80] Therefore, "the Jewish state," according to the

Führer, "is completely unlimited as to territory."[81] Following suit, in the words of Sayyid Qutb, the Jewish state is just a small part of a "universal Zionist conspiracy."[82] Similarly, Hamas views itself as "the spearhead of the struggle with world Zionism."[83] In keeping with such a worldview, on 17 January 2009, in an Egyptian Al-Rahma television broadcast, Muhammad Hussein Yaqoub declared, "If the Jews left Palestine to us, would we start loving them?... The Jews are infidels—not because I say so,... but because... Allah who said that they are infidels.... They are enemies not because they occupied Palestine. They would have been enemies even if they did not occupy a thing.... Our fighting with the Jews is eternal..., until not a single Jew remains on the face of the Earth"[84]—this in the name of God.

Conclusion: The Post-Holocaust Continuation of the Holocaust

The silence on the Islamic Jihadist exterminationist anti-Semitism inherited from the Nazis that has pervaded Holocaust studies is striking, if not scandalous. Indeed, it is part of a phenomenon that I have described as "Holocaust studies without the Holocaust." In the Jihadist discourse, there is a characteristic projection of their own evil onto the Jew that comes out in the allegations that the Jews have an exterminationist agenda toward the Arabs, that they were behind the 9/11 attacks, that they seek to conquer the world, that "whoever denies their religion deserves to be killed,"[85] and even that the Jews are consumers of blood. How is this last accusation a projection of the Jihadist evil onto the Jews? In February 2006 Hamas produced a video of a homicide bomber's final testimony to the world, in which he declared, "My message to the loathed Jews is that there is no god but Allah [and] we will chase you everywhere! We are a nation that drinks blood, and we know that there is no blood better than the blood of Jews. We will not leave you alone until we have quenched our thirst with your blood, and our children's thirst with your blood."[86] This most radical appropriation of the soul of the other person—the soul that is in the blood—was a defining characteristic of the Nazis' assault on the soul of the Jew, as well as the Jihadists' radical appropriation of God. Indeed, it is done in the name of God, albeit a false god.

Such an episode brings to mind a rabbinic interpretation of the meaning of *Amalek*, the name of the tribe who attacked the children and elders among the Israelites immediately upon the exodus from Egypt, a name that personifies the evil that threatens the Jews and the rest of humanity. *Amalek*, it is said, means "Am Lak," a "people" who "lick" blood.[87] Whether they lick the blood or dip their hands into it, as in the case of the Muslims who butchered Yossi Avrahami and Vadim Norjitz in Ramallah on 13 October 2000, the Jihadists thrive on the blood of Jews, honoring the words of al-Husseini: "Their spilled blood pleases Allah."[88] Jihadism not only *legitimizes* spilling Jewish blood—it *sanctifies* it in an undermining of the divine, absolute prohibition against murder (Exodus 20:13). Indeed, a defining feature of the evil both of National Socialism and Islamic Jihadism is the undermining of this prohibition, which means that Islamic Jihadism is not a throwback to a medieval mindset. It is as modern as National Socialism—but even more deadly.

We have seen both Nazi influences on Jihadism and Jihadist parallels to Nazis. Robert Wistrich sums up the point made here very well:

> Their Bible may be the *Quran* and not *Mein Kampf*, but the mental structures and world view behind their actions have striking analogies with German National Socialism. The Muslim fundamentalists—like the Nazis before and during the *Shoah*—rant against the 'anonymous powers' of globalization and the plutocratic West.... Like their totalitarian predecessors, they (falsely) claim to speak for frustrated, underprivileged, and impoverished masses betrayed by more traditional Arab and Muslim ruling elites and ruthlessly exploited by international capitalism.... Anti-Semitic conspiracy theories lie at the very heart of the Muslim fundamentalist and Arab nationalist world view today—linking together plutocratic finance, international freemasonry, secularism, Zionism, and communism as dark occult forces led by the giant octopus of international Jewry.... This mythical structure of thought is in many ways virtually identical with Nazi anti-Semitism.....[89]

If the Jihadist Bible is the Quran, and not *Mein Kampf*, then the Jihadist evil transcends the Nazi evil, inasmuch as the Quran is *Scripture*, a revelation from God, and not just the pronouncements of the Führer, no matter how godlike he may be. Establishing a *scriptural* foundation for their actions, the Jihadists can justify any action. *Eclipsing* God, the Nazis eclipsed the absolute obligation imposed from beyond, so that the inner will and imagination from within posed the only limits to their actions. Hence the Nazis did not do what was unimaginable—they did everything imaginable. By contrast, *appropriating* God, the Jihadists appropriate the authority to impose from beyond what they have determined to be the will of Allah, which is not a matter of human will but an absolute obligation. There we have the nuanced difference between how this evil defined the Holocaust then and how it seeks to bring about another Holocaust.

Thus we who claim to be Holocaust scholars and teachers collide with a fundamental question, the question put to the first human being: Where are you? It is the question that decides everything.

Notes

1. Quoted in David Welch, *Hitler* (London: UCL Press, 1998), 97.

2. See, for example, Hasan al-Banna, *Five Tracts of Hasan al-Banna: A Selection from the Majmuat Rasail al-Imam al-Shahid Hasan al-Banna*, trans. Charles Wendell (Berkeley: University of California Press, 1978), 97.

3. Ibid., 45-46.

4. Adolf Hitler, *Mein Kampf*, trans. Ralph Manheim (Boston: Houghton Mifflin, 1971), 632.

5. Christina Phelps Harris, *Nationalism and Revolution in Egypt: The Role of the Muslim Brotherhood* (The Hague: Mouton & Co., 1964), 152.

6. Richard P. Mitchell, *The Society of the Muslim Brothers* (Oxford: Oxford University Press, 1993), 55.

7. See Ziad Abu-Amr, *Islamic Fundamentalism in the West Bank and Gaza: Muslim Brotherhood and Islamic Jihad* (Bloomington: Indiana University Press, 1994), 1.

8. Matthias Küntzel, "National Socialism and Anti-Semitism in the Arab World," *Jewish Political Studies Review* (17, Spring 2005): http://www.jcpa.org/phas/phas-kuntzel-s05.htm.

9. Matthias Küntzel, *Jihad and Jew-Hatred: Islamism, Nazism and the Roots of 9/11*, trans. Colin Meade (New York: Telos Press, 2007), 3.

10. Mitchell, 295.

11. Küntzel, *Jihad and Jew-Hatred*, 10.

12. Ibid., 59.

13. Harris, 152.

14. Küntzel, "National Socialism and Anti-Semitism in the Arab World."

15. Harris, 177-78.

16. Küntzel, *Jihad and Jew-Hatred*, 56.

17. Ibid., 24.

18. Küntzel, "National Socialism and Anti-Semitism in the Arab World."

19. Mitchell, 32.

20. Küntzel, *Jihad and Jew-Hatred*, 46.

21. David G. Dalin and John F. Rothman, *Icon of Evil: Hitler's Mufti and the Rise of Radical Islam* (New York: Random House, 2008), 131

22. Klaus Gensicke, *Der Mufti von Jerusalem: Amin el-Husseini und die Nationalsozialialisten* (Frankfurt am Main: Verlag Peter Lang, 1988), 45-46; my translation.

23. Bernard Lewis, *Semites and Anti-Semites: An Inquiry into Conflict and Prejudice* (New York: W. W. Norton, 1999), 147.

24. Küntzel, "National Socialism and Anti-Semitism in the Arab World."

25. Jeffrey Herf, *Nazi Propaganda for the Arab World* (New Haven, CT: Yale University Press, 2009), 19.

26. Chuck Morse, *The Nazi Connection to Islamic Terrorism* (New York: iUniverse, 2003), 46. It should be noted, however, that, according to Gensicke, Eichmann and Hagen were unable to set up a meeting with al-Husseini; see Gensicke, 52.

27. Ibid., 109.

28. Gensicke, 59-60.

29. Lukasz Hirszowicz, *The Third Reich and the Arab East* (London: Routledge & Kegan Paul, 1966), 122.

30. See Lewis, 158.

31. Herf, *Nazi Propaganda for the Arab World*, 60.

32. Joseph B. Schechtman, *The Mufti and the Fuehrer: The Rise and Fall of Haj Amin el-Husseini* (New York: Thomas Yoseloff, 1965), 110.

33. Ibid., 306.

34. Gensicke, 165.

35. Schechtman, 159-60.

36. Dalin and Rothman, 50.

37. Schechtman, 160.

38. Jeffrey Herf, *The Jewish Enemy: Nazi Propaganda during World War II and the Holocaust* (Cambridge, MA: Harvard University Press, 2006), 173.

39. Dalin and Rothman, 55.

40. Herf, *Nazi Propaganda for the Arab World*, 200.

41. Ibid., 201.

42. Schechtman, 182.

43. Herf, *Nazi Propaganda for the Arab World*, 244; emphasis in original.

44. David N. Bossie, "Yasser Arafat: Nazi Trained," *Washington Times*, 9 August 2002.

45. Morse, 90.

46. Dalin and Rothman, 133.

47. Quoted in ibid., 106.

48. Hirszowicz, 219; emphasis in original.

49. Raoul Aglion, *The Fighting French* (New York: Holt, 1943), 217.

50. Quoted in Ronald L. Nettler, *Past Trials and Present Tribulations: A Muslim Fundamentalist's View of the Jews* (Oxford: Pergamon, 1987), 35; emphasis added.

51. Ibid., 28.

52. Hirszowicz, 27.

53. Ibid., 42.

54. Schechtman, 81.

55. Lewis, 140.

56. Paul Longgrear and Raymond McNemar, "The Arab/Muslim Nazi Connection," *Militant Islam Monitor*, 4 May 2004, http://www.militantislammonitor.org/article/id/73.

57. Küntzel, *Jihad and Jew-Hatred*, 30.

58. John Gunther, *Inside Asia* (New York: Harper & Brothers, 1942), 552.

59. Schechtman, 85.

60. Moshe Perlman, *Mufti of Jerusalem: Haj Amin el Husseini, A Father of Jihad* (Philadelphia: Pavilion, 2006), 45.

61. Dalin and Rothman, 134-35.

62. Lewis, 232.

63. Ibid., 195.

64. Quoted in Serge Trifkovic, *The Sword of the Prophet: Islam: History, Theology, Impact on the World* (Boston: Regina Orthodox Press, 2002), 188.

65. Quoted in Küntzel, *Jihad and Jew-Hatred*, 61.

66. Hitler, 232.

67. See Lewis, 194.

68. See Barry Rubin, *Revolution Until Victory?: The Politics and History of the PLO* (Cambridge, Mass.: Harvard University Press, 1994), 125.

69. Lewis, 265-66.

70. Küntzel, *Jihad and Jew-Hatred*, 5.

71. Ibid., 94.

72. Trifkovic, 190.

73. Küntzel, *Jihad and Jew-Hatred*, 95.

74. Osama bin Laden, *Messages to the World: The Statements of Osama bin Laden*, ed. Bruce Lawrence, trans. James Howarth (London: Verso, 2005), 9.

75. "The Covenant of the Islamic Resistance Movement (HAMAS)," 18 August 1988, http://www.jewishvirtuallibrary.org/jsource/Terrorism/Hamas_covenant_complete.html

76. Hitler, 493.

77. See Sayyid Qutb, *Social Justice in Islam*, trans. John B. Hardie (New York: Octagon Books, 1963), 167-68.

78. Alfred Rosenberg, *Der staatsfeindliche Zionismus* (München: Zentralverlag der NSDAP, 1938, 3.

79. Adolf Hitler, *Mein Kampf*, trans. Ralph Manheim (Boston: Houghton Mifflin, 1971), 56.

80. Ibid., 325.

81. Ibid., 301.

82. See Nettler, 49, 55.

83. Quoted in Dimitry Kapustyan and Matt Nelson, *The Soul of Terror: The Worldwide Conflict between Islamic Terrorism and the Modern World* (Washington, DC: International Affairs Press, 2007), 147-48.

84. Muhammad Hussein Yaqoub, "We Will Fight, Defeat, and Annihilate Them," Al-Rahma TV, 17 January 2009, http://memri.org/bin/latestnews.cgi?ID=SD227809.

85. Bin Laden, 190.

86. Itamar Marcus and Barbara Cook, "Hamas Video: 'We will drink the blood of

the Jews,'" *Palestine Media Watch*, 14 February 2006, http://www.pmw.org.il/latest%20 bulletins%20new.htm#b140206.

87. See Moshe Weisman, ed., *The Midrash Says*, Vol. 2 (Brooklyn: Bnay Yakov Publications, 1980), 158.

88. Tom Knowlton, "Nazi Roots of Modern Radical Islam," 23 May 2014, http:// www.bbsradio.com/cgi-bin/webbbs/webbbs_config.pl?md=read;id=6846.

89. Robert S. Wistrich, "Islamic Judeophobia: An Existential Threat," in David Bukay, ed., *Muhammad's Monsters: A Comprehensive Guide to Radical Islam for Western Audiences* (Green Forest, AR: Balfour Books, 2004), 196.

CHAPTER 6

The Abuse of Memory as a Fig Leaf of Hate: Why Have the Lessons of the Holocaust Not Contained Contemporary Antisemitism?

SHIMON SAMUELS

Uniqueness

Is the Holocaust Unique? This question set the lines for an acrimonious debate in the 1980's between particularists and universalists. The former feared debasement of the Holocaust by invidious comparison.[1] The latter placed the Holocaust alongside non-Jewish experiences of mass extermination as part and parcel of the global context of genocide. This writer views that debate, *ipso facto*, as dishonoring the memory of the respective victims of each genocide. Each case is specific as a threshold phenomenon, while each also adds its unique memory as signposts along an incremental continuum of horror. We focus here on the relevance of the Holocaust as a preventive instrument against its recurrence, that is, a benchmark for minorities, a yardstick for contemporary atrocity, and—as convincingly demonstrated by the late Franklin Littell—an early-warning system for mass murder.[2]

The Holocaust's uniqueness within Jewish history is only a question of degree. Two thousand years of antisemitism—successively political, theological, and racial—climaxed in the Nazi Final Solution. The durability, persistence, and pervasiveness in time and space of ever-mutating Jew-hatred have made the Holocaust a unique baseline among genocides. Nevertheless, the steps to the Final Solution provide a paradigm. Its stations proceed from incitement to an ideology of hate, its dissemination from a political power base, its inculcation bound together with paramilitary training, the de-legitimization of targeted enemies, legislation to validate their social exclusion and incarceration, their deportation and eventual extermination. This paradox has been succinctly summarized by Henry Knight as "The Holocaust is never not Jewish but always more than Jewish."[3]

For two millennia of exile, Jewish history was characterized by constant precariousness. The decade 1938–1948 represented the extremes of nadir to apogee along the Jewish timeline—from utter powerlessness and almost extinction to a return to sovereignty and history. A lachrymose interpretation of these 2,000 years may be a prescription for paranoia. Yet, whether acknowledged or not by the Diaspora, the Jewish State is a psycho-political shattering of the image of marginalization in the communities of exile. For the first time since the Second Temple, "Let My People Go" is a reality, from the Soviet Gulag to the Rivers of Babylon. To be a Jewish victim of oppression today is an act of choice. The battle for Jewish survival is a function of power politics.

Our sages have long debated two distinct modes for interaction with the world: "*Am Levadad Yishkon*"—a people that dwells alone, i.e., ostracized, marginalized, ghettoized, victimized, introverted, etc. or "*Or Lagoyim*"—a light unto the nations, i.e., a barometer, an alarm bell, a participant, and even a role model.

At the 1938 Evian conference on refugees, the world was not silent. Each nation's representative explained why Jewish fugitives from Nazism were unwelcome. Only the Ambassador of the Dominican Republic offered places for Jewish agriculturists. In 1971, I drove the 150 miles across that Caribbean island from the farm cooperative established by Jewish refugees of the Holocaust at Sosua[4] in the North, to an Israeli rural training project at Azua in the South. To have joined with the Israeli technical assistance team in building the village church for Dominican "campesinos" was, for me, a dramatic and personal act of transition between the modes from object to subject, from voyeur to actor.

Pastor Martin Niemöller confessed a betrayal of personal responsibility: "When they came for the Jews, I was not a Jew, so I did not protest. When they came for the Communists, neither was I a Communist. When they came for the Trade Unionists, nor was I a Trade Unionist. When they came for me, there was no one left to protest...." He might have said,

"What starts with the Jews does not end with the Jews, for hatred is indivisible." So, too, with the Holocaust. For the last forty years, curricula development and research into the Holocaust have been accepted into mainstream academic programs in North America and Western Europe.

Figleaf

A delicate balance must be maintained between the particular and the universal to prevent the anthropologization of the Holocaust, i.e. a mourning for Jews murdered 70 years ago may camouflage a prejudice against today's Jewish neighbors. Indeed, this parallels anti-immigrant groups in Europe brandishing the flag of Palestine to cover up their wish to empty the streets of their Arab neighbors.

The Stockholm Forum on the Holocaust was organizing teacher seminars in Russia. Invited to join one in Archangel, I contacted the local Jewish community President. He knew nothing of the seminar. The Swedish organizer responded as to why they were not invited: "We are teaching Holocaust, what has that to do with contemporary Jews?"

Containment of Contemporary Hate

This then raises an uncomfortable point: the massive investment in Holocaust memory has neither prevented nor mitigated the resurgence of anti-Semitism, Gypsophobia (Romaphobia), homophobia, or even Skinhead violence against the disabled. The signpost itinerary in today's Berlin of memorials to each of these groups of victims in the Nazi death camps has in no way ended prejudice against them. Indeed, it is rising.

The Lessons of the Holocaust as an Arm against Recurrence

If Holocaust education is to be an instrumental pedagogy, and it is to serve as the touchstone for anti-racist and human rights sensitization, the educator has a deprogramming responsibility to return to the touchstone itself: today's victims of resurgent antisemitism and also Gypsophobia. The lessons of the Holocaust must re-couple the fate of its victims with their survivors and heirs targeted in our time.

Perhaps teaching the facts has been inadequate. Should we not now move the emphasis to defining, drawing, and applying the lessons of the

Holocaust to a practical global agenda focused here, inter alia on: language—memory—justice—restitution—technology? I will, throughout, propose brief applications to the cases of Rwanda, Kosova, and Halabja.

Language

Every genocide covers itself in euphemism: the Nazis used "special treatment" for deportation, in Rwanda the Tutsis were identified on Hutu radio as "cafards" (roaches). In the immediate post-war period, the images of the Holocaust acted as protective "teflon" against blatant expressions of antisemitism in the West. Indeed, open identification with such positions became distasteful and even legally actionable. For the past thirty years, this "teflon" has been eroding. Remaining pangs of conscience for active or passive collaboration in countries occupied by the Nazis have been assuaged by a projection of guilt mechanism, i.e., the use of Holocaust language, which began in European media, to describe the Middle East conflict.

In 1983, I shared a panel at the International Society of Political Psychology in St. Catherine's College, Oxford, with a Lebanese researcher. We each respectively exposed anti-Semitic and Islamophobic stereotyping in the European press during the 1982 Israel-Lebanon war.[5] European collaborators and bystanders in the Nazi period could now breathe freely, whispering, "Look at them today, we were not that bad?" Rabbi Abraham Joshua Heschel has said that "Auschwitz was built not with stones, but words." As children we would sing the ditty, "Sticks and stones may break my bones but words will never hurt me!" We were so wrong; words can kill! The torrent of Holocaust language, now turned against Jews, could be directly correlated with a dramatic growth in antisemitic incidents and especially terrorist acts against Jewish institutions.[6]

The 1989 fall of the Berlin Wall and the end of the Soviet empire released the pent-up ghosts of classical antisemitism in countries where the Holocaust had succeeded, i.e., "an antisemitism without Jews" or "a phantom pain syndrome" (the limb has been amputated but the body still seeks to scratch). The last vestiges of the ravaged communities of Eastern Europe became the scapegoats for the pain of withdrawal from the central economy and the transition to market capitalism. Yet East European antisemitism has less to do with "genetic Jews" than with the abstract image of "generic Jews"—a euphemism or code-word for "imported," "foreign," "Western," etc. "The Protocols of Zion"—a Tsarist forgery, claiming a world Jewish conspiracy—resurfaced in every post-Communist country, feeding a persistent disposition to hate that which is most feared—the unknown! To make sense of it, a conspiracy theory of invisible enemies of the nation is the line of least resistance. Antisemitism in almost "Judenrein" post-Holocaust Eastern Europe is a diagnostic code to undemocratic conditions and behavior and a threat for all minorities. In the absence of real Jews, antisemitic prejudice still persists as a vital element of political discourse.[7]

The word "Jew" represented anything alien to the "Volk," from Western media to pop music, human rights to technology. Ignorance, frustration, envy, rancor, fear of the new and the different are the bases for the conspiracy theories that are the building blocks of xenophobia. Post-Kosovo Serbs explained their situation as the result of American/NATO interventionism, German revanchism, Islamic fundamentalism, the Vatican, and even Zionism. Remove German revanchism and the Vatican for the Croat. The litany has its variants throughout East-Central Europe. There may be no Jewish presence, but the "phantom missing limb" still seeks to be scratched.

Memory

Ibuka, the name of the Rwandan NGO, born of the genocide, means "Memory" in the imperative. We work closely with its leaders on commemoration and justice. "Zachor"—Thou shalt remember!—is Judaism's categorical imperative. Instrumental memory draws lessons for survival. "Memoricide" (twice murdered by denying the memory of the victim) is an abomination. Holocaust denial or so-called "revisionism" is genocide compounded by memoricide. A political transvestitism has focused extremist agendas on the Holocaust; for example, the French denier Robert Faurisson, though identified with the extreme right, published his denials of the gas chambers in Trotskyite publications. The far right aimed to absolve Germany: "if the Holocaust was a Jewish lie, then Germany was its first victim. "For some the intent was: "Let us make it a reality."

The Simon Wiesenthal Center began a campaign to obtain a plaque in memory of the eighty-seven Jews brought west from Auschwitz to Struthof-Natzweiler. There, they were gassed to supply skeletons at the request of the Anatomy Department of nearby Strasbourg University. That campaign for integrity to history will not be over until plaques are erected at Struthof for all its other victims: Algerian Moslems, Soviets, Spanish Republicans, Roma, and homosexuals.

Memory is to be applied: At the inauguration of the Lyons Museum of Resistance and Deportation, Suzanne Lagrange, recounting her deportation to Auschwitz and the murder of her father before her eyes on arrival, was interrupted by a young German in the audience who wished to apologize for Nazi Germany. "Sit down, we do not believe in trans-generational guilt," she said. He took his seat, whereupon Mme. Lagrange turned on him. "Now apologize," she rebuked him. "I don't understand. You said...," protested the young German. "I said you bear no responsibility for the crimes of Nazi Germany, but you share responsibility for the neo-Nazi crimes of young Germans today! Germany is not the bearer of collective guilt. But it must acknowledge its collective shame, thus endowing it with a special sensitivity."

The opening of both World War Two and Communist-period archives were, for a new generation of political leadership and opinion molders, a painful crisis of memory with perceptual withdrawal symptoms (what is termed in psychology "cognitive dissonance"). Absorption of new and contradictory information, resulting in the deconstruction of anchored myths, predispositions, and prejudices, requires the reformulation or reinterpretation of collective memory, i.e., "cognitive dissonance." This can take two forms: Negative: neurotic grappling to unreality, a search for scapegoats, further denials, and an entrenchment of extreme positions; and, Positive: exposure of truths to lance a long-festering boil, thus allowing the pus to drain. The cleansing of the wounds is an act of catharsis and a rejection of revisionist escape-routes, which were constructed to assuage conscious or unconscious scars of guilt.

Such transparent fine-tuning of the psychological underpinnings of national collective memory may be opportunities for conflict resolution based directly upon the lessons of Holocaust denial. At the 1994 Buenos Aires inauguration of the Wiesenthal Centre's Holocaust exhibit, The

Courage to Remember, journalists asked its relevance to Argentina's recent "dirty war" and its "disappeared" victims. I spoke of the same exhibit's successful tour of China, where visitors, who knew nothing of Jews or Nazis, viewed it through the prism of their own experience: the Tanaka Plan, the Nanking massacre, Japanese war crime medical experiments, etc. The Courage to Remember became a memory trigger to whomever peers into its mirror. The same applied to the Argentine visitor, who could see it in the context of the General's dictatorship and the "Dirty War."

Memory requires shrines as focal points. These memorials must be maintained and protected. Some became museum sites, like Yad Vashem or Auschwitz-Birkenau. They serve to combat denial.

The Wiesenthal Centre proposed to Ibuka that, just as in the case of Auschwitz, the memory of the thousands of corpses in the hecatomb of Morombi be submitted for inscription by the UNESCO World Heritage Committee.

According to the Talmud, "He who saves a life has saved a universe." Jews call these saviors "Righteous Gentiles," who must be eternally acknowledged and commemorated for putting their lives in peril to rescue another. In the case of Rwanda, of the 3,000 "Blue Beret" United Nations Peacekeepers who were withdrawn as the genocide began, some 250 chose to remain. The movie "Hotel Rwanda" portrays how 11 saved 800 during the100 days' nightmare. We suggested that the new Rwanda locate and honor these heroes together with the few Hutus who hid Tutsis. Similarly, I climbed in the footsteps of Yugoslav Jewish fugitives through the mountainous border terrain, where Kosovar Muslim rescuers led them to safety in Albania. My guide was the grandson of the Righteous Gentile—a businessman who had made the Haj to Mecca—who conceived, led and financed their escape. This wartime operation is now known as the "White Hats," for the Albanian egg-shaped headgear which was their cover. Similar stories and photos of Muslim Bosnian rescuers of Jewish fugitives from Croatian Ustasha Nazi allies, are even more dramatic. The circle is closed by the similar work of the Jewish 'La Benevolencia' in the 1990s, saving Bosnians from Serb brutality and deportation to Srebenica. The commemoration of these episodes of reciprocal courage and mutual respect between Muslims and Jews may be valuable lessons to reinvigorate that challenged relationship.

Justice

We are witnessing an evolving jurisprudence on genocide, war crimes, crimes against humanity, and human rights. Real-time media reporting, a shrinking world village, market interdependence, and the ineluctable imperative toward transparency are telescoping time and space. Despite the dangerous politicization of the International Criminal Court, there is growing understanding that conflict resolution requires psychological closure that, in turn, is conditioned upon collective satisfaction that justice is seen to be done.

The late Simon Wiesenthal, on entering a courtroom in the trial of a mass murderer, would demand the removal of the blind statue of justice holding the scales that symbolize a balance between crime and punishment. How many seconds would the accused serve for each of his victims, Wiesenthal would scoff. Yet he believed that justice was necessary for closure and a pedagogical lesson to the younger generation that, even seventy years later, they would still be responsible for their crimes. "Longevity does not endow impunity."[8]

Tutsi justice in post-genocide Rwanda differed. The "Gachacha process" penned the captured perpetrators in open-air camps. They wore unmistakable pink tee-shirts, which if removed, in or out of the prison camp, carried severe penalty. Justice was a truth and reconciliation process. The new regime sought justice but also reunification. Wiesenthal, while still in Mauthausen—already liberated by American forces—would accredit "para-notaries" to take testimony to ensure that, even if the witnesses were to die, the facts they certified would remain valid for litigation. Gachacha adopted the same system due to the risk that witnesses might be killed to forestall their court appearance.

Simon Wiesenthal, while still in the liberated camp, began to scrupulously collect documents. This emphasis is a theme of every genocide. At a 1997 seminar on Documentation, held by the Soros Foundation at the Central European University in Budapest, experts recounted hair-raising tales of archives targeted for arson or terrorism and the murder of researchers in the ex-Yugoslavia.[9] The Holocaust, as the most documented of genocides, set baselines for the perils and pitfalls in constituting archives and determining rights to access them. The assembling of documents in the "machete genocide" of the Tutsis was a similarly dangerous task, and is now taken seriously as Rwandan genocide denial increases.

Restitution

Organizing a 1996 conference in Geneva on "Loot and Restitution: The Moral Responsibility to History," I could not imagine the volume over the next four years of World War Two assets-related restitution enquiries, claims, and negotiation. Media and judicial pressure demanded transparency, and most combatant and neutral nations successively established national archival research commissions to investigate banks, insurance companies, museums, and private industry.

The Washington, D.C., conference on Holocaust Assets in December 1998 defined the array of problems and set the scene for the final phase—that of enforcing settlement, the close of commitments, the fulfillment of promises. In the spirit of the Biblical injunction of Leviticus, Chapter 25, verse 10: "In the fiftieth year... thou shalt restitute to each his property."

Why over fifty years until Pandora's emergence? Most Holocaust survivors, for self-rehabilitation, had closed a curtain. Those returnees who submitted claims were met, at worst, with violence, or at a poor best, with banker obscurantism. The prevailing exigencies of resettlement in lands of freedom, the establishment and support of a Jewish state and, for those who stayed behind, the new challenges of survival under Communism, vitiated immediate post-war indemnification demands. The weakness of the Jewish lobby, and its ideological divisions over reparations from the new Germany, was to limit strategic approaches to the issue. With the onset of the Cold War, Jewish material claims from the West were frozen as energy was devoted to the needs of their brethren under Communism and in other lands of oppression. The fall of the Berlin Wall and the consequent rollback of the Soviet Empire led to the opening of archives, first throughout Eastern Europe, with an imperative to transparency that moved ever westward. From 1989 to 1995, the focus of fiftieth anniversaries drew from the mouths of survivors belated testimonies for the grandchild generation.

Holocaust museums, *Schindler's List*, global village communications technology, real-time genocidal reporting, and a fascination with the events of the 1930s set the scene and the tone. The catalyst was the political and juridical clout of the U.S. Congress and Federal class action suits against American affiliates of European holders of looted assets. Were this to have remained a uniquely Jewish issue, the price might have invalidated its purpose, as it only led to the awakening of dormant antisemitism. The restitution campaign had not only its own intrinsic justice but served as the springboard for a moral pedagogy, including the caveat that the targets of research—World War Two neutrals and combatants—are not the bearers of collective intergenerational guilt. Indeed, the enquiry process required the co-optation of all elements in societies eager for the truth.

The restitution issue was not exclusive to Jewish claimants, but of concern to a community of World War Two victims, now evident in Slavic forced/slave labor and Sinti and Roma claims processes. Indeed, in 1995, I conducted research on the Tripartite Gold Commission in the French Finance Ministry archives. This revealed Nazi "mix and melt" of "monetary gold" (looted from occupied Central Banks) and "non-monetary gold" (stolen from Holocaust victims and mainly comprising "tooth gold" extracted from the mouths of corpses after the gas chamber). Following the release of those findings, I was asked for information on lost gold by officials from Hungary, Italy, Spain, and Turkey.

Such claims are also a contribution to an evolving jurisprudence in the war crime of looting. A CNN financial analyst emphasized this during Kabila's march on Kinshasa. "It took a Holocaust bank scandal to open Mobutu's accounts..." Based on this precedent, the British Society of Black Lawyers began campaigning for both a high school curriculum on the history of colonialism and compensation for slavery by forgiving African debt. Similarly, Ethiopian refugees have approached New York Holocaust Class Action lawyers to consider restitution action for their lost assets.

The restitution campaign had shaken to the core national myths of World War Two neutrality and resistance, questioning human behavior and disestablishing collective memories. On a 2012 solidarity mission to the Kurdish Regional Government (KRG) of Iraq, the Wiesenthal Centre became an advisor on restitution—not material but medical—for the survivors of the Halabja and broader "Anfal" ("Spoils"—an Iraqi euphemism for genocide), victims of Saddam Hussein's 1988 poison attack. In 1991, the Wiesenthal Centre had issued a report—"the Poison

Gas Connection"—identifying the corporate suppliers of chemical precursors used in these atrocities. Together with the KRG, the Centre had prepared an exhibition on Halabja. Five thousand had perished that day, but of the 27,000 wounded, many today have 80-90 % incapacity in their lungs or vision. The Centre advised a legal team on documentation and restitution for suits to provide funding for medical treatment, mainly in Europe. Poison gas was the tool of mass murder in the Holocaust. Its lessons serve justice and compensation for the Kurds also.

Technology

At a 1988 anti-racist conference in the Netherlands, Turkish migrant workers' groups attacked me for holding a seminar on "The Holocaust Experience as an Early Warning System." They claimed that the Holocaust only served Zionist interests and was irrelevant to their needs. I shared with them a number of neo-Nazi computer games that I had just obtained from Germany. These included "The Aryan Test," "The Führer Lives," and "KZ Manager." The latter game required the player, normally of high-school age, to select among a series of victims: Jews, Turks, North Africans, Pakistanis, homosexuals, handicapped, Communists, or Jehovah's Witnesses. Given an initial 2500 deutschmarks, the child would choose victims according to a tariff, purchase Zyklon-B gas canisters, proceed to exterminate them, sell the hair and gold-teeth to recoup capital, and buy new victims, etc. The language and modalities of the Holocaust were now addressed to contemporary targets.

The Netherlands migrant groups were shocked into a new mindset regarding cooperation with Jews. In fact, these very groups, in 1998, elected me to the Board of the European Network Against Racism (ENAR) and, at its 1999 meeting in Helsinki, endorsed the Wiesenthal Centre's call for "German industry to compensate their former slave and forced labourers."[10]

The child player of these games is also a victim. Desensitized to hate, he becomes vulnerable recruit potential for neo-Nazi circles, just as today young Muslims can be radicalized to Jihadism through social networks. Our exposure of these games led to a first international conference at UNESCO in 1992 on "Educating Against Prejudice," and to an Istanbul television debate on "The Turkish Victim of neo-Nazism in Today's Germany." Two thousand floppy disks of "Race War," a game produced by the Nebraska-based American Nazi Party's Gary Lauck, were held by Amsterdam airport Customs in 1992.

Twenty years of Lauck's mailings and postage-stamp licking can now be downloaded in five minutes over the World Wide Web. The Wiesenthal Centre's latest CD-ROM, Digital Hate 2014, is based on over 30,000 sites in over a dozen languages, a figure that is growing exponentially each year. The first such site was launched in 1995.

Simon Wiesenthal characterized the Holocaust as the meeting point between ideology and technology. Indeed, the Los Angeles-based Museum of Tolerance of the Simon Wiesenthal Centre is a hi-tech human rights laboratory directed to the Internet generation. The Museum's "Tools for Tolerance" programs provide sensitization to pluralism courses for law enforcement agencies and the military. Technology has empowered the forces of hate. Terrorists, political extremists, racists, and Holocaust deniers have invaded cyberspace to sow the seeds of prejudice with impunity. For the hate-monger, the Jew is only a tactical target; his strategic objective is democracy itself.

In 2008, I was invited by the C:100 Islam and the West in Dialogue, of the World Economic Forum, to present a "Website Tracking" PowerPoint on Antisemitism and Islamophobia. The findings were displayed in Davos and Sharm al Sheikh. While antisemitism came from both Islamist and extreme right, the study showed that both Islamophobic and Islamist sites were rivalling mainstream Muslim sites in popularity.[11]

The Wiesenthal Centre, following the Mohammed Merah murder of children in the Jewish school of Toulouse, met with Muslim leadership of the city. Sharing with them CDs of such websites, we suggested that they watch where their children were surfing and, if possible, have a meeting of Muslim and Jewish parents to watch together. As all—Christians, Jews, Muslims, women, children, disabled, gay -are targeted on the Internet, it is the perfect platform for solidarity.

Technology, however, is neutral, it may be abused or productively and creatively used. This technology should be, in fact, an agent for both Holocaust education and the application of its lessons to cutting-edge dilemmas and challenges.

Conclusion

The experience of the Holocaust must serve as a weather vane or windsleeve, to sound the alarm and train society's ears to the sounds of impending danger. "What starts with the Jews..." is an instrument of measure, a barometer for democratic health, and the lessons of the Holocaust provide an early-warning system to combat contemporary intolerance.

The Simon Wiesenthal Centre has defined this engagement on three levels:

- "monitoring" of the trans-ideological and international linkage between all actors that threaten the democratic condition;
- "counteraction" through coalition-building, networking, exposure through the media, legislative, judicial, and governmental authorities, and international organizations;
- "prevention" through contributing to an expanding moral pedagogy on human rights.

The examples drawn in this paper from the lessons of the Holocaust point to demands for greater media responsibility, more humane treatment of refugees, improved professional accountability of insurance companies toward beneficiaries, an exercise in prudence for art dealers and museum curators, a reminder of client-first good practice for the banking industry, and more acute governmental sensitivity to the posterity power of archival transparency.

Simon Wiesenthal conditioned the granting of his name, in his lifetime, to an institution that would guard memory and employ vigilance to assist in preventing the Holocaust's recurrence for any people. Following the "machete genocide," the Rwandan government of reconciliation sought advice from three Jewish experts, respectively, in regard to the:

- rehabilitation of survivors,
- the apprehension of criminal perpetrators, and
- the establishment of mechanisms for commemoration and education.

The Holocaust has taught us that no closure can be possible without serving rehabilitation, justice, and memory. At the November 1999 "Holocaust Phenomenon" conference in Prague, Yehuda Bauer was quoted to have said, "even as the mass murder of Jews was ended by the defeat of the Nazis, the source of the Holocaust remains the same. Genocide Avenue is marked with many chronological signposts and should provide a solidarity platform for all massacred peoples. Each signpost exposes the emptiness of such expressions as "Never Again." But solidarity among the victims of genocides can act as a lever against the identity theft of the narratives of victim peoples; in other words, to contain the subsequent denial, banalization and trivialization common to all victimologies.

Simon Wiesenthal, in 1995—the UN "Year of Tolerance"—was Austria's representative at the 50th General Assembly. There, he spoke out on Srebrenica and Rwanda, calling for the prosecution of the perpetrators. In Kigali, in 1996, I sat among an intergenerational gathering of native American, Armenian, Jewish, Cambodian, Bosnian and Tutsi survivors in a shared circle of communion. Between them, there was no pecking-order of tragedies, no competition in suffering, no theft from each other's narrative, and total respect within that commonality between all the victims.

The year 2013 marked the 25th anniversary of Saddam Hussein's gassing of the Kurds of Halabja. Speaking to Kurdish survivors on a solidarity visit, I explained that, "As a Jew, once exiled from the Land of Israel to Babylon, here, a few kilometres from the border of today's Iran, we wrote a book called the Talmud, which states, "If I am not for myself, who will be? But if I am only for myself, what am I? If not now, then when?" We are here for you, just as I believe you will be there for us.

Halabja, Morombi, or a twenty-minute drive from here (Paris), Drancy, a way station to Auschwitz for over 76,000 French Jews. These today are monuments, signposts on the Avenue of Genocide that must serve as warnings, not as precedents.

Notes

1. This paper draws on and updates my chapter, "Applying the Lessons of the Holocaust," included in the 2001 edition of *Is the Holocaust Unique?: Perspectives on Comparative Genocide,* edited by Alan S. Rosenbaum, Westview Press, 2001. I have long considered that chapter as a credo and objective that has informed my career. Therefore, its essence will be adapted for the Arab reader in the Arabic language edition

of *Antisemitism—The Generic Hatred: Essays in Memory of Simon Wiesenthal.*

2. Franklin Littell, "Essay: Early Warning," *Holocaust and Genocide Studies,* vol. 3, no. 4 (1988), pp. 483-490.

3. In a conversation with Henry Knight at the 2011 ASC in Rochester, New York. To maintain its pristine unique character and distance itself from the banalization of the term "Holocaust" (as in such obscenities as the title of a pornographic movie, "The Naked Holocaust"), or even political-agenda amalgams (such as animal rights activists on "the pet Holocaust"), there is an increasing use of the Hebrew "Shoah" to replace the popularization of the term "Holocaust."

4. Shimon Samuels, "Sosua—Moshav in the Caribbean," The American Jewish Yearbook, New York, 1972.

5. Shimon Samuels, "West European Media Antisemitism in the Lebanon War: Political Campaign or Mimetic Effect?" presented at the International Society of Political Psychology 1983 conference at St. Catherine's College, Oxford.

6. Shimon Samuels, "Antisemitic Incidents and Anti-Jewish Terrorism in Western Europe 1980 -1982—The Dam Breaks," ADL Eurobriefs, Paris, September 1982, Anti-Defamation League of B'nai B'rith.

7. In a conversation with Sewerin Blumsztajn.

8. "One Person's Commitment to Never Forget," Response, p. 4, September 1989, Simon Wiesenthal Centre, Los Angeles.

9. Based on a seminar held by the Soros Foundation at the Central European University in Budapest in 1997, in which the author participated.

10. ENAR is an umbrella body for over six hundred anti-racist NGOs in the then-fifteen and now twenty-eight member States of the European Union, established in cooperation with the European Commission.

11. "Islam and the West: Annual Report on the State of Dialogue," World Economic Forum, Davos, 2008, *Islam and the West: The Internet Dimension,* Shimon Samuels, pp. 78-79.

Part III

The Event

CHAPTER 7

Against the Odds: American Jews & the Rescue of Europe's Refugees, 1933-1941. Researching the Mayer Lehman Charity Fund

KAREN S. FRANKLIN

> "Mr. and Mrs. Sinn and Margot, their younger daughter, were fortunate enough to have secured their visas before July 1, 1941, but it was exceedingly difficult to get passage for them as they were trying to get away just at the height of the exodus from Germany. Their visas would have expired on August 24, 1941, and they sailed from Lisbon on August 20th! The Sinns arrived in New York on September 1, 1941...
>
> Else was employed when her family arrived and Margot soon got work running a power machine. Both girls have been constantly employed and Mrs. Dryfoos's last report [from the Employment Department of the National Refugee Service] stated that their combined earnings were $36.00 weekly. The Lehman Fund supplements the Sinns' income to the extent of $41.00 a month, but that is to be decreased this coming September...
>
> The cost of transportation to the United States for Mr. and Mrs. Sinn and Margot was $2004.35."[1]

In 2008 while conducting research for *The Morgenthaus: A Legacy of Service,* an exhibition for the Museum of Jewish Heritage—A Living Memorial to the Holocaust in New York City, I came upon a copy of *The Fourth Report of the Mayer Lehman Charity Fund.*[2] I had not heard of the fund and wondered what the history of the document was and where the first three reports were. I spent the next six years searching for the answers.

At the same time as I was researching the Fund, I learned that the Museum of Jewish Heritage was preparing an exhibition that would frame the larger story of American efforts to assist European refugees. My research about the Lehmans became part of the Museum's exhibition *Against the Odds: American Jews and the Rescue of Europe's Refugees: 1933-1941*. The exhibition opened in May 2013 and ran through February 2015.

The historical context of the period was outlined in an introductory text panel in this exhibition:

> When the Nazis came to power in Germany in 1933 and began to persecute the Jews, they touched off an international refugee crisis that escalated through the 1930s.
>
> Most countries refused to accept large numbers of Jewish refugees. Many German Jews hoped to come to the United States, but laws passed by Congress in the 1920s had ended the era of open immigration. The new policy set strict quotas that made no special allowances for refugees.
>
> Jews in flight from the Nazi regime reached out to relatives, friends, and even strangers in America, whose sponsorship was essential if they hoped to secure U.S. visas. (*Against the Odds* tells the story of American Jews who answered their call for help.) Working within the limits of American immigration law, they overcame obstacles to bring thousands of Jewish refugees to safety.

The Lehman Family and Governor Herbert H. Lehman

The Lehmans were instrumental in assisting over 200 individuals, most of them relatives, by providing financial support to those still in Europe, affidavits (documents required for an American visa, that ensured that the American sponsor would support an immigrant financially, if required), expediting documents, and providing employment opportunities prior to, during and following the Second World War. Much of this was possible through the work of Governor Herbert H. Lehman.

Herbert H. Lehman was the youngest son of Mayer Lehman. A gifted and eloquent speaker, the young Lehman was Governor of New York State from 1933 to 1942. In the 1930s, Lehman was an advocate for change in immigration policy. In 1934, he wrote to President Franklin D. Roosevelt, appealing to him to raise the immigration quota for German Jews: "It is imperative that the opportunity for immigration be given to as many of the persecuted Jewish citizens of that country as is possible."[3] His appeal to Roosevelt was not successful; nonetheless, he used his personal and political connections to assist refugees, expediting paperwork, providing jobs, and allocating resources.

Because of his highly visible position as a man of power and wealth, and as a Jew, Governor Lehman's office was flooded with requests by desperate unrelated individuals, Jewish and non-Jewish, and by family members, who begged for help in fleeing Europe and establishing lives in the United States. In April 1937, well before the surge of requests would arrive, the Governor wrote his assistant, Carolin Flexner, "I wish I could help all the worthy people in Germany who desire to emigrate. It is obviously impossible for me to do so as I am already contributing as much as I possibly can afford… I have a stack of letters here which I have not even sent you."[4] On November 29, 1938, he wrote to a Mr. Max Moser, who had asked for assistance in bringing his relatives to the United States: "I have received hundreds if not thousands of requests…" He also responded that he had just learned that his own family had been sent to camps.[5]

Governor Lehman directed most of the requests to Carolin Flexner. He also asked his niece, Dorothy Bernhard, a daughter of his brother Arthur Lehman, to oversee the overwhelming administrative tasks required to coordinate the response to relatives who requested aid. They received assistance through a family foundation, the Mayer Lehman Charity Fund.

Mayer Lehman Charity Fund

The Mayer Lehman Charity Fund had been established in the 1920s to support family members in Europe. Governor Lehman and Dorothy Bernhard took on the task of raising money to replenish the fund so that they could facilitate the immigration and resettlement of those relatives fleeing for their lives. Lehman sent solicitation letters to family members on November 17, 1938: "We feel that under the circumstances a substantial fund should now be provided by members of the family so that these people... can be supported for at least a number of years. We have already given affidavits for a very large number, many of whom have come to this country."[6]

Carolin Flexner and Dorothy Bernhard worked together in coordination with numerous social service organizations including: the National Refugee Service, National Council for Jewish Women, Jewish Social Service Association, and the German-Jewish Children's Association. The resettlements took place not only in New York, but also in Detroit, San Francisco, Washington, and elsewhere.

Between 1939 and 1952, Dorothy Bernhard wrote at least seven periodic letters or reports to the family, describing the activities of the organization.[7] The Fourth Report was one of the most detailed, documenting the stories of 89 individuals. At the time it was written, circa June 1942, 39 individuals for whom the family had provided affidavits were still in Europe. Not all could be rescued; among those who received affidavits but ultimately perished were Seligman and Hedwig Koschland and their four children, Justin and Lena Adler and their two children, and Eva Thalheimer, a first cousin of Mayer Lehman.

Included among the first four reports are the stories of Max Neugass, who arrived in Miami, Florida in June 1941 after detention in Casablanca, Morocco; Ilse and Adolf Baer, whose escape took them to Egypt and Palestine, and then to Brazil before reaching California, and Julius Hirschberger, who sent "imploring letters" from Belgium.[8]

Many of those newly arrived in the US took any job they could find; work in a delicatessen, janitor in a Home for the Aged, household help, manager of a cigar stand, and factory positions were among those listed in Dorothy Bernhard's reports. Dr. Erich Kaufmann was one of several physicians listed by Bernhard; he received a New York state license to practice medicine a few months after his arrival in New York in 1938. He had received an affidavit from the Lehmans but did not receive financial assistance after he arrived.[9] The reports list disbursements of loans to establish businesses with the Fund's assistance. Some of these enterprises were more successful than others. The later reports describe Dorothy Bernhard's continuing relationship with the families through social service organizations that administered support, and as the immigrants adjusted to their new situations.

The Lehmans also worked together with Edith Altschul Lehman's brother, Frank Altschul, to coordinate political efforts and to facilitate the immigration of other relatives and business associates. Altschul himself provided affidavits for dozens of his wife's Viennese family members.

The Governor and influential Lehman cousins used political pressure to obtain the release of their mutual relatives Hans Gerst and Ernst Silbermann from Dachau in November 1938.[10] Lehman was particularly interested in the family because he was a first cousin of the mother of Hans Gerst's wife, Irma.

Hans Gerst and Ernst Silbermann were taken into "protective custody" with other Jews from Bamberg on November 10, 1938. Silbermann's father made a personal appeal for their release on November 12 but received a negative response on November 21. Additional appeals also went unanswered until U. S. General Consul S. W. Honaker wrote a letter to the Secret State Police in Nuremberg stating: "I hope you will take into consideration the special interest shown by prominent people in the fate of Messrs. Hans Gerst and Ernst Silbermann. I take this opportunity to reiterate the fact that Hans Gerst and Ernst Ludwig Silbermann are relatives of very prominent people in the United States. I have received documents from the Assistant Secretary of State in Washington that... (they) have permission to enter the United States, as soon as they reach their turn on the waiting list."[11] As a result of Lehman's pleas to Honaker, Gerst and Silvermann were able to flee to England and later to the United States.

Additional research yielded information on dozens of other individuals who were assisted by other family members and associates. Carolin Flexner, of limited means, personally provided an affidavit for a family and privately assisted a number of refugees. Dorothy Bernhard also developed strong personal relationships with many of the families with whom she was in contact.

As the requests poured in, some guidelines for who would receive an affidavit had to be established. Family came first (visas were more likely to be issued by the State Department to close family, and to those who were likely to be self-sufficient). If a family relationship was not already known to Dorothy Bernhard, an explanation or family tree was requested. Those whom Bernhard described as "distantly related" were individuals who had connections that can now be established from the mid-18th century. Because they were helped it was inferred that Dorothy Bernhard must have been aware of the relationship at the time, but the only way to confirm the connection was by researching existing family trees back some two generations. Even with this new information, it was still not clear how some "distant connections" were related.

Many of those requesting affidavits were "elderly" (over the age of 60). Because they were unable to show that they would not require future financial assistance, and because Governor Lehman was aware that the number of affidavits he could provide would be limited, requests from elderly relatives were almost all denied, even if a child or grandchildren had already obtained the precious affidavit. It was an agonizing decision for Governor Lehman, who was at the time around 60 years old.

Thrown into the task of selecting those who would receive assistance, then preparing the extensive documentation and advocating through the maze of restrictions and roadblocks set by governments on both sides of the Atlantic, Governor Herbert H. Lehman surely felt both the privilege of power in his ability to leverage his office and the hopelessness of the overwhelming need. The hundreds "if not thousands" of requests included those like that of Jakob Blum, a distant cousin, on July 7, 1939, "Therefore I entreat you with all my heart. Please give me a help. All our self confidence is broken already... I promise never to ask anything of you for myself or my family, I only beg you to be a warrantor for us in such a way as might enable us to immigrate into your country."[12] (The Blum family was turned down for an affidavit by the Lehmans, but came later with one provided by the movie producer, Carl Laemmle.)

Conclusion

The work of Governor Herbert H. Lehman, Dorothy Bernhard and Carolin Flexner in supporting the families brought to the United States, and those who oversaw the fund in ensuing years, extended well beyond facilitating the process of immigration. Through the Mayer Lehman Charity Fund, relatives in financial need were supported until at least 1974.[13] Although there were many American Jewish families who took on responsibility for the lives of their European brethren, few were as engaged as the Lehmans. To my knowledge this is the only family that continued support for a foundation that assisted refugee relatives for over 40 years.

The exhibition at the Museum of Jewish Heritage, *Against the Odds: American Jews and the Rescue of Europe's Refugees: 1933-1941,* dealt with the American role in rescue and American political obstacles to immigration and resettlement. A more focused view into the role of one family that took on the task reveals the personal sacrifice as well as the reward in the work.

In 1957, Carolin Flexner was asked in an interview whether all the Lehman family members got out of Germany. She replied, "I think so, yes. I don't think they have ever heard of any people who were killed." [14] Flexner surely knew the fate of many family members for whom affidavits could not be given, or for whom such aid would be useless because their American immigration quota number was too high. That one of the relatives, Guenther Boettigheimer, had been deported into Germany and "was lost" was even stated in the Fifth Report of the Mayer Lehman Charity Fund. To have had the burden of participating in the decision-making process for who might receive life-saving documents and who would not, must have been a role that was very painful to bear and too unbearable to remember.

Two Families

The Boettigheimer Family

Prior to 1940, the Boettigheimer family, Guenther, Betty, and their son, Bernd, lived in Kleineichozheim, Germany, a small town about 50 miles east of Mannheim. Betty was very distantly related to the Lehmans through the Neugass family; their closest mutual ancestor was born in 1766.

Dorothy Bernhard's efforts to assist the family in reaching America's shores are detailed in The Fourth Report of the Mayer Lehman Charity Fund. She sent applications for affidavits in January 1939, again in December 1939. In October 1940, the family was sent to Camp Gurs in southern France, along with about 7,500 Jews from Baden. Early in the research, I discovered pages of testimony filed at Yad VaShem that stated the entire family had been murdered at Camp Gurs.[15] Subsequent research proved otherwise.

In March 1941, Guenther, Betty, and Bernd Boettigheimer were transferred to Rivesaltes, a transit camp for deportees. Dorothy Bernhard and Betty Boettigheimer's siblings in the United States continued efforts to secure affidavits and the family's immigration. Their attempts are also documented in letters from Dorothy Bernhard to various social service and government agencies found in Hebrew Immigrant Aid Society (HIAS) files at YIVO Institute for Jewish Research in New York and from private family letters.[16] On July 17, 1941, the family had an appointment to appear before the United States Consul at Marseilles to receive their visas. On July 1, however, the United States State Department voided previous applications and all visa applicants had to submit new forms with more detailed biographical information, character references, and financial documentation. As she was required with all family members attempting to flee Europe at the time, Dorothy Bernhard had to begin the paperwork all over again; she continued to press for their release.

By August 8, 1942, a final appeal to the Department of State in Washington, D.C., for visas for the Boettigheimers was denied. It was too late for Guenther Boettigheimer. He had already been transferred to the internment Camp Les Milles. He was later moved to Drancy, and on August 14,1942, he was deported to Auschwitz.

Correspondence in the HIAS files indicates that the family appealed with greater urgency to bring Bernd Boettigheimer, who would have about eight years old, on a children's transport to the United States. Dorothy Bernhard deposited money with HIAS for this purpose, but the arrangement could not be made.

According to information obtained from the Memorial de la Shoah in Paris, France, Betty Boettigheimer was released from Rivesaltes on July 17, 1942. We know that she went into hiding, but it is unclear how or where. The Lehmans believed that she had also been deported.

It was a year into the research when I learned through a cousin of Betty that Bernd had survived the war and was living in New Jersey under a different name. In 1942 he was placed into the Brout-Vernet-Chateau des Morelles orphanage by the Oeuvre de Secours aux Enfants (Organization to Save the Children, a French Jewish humanitarian organization). The orphanage was identified in an index on the Jewish genealogy web site, JewishGen.org. A refuge for several hundred children during the Second World War, the orphanage is located in central France.

Guenther Boettigheimer, courtesy of the family

It is unclear where mother and son resided after the war. Dorothy Bernhard writes in the Fifth Report of the Mayer Lehman Charity Fund, which describes the work of the organization between June 1, 1942 and March 1, 1947, "Mrs. Strauss [Betty Boettigheimer's sister] informed me that she had traced Mrs. Boettigheimer and Bernd, but that no word had been heard from Mr. Boettigheimer, so it was presumed that he had been deported into Germany, and that he was lost." [17] Bernhard did not know when she wrote the report that Betty and Bernd Boettigheimer had arrived from Marseilles in New York two months earlier, on January 3, 1947. A cousin, who as a child met Bernd upon at his arrival in New York, later recalled, "I'll never forget meeting him at the pier. He was wearing shorts! In January! I guess he didn't have anything else to wear."[18]

The Ehrmann Family

Hugo, Elizabeth, and their children Karola and Kurt

After much research to identify the descendants of Kurt Ehrmann, I found his sons, Dr. David Ehrmann and Dr. Paul Ehrmann. David Ehrmann wrote the story of his father's life in an e-mail:

> Our father, Kurt Ehrmann, was born on July 11, 1922 to Hugo Ehrmann and Else (Schaeler) Ehrmann. He was raised in Koln-Sulz and attended school in Koeln and later in Aachen. Between the ages of 10 and 14 years, it is our understanding that he was preparing to pursue a career in agricultural science. He had a younger sister, Karola (Carole) who was his only sibling. He was sent on the Kindertransport from Germany and his embarkation card is date-stamped with a January 06, 1939 arrival date in Harwich, England. He apparently spent some time in Dovercourt. From there, he was taken in by a family who owned a farm. He was given a great deal of physical labor during that time. He was subsequently labeled as an "enemy alien" by the British Government and was deported with approximately 200 additional German men (age 18 years or older). He was under the impression that he would be taken to Canada (aboard the ship Dunera). Rather, the ship docked after approximately six weeks at sea, first in Sydney and then Melbourne. Our father disembarked in Melbourne where he was placed in a temporary internment camp. Subsequently, he was conscripted into the Australian army and was deployed to New Guinea where he was in active combat with the Japanese. He survived a gunshot wound to the leg and ultimately arrived in San Francisco in 1946 aboard the steamer Matson.
>
> Our father came to Detroit in 1946 where he was reconnected with my grandparents and aunt. He was never formally schooled after his

> departure from Germany, but he worked tirelessly in the wholesale, then retail, clothing industry. He married our mother, Elsie Lewis in 1952. Elsie Lewis was the daughter of Elias Lewis (born and raised in Buenos Aires, Argentina) and Ida Eisenberg (from Horoduk). We were shown a silver bowl that was said to be a wedding gift from the Lehman family. Paul Ehrmann was born in 1953; David Ehrmann was born in 1956. Our parents' priority was to provide their sons with education. Paul is a practicing family physician in Royal Oak, Michigan and David is an endocrinologist at the University of Chicago.
>
> Our father had a myocardial infarction (heart attack) at age 38 years. He survived this, but succumbed to heart disease at age 52 years, in 1974. This was a devastating loss to the family even to this day.
>
> We understood that our grandparents (Hugo and Else) as well as our aunt (Carole) contacted the Lehman family while in Germany with a request for sponsorship to the United States. This contact was made as a consequence of an apparent relationship between our grandmother and the Lehman family. Miraculously, my grandparents and aunt were able to leave Germany as a result of the kindness and resources provided by the Lehman family.[19]

The relationship between Herbert H. Lehman and Elizabeth Schaeler Ehrmann was remote: they shared an ancestor who was born in 1743. Dorothy Bernhard was hesitant to take on the case in the beginning because she doubted that the family was related, and because it was not clear that the family could be self-supporting. She was swayed to intercede by a single letter, dated October 31, 1937, by a young man who introduced himself as Kurt Ehrmann,

> I am… 15 ½ years old, healthy, tall and vigorous, briefly an enterprising fellow who does not shirk any kind of work. I should like to emigrate, but as I am lacking an opportunity, I ask you kindly to help me realize my desire… I am writing this letter without my parents knowledge because I should like to build a future with my own strength.[20]

Bernhard was successful in assisting Kurt's parents and sister, who arrived in 1940, but Kurt was not with them. After some delay in paperwork, Kurt had already left the country on a Kindertransport to England.

In addition to the difficult physical labor he underwent in England, he was also interned in a Huyton Alien Internment Camp, known for its deplorable conditions. It was from this camp that he was sent to Australia.

During this period his parents, who had by then settled in Michigan, were desperate to provide an affidavit for him, and Dorothy Bernhard did everything in her power to intercede. Even with her assistance, the barriers proved insurmountable. Already almost 60 years of age and in poor health, Hugo Ehrmann, recently arrived, was unable to find a job and, "Kurt is being detained until evidence has been presented that his father is self-supporting."[21] Kurt could not obtain the required visa to enter the country unless his father could prove that he was employed. Despite the Lehmans' intervention and willingness to provide financial assistance, Kurt was unable to reach America's shores until after the war.[22]

Notes

1. Dorothy Bernhard, Fourth Report of the Mayer Lehman Charity Fund: June 1, 1941 to June 1, 1942; Section I (A) pp 3-4. The dollar value of the tickets today would be over $33,000.

2. The report was in the possession of Dr. Joan Morgenthau Hirschhorn, the daughter Henry Morgenthau, Jr., Secretary of the Treasury in the Roosevelt administration, and his wife Elinor Fatman. Elinor was a granddaughter of Mayer Lehman, a founder of the firm that was to become Lehman Brothers. Dr. Hirschhorn was intrigued by the Fourth Report, and had always been curious about its history.

3. November 1, 1934 Document ID: ldpd_leh_0784_0102, Lehman Special Correspondence Files, from the Herbert H. Lehman Collections, Columbia University http://lehman.cul.columbia.edu/lehman/document_id=ldpd_leh_0784_0102&itemNo=1

4. Herbert Lehman Papers, Rare Book & Manuscript Library, Columbia University in the City of New York Box 1198.

5. Letter to Mr. W. M. Moser, http://lehman.cul.columbia.edu/lehman/document_id=ldpd_leh_0801_0040?&q=file_unittitle_t%3A%22Rossbach%2C+-Max+J.+H.+and+Mrs.+%28Mabel+Limburg%29%22+AND+unitdate_iso%3A%5B1938-11-01T23%3A59%3A59Z+TO+%2A%5D;&items=82&itemNo=.

6. Herbert Lehman Papers, Rare Book & Manuscript Library, Columbia University in the City of New York, Box 1197.

7. Herbert Lehman Papers, Rare Book & Manuscript Library, Columbia University in the City of New York, Box 1198.

8. Third Report, Section IV, page 2 Herbert Lehman Papers, Rare Book & Manuscript Library, Columbia University in the City of New York, Box 1198.

9. First Report, page 1, Second Report, Section 1, page 2 Herbert Lehman Papers, Rare Book & Manuscript Library, Columbia University in the City of New York, Box 1198.

10. A letter written by Governor Lehman on November 15, 1938 to the Honorable A. A. Berle, Jr., Assistant Secretary of State, requesting that the case be expedited, can be found in the Columbia University Herbert H. Lehman Collections. Herbert Lehman Papers, Rare Book & Manuscript Library, Columbia University in the City of New York, Box 1199 Gerst File.

11. Karl H. Mistele, *The End of a Community*, Bamberg 1988; US in English, 1995, pp. 48-51.

12. Letter from Jakob Blum to the Honorable Governor Lehman 7 July 1939, Nuremberg, Herbert Lehman Papers, Rare Book & Manuscript Library, Columbia University in the City of New York, Box 1195.

13. Letter from Edith Altschul to Helen Buttenwieser, Box Edith Altschul Lehman Collection 1856-1976, Series III, Box 8, Folder 8, Rare Book & Manuscript Library, Columbia University in the City of New York.

14. "Reminiscences of Carolin A. Flexner: Oral History, 1957 Call Number: NXCP87-A861; Columbia University Butler Library, p. 15.

15. Bernd Boettigheimer Page of Testimony item ID: 4426448 by Alex Salm Guenther Boettigheimer 4423942 by Alex Salm; Betty Boettigheimer; 4426447 by Alex Salm, also Betty Boettigheimer 3784071 from the Gedenkbuch—*Opfer der Verfolgung der Juden unter der nationalsozialistischen Gewaltherrschaft in Deutschland 1933-1945*, Bundesarchiv, Koblenz 1986.

16. Archival material from the Herbert H. Lehman Collections at Columbia, (footnote 1195), and HIAS collection at YIVO (RG.246 for Boettigheimer, Betty & Guenther #A-28101) provided details about the immigration of the family.

17. Fifth Report, Mayer Lehman Charity Fund, page 10, Herbert Lehman Papers, Rare Book & Manuscript Library, Columbia University in the City of New York, Box 1198.

18. Interview with Herbert Jakob Weingartner, December 8, 2012.

19. Email from David Ehrmann to Karen S. Franklin, April 4, 2013.

20. Herbert Lehman Papers, Rare Book & Manuscript Library, Columbia University in the City of New York, Box 1195.

21. Cecelia Razofsky, 31 Jul 1940, HIAS papers.

22. Archival material from the Herbert H. Lehman Collections at Columbia, (footnote 1195), and HIAS collection at YIVO (RG.246 for Ehrmann, Hugo & Elizabeth #A-35540) provided details for the immigration of the family.

CHAPTER 8

The Role of Greek Jews in the Sonderkommando Revolt in Birkenau

YITZCHAK KEREM

One of the largely untold stories of the October 7, 1944 Birkenau revolt, is the role of the Greek Jews, who were among its organizers, heroes, victims, and survivors. Holocaust historian Gideon Greif wrote that, "According to diverse sources, the Greek Jews were those that were the initiators of the Sonderkommando revolt, that broke out on the Sabbath day, 7 October 1944."[1] Corfiote-raised Greek military officer Lieutenant-Colonel Yosef Baruch, a demolition and explosives expert, was among the organizers of the overall camp revolt committee and had hidden gun powder and explosives in the walls of Crematorium 2 where the revolt was intended to begin. Yosef Ben described the role of Baruch in the Sonderkommando revolt and his inspiration for revenge and revolt:

> The plans to blow up 4 Crematoria in Auschwitz were sewn together amongst the Sonderkommando apparently in June 1944 and for this need connections were made between the Greek Jews of the Sonderkommando and the other Jews who served with them. From the testimonies we have Yosef Baruch—a former Lieutenant-Colonel in the Greek army—who was assigned to the Sonderkommando in the month of May 1944, was among the initiators of the plan for the Sonderkommando rebellion. On 30 June Yosef Baruch identified the corpses of his parents, residents of Corfu, and that of his friend the lawyer Yom-Tov Yakoel, among the bodies that were taken out of the gas chambers and his wrath flamed up within him that this miserable position was cast on him. In the need to plan for a revolt, Baruch alligned himself to the kapo Kaminski, a Polish Jew, who in practice began to coordinate the preparations for the revolt. The plan for the revolt was to blow up all four Crematoria on 15 August 1944. But

> two hours before the set time, when the preparations were underway, they announced suddenly a transport of 4,000 Polish Jews that arrived accompanied by a group of S.S. There was a fear that the presence of so much German army in the camp would lead to a disaster for the revolt, and thus, it was decided to postpone the date. That was the first failure to carry out the uprising.[2]

When the Sonderkommando workers in Crematorium 2 were locked in a room by the Germans at the beginning of the revolt in Crematoria 1 and 4, Baruch was neutralized from all activity.

The Greek Jews started the revolt in Crematorium 4 by lighting mattresses, killing several German soldiers, and running with the other inmates the relatively short distance to Crematorium 3. There, with other Sonderkommandos, they continued to kill German soldiers, but the building was surrounded. Before they surrendered, they sang a Greek partisan hymn, one verse of the German national anthem, and Yitzhak Baruch, a Salonikan Jew of Skopjan descent, placed a bomb in the furnace to blow up the crematorium. Those surviving were quickly executed.

French and Hungarian Jews also participated in the revolt in Crematoria 3 and 4. While there had been at least two previous aborted attempts at a general camp uprising, and an additional initiative had been called and cancelled, this time the Greek Jews decided that they would go through with the plan and took the lead to instigate the revolt in these two crematoria. The XI Sonderkommando workers knew that their time had come and they were doomed by the Nazi effort to eliminate all witnesses to the death process; they chose, instead, to initiate and participate in the 7 October 1944 revolt in Birkenau. Bowman remarked:

> ... The Eleventh Sonderkommando is unique among the sequence of squads that worked in the crematoria and rightly takes a special place in the historiography of Auschwitz. Yet its actual history is still somewhat confused, particularly regarding the role of the Greeks. We have, for example three photographs of the Sonderkommando at the burning pits taken during the summer of 1944 and smuggled out of the camp in an attempt to inform the world of the systematic slaughter occurring in Birkenau. According to survivors, a Greek Jew identified as Aleko actually snapped the pictures.[3]

He was identified as Aleko Alexandreas, a partisan pseudonym. Molho and Nehama identified him as Albert Errera,[4] but that assertion remains conjecture for lack of any substantive proof. Errera, from Larissa, Greece,[5] had been a Greek naval officer and later joined the leftist-leaning ELAS partisan movement; caught by the Germans in Greece and subsequently deported, he had unsuccessfully tried to escape as a Birkenau Sonderkommando worker (as enumerated by Bowman below) sometime in the summer of 1944 while sent to dump ashes in the Vistula River, and was executed shortly afterward in Birkenau.

The Greek Jews in the Sonderkommando were incensed by the Nazis gassing their close relatives, leaders, like attorney Yomtov Yakoel of Salonika, arrested in Athens and chosen for death while being a Sonderkommando and previous groups of Greek Jews who refused to work as Sonderkommandos, forcing Jews into the gas chambers, pulling out the dead bodies, putting the corpses into the furnaces of the crematoria, and serving as accomplices in the death process.

There are two differing versions of the revolt, one only involving the Ashkenazim, particularly in Crematorium 1, and the other involving the Greek Jews in Crematoria 3 and 4; mostly told by Greek Salonikan survivors in Crematorium 2, who in the end did not revolt, Langbein combined both groups in the organization of the revolt:

> Despite all this, Kaminski and two Greeks who had participated in earlier discussion of these plans with Porebski decided to organize a rebellion of the Sonderkommando, who had nothing to lose. The name of one of the two Greeks has been passed along; Eduard de Wind writes about Errera from Larissa and Albert Menasche mentions Alexander Hereirra. While Paisikovic does not remember the name, he does recall that a very intelligent Greek,who was known on the detail for his beautiful singing, took part in the preparatory work.[6]

Kaminski and Lemke, Kapo of Crematorium 2, had been the overall camp revolt committee leaders; above them, the Kapo Mitek Morava, who oversaw the Sonderkommando in Crematoria 2 and 3.[7] All three were from the Bialystok region, and it can be assumed that Yosef Baruch had been in contact with all of them about the revolt plans. Greek Sonderkommando workers in Crematorium 2 recalled that Baruch met with Kaminski and other organizers at night outside the crematorium building. Other Greek Jews active in planning the revolt were Yosef Levi, Moris Levi, Yitzchak Baruch, and Sam Carasso.[8]

The unsuccessful escape of Albert Errera, a Sonderkommando worker from Larissa, Greece, and a former Greek naval officer, also angered the Sonderkommando and inspired many Greek Jews and other Sonderkommando to revolt. Steven Bowman wrote:

> Alberto Errara, a former officer in the Greek army, was part of a squad sent to empty the ashes from the crematoria in the Vistula. He attacked the guards and leaped into the river but was wounded during the attempted escape. Later he was captured and brought back to the camp and executed before the assembled prisoners according to standard policy.
>
> Errara's action, according to Leon Cohen who survived to write his memoir of the Sonderkommando and the revolt, impressed the Russian prisoners and convinced them to join in the revolt.[9]

Many of the Greek Jews in the Sonderkommando had military backgrounds; some were officers. They had done two years basic service and many fought in the Albanian campaign against the Italians from October 28, 1940 to early April 1941 when Greece finally capitulated. Numerous Sonderkommando prisoners from Greece were partisans caught by the Germans in the Athens area or in mountainous regions to the northwest in Attica. A group of Jews from Ioannina, whose parents persuaded them to return home from the partisans at the demand of the religious leader Shabetai Kabili who had been pressured by the Germans to do so, were thus duped when arrested in Ioannina and later deported to Birkenau from a detention camp in Larissa, Greece.[10] Others were from Preveza, Arta, Athens, Larissa, and Corfu. At least twenty of them were Romaniote Greek-speaking Jews from the Epirus region in northwest Greece or Corfiote Italian origin, and not Judeo-Spanish Sephardim from Salonika in northern Greece. A few were Salonikans who were veterans in Auschwitz, or caught in Athens in hiding, or among the partisans in the Attica region. Two Jews in the Sonderkommando named Mizrachi were born on the island of Chios, but probably were deported to Birkenau from Athens. Most of the Jews in the Sonderkommando at the time of the revolt were Jews deported from Athens, Epirus, or Corfu in spring 1944, or were Salonikan Jews who had fled to Athens in early 1943 to avoid the Salonikan deportations in spring 1943. A spirit of resistance, despite the odds, prevailed amongst the Greek Sonderkommando workers in Birkenau in the late spring, summer, and early autumn of 1944.

Greek Jews numbered at least one-third of the XI Sonderkommando in Birkenau, which totaled 663 workers in 4 crematoria.[11] In July 1944, Greek Jews were needed in the Sonderkommando for transports of Hungarian Jews. Some 400-436 Greek Jews were selected for the Sonderkommando, but refused and were sent to their deaths in the gas chambers. Previously, one hundred Greek Jews from Athens in May 1944 had refused to perform the Sonderkommando tasks and likewise were sent to their deaths in the gas chambers.[12] Most of the Greek Jews were in Crematoria 3 and 4, but at least two dozen were in Crematorium 2. In Crematoria 2 and 3, the prisoners slept on the second floor loft. Bowman noted that, "despite the isolation of this commando at the end of June 1944 by Haupstscharffuhrer Moll, contact was maintained with the Resistance in the main camp via crematorium1 (in Auschwitz I), usually through the ration carriers and injured prisoners who frequented the hospital."[13]

According to the written testimony of Leon Cohen, who wrote vividly and in detail of the Greek Jews in the Sonderkommando revolt in Birkenau,

> On 7 October, during the hours of the afternoon, the people were amassed in the hall of the crematorium and ordered to go to disinfection. That moment one of the Greeks gave the sign to revolt and voiced the code 'on them'. Immediately the Greeks in crematoria 4 jumped on two soldiers that accompanied them and took their rifles. The non-Greek prisoners, not only not helped, but tried to take the guns away from the Greeks and return them to the Germans. After several shots in the air, which caused panic amongst the prisoners, a group that numbered 25 Greeks went out, and ran the distance to Crematorium 3 (250-400 meters). They jumped on the guards and took control over Crematorium 3. Yitzhak Baruch, a Salonikan whose family came from Skopje, managed to place the bomb that blew up the furnace before

> the Germans arrived. After back up was called and the soldiers tried to burst into the building, fire was ignited as planned, and the whole crematorium went up in flames with all the Greek prisoners inside. In the revolt twenty guards were killed, Crematorium 3 was destroyed, and damage was caused to Crematorium 4. As such half of the death machine in Birkenau was closed down. Before their death, the revolters managed to sing a partisan song and one verse of the Greek national anthem. Several survivors fled before the doors were closed, and managed to hide in Crematorium 4; the Germans arrived and killed everyone.[14]

Photini Tomai added that, in addition to singing the Greek national anthem, the Greek Sonderkommando revolters raised a makeshift Greek flag in the air.[15] The physician Albert Menasche, a former Salonikan inmate in Birkenau, published a memoir on Birkenau in 1947, including many recollections of the Sonderkommando and the revolt. While the depiction may be questionable regarding many of the details, noteworthy of mention is that there were Greek Jews in Crematorium 3 amongst the revolters and that during the revolt they sang the Greek national anthem:

> The personnel of Crematorium III had revolted during their work. The revolt had begun by the killing of a German *Capo* who had been thrown alive into the furnace. The German sentinel was also killed, after which the furnaces were ignited. I am not in a position to give exact details either on the type of explosives used or on the manner in which the *Sonder* obtained them. But, from Crematorium III, the revolt spread to the other crematoria.
>
> The workers of Crematoria III attempted an escape but were forced to retreat before the on-coming German troops. Singing the Greek National Anthem, three hundred Greek Jews buried themselves beneath the debris of their crematorium. The revolt lasted all afternoon. The entire *Sonder* was massacred. It is possible that some prisoners were able to escape in the general uproar but I can not state this with any degree of certainty.[16]

According to Bowman, the revolt began in Crematorium 4 after the roll call of 300 Greek and Hungarian Jews, when the prisoners rioted, threw stones at the guards, and there was shouting. Within minutes fifty-five German guards arrived and began shooting at the prisoners. He added that the guards killed all the prisoners.[17] Unlike the testimony of Leon Cohen, he does not mention that a group of Greek and other Jewish prisoners ran to Crematorium 3.

Leon Cohen recalled that the Greek Jew Marcel Nadjari had fled from Crematorium 4 and ended up being forced into Crematorium 2:

> Suddenly, the door of our cell was opened and one of our Greek comrades from No. 4 was kicked inside. Still alive but covered in blood and dragging a broken leg, he fell on the floor. He gave us a full account of the Crematorium 4 incident. He told us that when the morning shift had taken over, his fellow prisoners were ordered to leave for another camp where they would reinforce the Sonderkommando. All their belongings were to be packed after breakfast. It was unanimously decided to keep the original plan and, during the midday meal, to notify the others in the kitchen. To their surprise, the Crematorium prisoners had an identical story. There could no longer be any doubt that the Germans had decided to get rid of all the prisoners from both crematoria. Faced with imminent death, they once again decided to stick to their original plan.[18]

Marcel Nadjari (transliterated Natzari from the Greek spelling) left notes, drawings, and recollections from his Sonderkommando experiences in Birkenau in Crematorium 4. His diary, in the form of a thirteen page document, had been buried in a bottle under an oak tree near the changing-rooms of Crematorium 3, was found by Polish workers in Birkenau within a leather bag on 24 October 1980 when they were cleaning the shrubs between Crematoria 2 and 3, and was taken to the Auschwitz-Birkenau Museum.[19] There in Crematorium 4, Nadjari was with other Greek Jews deported from Athens in 1944 like Yaakov Viko Brudo, Maurice Aron, and Isaac Baruch.[20] The latter must have run from Crematorium 4 to 3 in the revolt before he placed the bomb in the furnace that blew up Crematorium 3. Nadjari cited that there were 26 Greek Jews in Crematorium 4, out of a total of 200 workers; including Polish Jews and Russian political prisoners.[21] In 1947, Nadjari added written details and sketches of his Holocaust experiences in an historical chronicle when he served as a soldier in the Greek army during the Greek Civil War in the General Military Hospital of Thessaloniki. After he left Greece and migrated to the United States in 1951, he told relatives that he had left a diary behind in Birkenau. He died of a heart-attack in 1971 at the age of fifty-four, before the dairy was uncovered.

In his diary, Nadjari expressed devout patriotism to Greece. On page two of the diary, he wrote, "To my beloved ones ... and finally to my beloved country *Hellas* (Greece) to which I was always a loyal citizen."[22] On page 11 of his diary, written while he was in the Sonderkommando in Birkenau, he wrote some poignant statements as a victim of the Germans solely for being a Jew, "At Birkenau ... it does not matter to me that I will die, but only that I will not be able to avenge myself, the way I would like and know ... and if by any chance you receive a letter from our relatives abroad, please write to them immediately and say that the Nadgary family was wiped out by the civilized Germans ("New Europe" as they for some reason call themselves) ... My last words shall be: [Long live Greece.] Marsel Natzari."[23] Finally, on page 13 of the diary, he concluded, " ... [*Esteemed Greek Embassy* will receive ... from a Greek ... Emmanuel or Marcel Nadjary from Thessaloniki, address, street] Italias [no. 9, Thessaloniki. Please send my letter to the address: Dimitrios Athanasios Stefanikis 4 Krousovou Street, Thessaloniki, Greece. This is my last wish. I am condemned to death by the Germans, because I am of Jewish religion. Thank you]."[24]

According to the late researcher Yosef Ben, it was Yaakov Brudo, a name of Salonikan Jewish Sephardic origin, who called out to rebel in Crematorium 3, and led the cry to attack the German guards.[25] The Germans had decided to gas another 300 Sonderkommando workers, Greek and Hungarian Jews. The prisoners threw into the furnace the French kapo who had begun to read out the names of the Hungarian and Greek Jews selected for gassing, and then killed German guards. Some fifty Polish Jews fled from Crematorium 3 according to Ben's description, but it is more logical that those were Poles in Crematorium 1 who revolted simultaneously and who were among a group of anywhere between 30 and 230 Russian political prisoners and Polish Jewish prisoners who escaped, although most were killed in a battle shortly afterward in the general vicinity. It is known that about thirty of them survived and reached Dachau.[26]

Other Greek Jews participating in the revolt, but who were killed in the process, were Maurice Levy,[27] Errikos Nechama Kapon,[28] Joseph Levy, Maurice Aharon, Sam Carasso,[29] and Edgar Levy, who was known to have been involved in igniting the fire and then being part of the revolt in Crematorium 3 when it blew up. Kabeli, who had been in the Sonderkommando for a year, survived, and later was a professor of literature at the University of Athens, mentioned the following Greek Jews who participated in the organization of the uprising; (Joseph) Baruch, Brudo, (Sam) Carasso, Arditti, and (Albertos?) Djahon.[30] Kabeli assessed that 135 Greek Jews were among the Sonderkommando revolters who died in the revolt, but such an estimate is unsubstantiated.

One Salonikan in Crematorium 3, Isaak "Hugo" Venezia, stepped outside due to the smoke, sat on the outer wall, fell off, and joined the Sonderkommando inmates in Crematorium 2. Shlomo Venezia, who was in Crematorium 2 with his brother Maurice, wrote about Isaak Venezia, who was not related to him; "He managed to get across to our crematorium, I myself didn't see him, but my brother personally told me what he had heard. He said that the men of Crematorium IV had set fire to mattresses and thereby triggered the revolt before the scheduled time, convinced as they were that someone had betrayed them. It seems they'd had time to kill three Germans before reinforcements arrived. They set fire to the Crematorium and tried to escape. But almost all were killed on the spot."[31]

Isaak Venezia survived with the latter prisoners, but died in Gleiwitz in the Death March. His recollection had been depicted in the memoirs of Leon Cohen, written initially in Hebrew in the early 1980s. Most of those Greeks who survived in Crematorium 2, were interviewed in the USA and Israel from the 1980s onward. These accounts have been analyzed and incorporated in the scholarly research, all separately, of Kerem, Bowman, and Greif in depicting the role of the Greek Jews in the Birkenau Sonderkommando revolt. In interviews with numerous Greek former Sonderkommando workers, like Daniel Benahmias and Rene Molho in the Oakland area, the Gabbai brothers in Los Angeles and Tel Aviv, and Pepo Zakar, Shaul Hazan, and Leon Cohen in the Tel Aviv area, most told me that the signal to start the revolt was smoke in the chimney from the adjacent Crematorium (number three), but when this happened the Germans very expediently and quickly whisked all the Sonderkommando workers of Crematorium 2 in a small room for over a day. Joseph Baruch had coordinated plans with the general revolt organizers at night, and he had made improvised bombs with gunpowder, which he hid in the walls of Crematorium2, and were never used. They also had amassed grenades, which they never used.[32]

According to Daniel Bennahmias, it was from Joseph Baruch that "he learned not only about the plan to blow up the sauna and liberate the camp, but also what was expected of him. He was informed that within a week someone would start a fire, that smoke would pour out of a window in Crematorium IV, and that this would be the signal to look out for. For the time being, and for the sake of security, however, the exact day of the rebellion had to be withheld, but it was understood that the signal would be given between the hours of two-thirty and three in the afternoon. Clearly, then, the action was to coincide with the changing of the guards, an event that took place at the base of the sentry posts, inasmuch as the guardhouses themselves were perched high above ground level."[33]

Leon Cohen claimed that the Sonderkommando in Crematorium 2 were dejected that they were not an active part of the revolt, and they felt betrayed by the Sonderkommando of Crematorium 1, since they did not receive the agreed upon signal of a burning rag to be thrown out of the window.[34] Each Sonderkommando worker had a pre-designated task for the revolt, but those in Crematorium 2 did not carry them out. They did not revolt because they did not receive a signal. Those in Crematorium 2 thought that those in Crematorium 1 succeeded in running away when they viewed from afar that the courtyard in the latter was empty, but they did not know that most were executed for revolting. They heard shooting from other crematoria. When they finally saw smoke from Crematorium 3, the courtyard in Crematorium 2 was filled with German soldiers with their fingers on the triggers of their machine-guns. The Greek prisoners rushed to straighten out the mattresses and blankets, which they had planned to burn to start their part of the revolt, and as the German soldiers put the butts of their guns in the backs of Greek and other Jewish Sonderkommando prisoners, they all lined up. All the Sonderkommando workers of Crematorium 2 were put in a closed room for a day and were neutralized from any possibility of revolting. The gunpowder that Yosef Baruch had amassed to make bombs for the revolt remained in the walls of the second floor of Crematorium 2, where the Sonderkommando slept.

In Crematoria 4 and 5 there were newly arrived Greek and Hungarian Sonderkommando workers. Those in Crematorium 5 did not revolt, were not punished and, according to Mois Mizrahi, they were assigned the task of cremating the bodies of those killed in the revolt. Approximately 250, mainly Greek and Hungarian Jews, were shot from Crematoria 3 and 4, and as many as another 200 from Crematorium 1, totaling some 450 dead.[35] Outside Crematorium 2, among the dead bodies of the revolting Sonderkommando, was the Greek Jew Aaron Barzilai.[36] When the Sonderkommando of Crematorium 2 were locked up, some ten or fifteen of them were taken out to remove the corpses of the Sonderkommando that bordered Crematoria 1 and 2. Danny Bennahmias was among those who had been ordered to deal with the bodies:

> In this location, between ten and fifteen persons had been killed. All had been shot. Among them was a fellow by the name of Aaron Barzilai, a Greek Jew of about forty years of age. Danny and the others brought the bodies to Crematorium 1 and placed them in front of the ovens, under the supervision of a guard.[37]

In his memoir, Errikos Sevillias of Athens, a survivor whose written account was discovered after his tragic death in a motorcycle crash in 1974, noted that he was in the Sonderkommando in one of four crematoria and did not specify which one, but initially was in the D Camp, that had been built in 1943 specifically for the Jews of Salonika, and was in the vicinity of the Kanada Kommando, where the belongings of those gassed were sorted and was located between crematoria 3 and 4. He noted that both of his brothers-in-law, Jaime Kohen and David Persiades, were killed in the revolt. He depicted the revolt as such:

> When midday had passed we began to wait anxiously for the signal to be given. All of us were nervous, but all of us had made up our minds. At 2:00, as we were working, we heard shouts from the crematorium. It was nerve-wracking. Suddenly we could see the inside workers pouring out with hatchets in their hands, cutting through the fence, and running out of the crematorium. We were completely stunned and

stood watching them, not knowing what to do. It was only 2:00, and they had arranged things to begin at 4:00. We understood that something bad had happened, probably betrayal. In the meantime many SS arrived and were killing whomever they found before them with their machine guns. Our work group didn't budge. I hid under some wood stacked nearby and remained there motionless since they were shooting anyone who moved. When the Germans had finished with the inside workers they ordered us all to get to our feet. When I got up out of my hideout I saw that there were so many dead that they covered the ground and the Germans still had their machine guns raised. They were looking at us in such a wild way that I was sure they were going to kill us. It was the only time I thought of my wife and child and my eyes filled with tears.

When we were all up they ordered us into a column and made a check. Then I relaxed. From the fifty men who made up our work group only thirty-eight remained. Twelve had been killed with the others in attempting the escape. Soon after this they led us back to camp. As I moved forward through the dead I stole glances, hoping I wouldn't see my relatives; I saw none. Just as we were passing the entrance to the crematorium, however, I could see that they had all of the surviving inside workers with their hands held high. Among them were my brothers-in-law. My heart froze inside me as I knew they would be killed for being co-responsible with the others. The next morning we learned that they had killed everybody who was on duty at the time; among them were my relatives. I fell into a deep depression over this loss and, because of the weakened state of my nerves, I wept continuously.

We later learned that the betrayal had been made by one of the prisoners who thought that he would be rewarded, thereby saving his neck. He had told the plan to a German Capo, who quickly informed the others. When the inside workers saw that they had been betrayed, they understood that they were lost. They grabbed the Capo and threw him into the oven alive. Then they seized hatchets and ran out to escape. Since they had been warned, the Germans were ready for them and what happened, happened. The plan failed because of the stupidity of one traitor, but he got what he deserved; he was killed with the others.[38]

Only 26 Greeks from the Sonderkommando survived the revolt.[39] These were mostly the Greek Jews in Crematorium 2 who were locked in a room by the Germans when the revolt had started. Tomai published a list of some 60 Greek Jews who took part in the uprising of 7 October 1944. Less than a dozen of the names were those locked in Crematorium 2. Unaware of the Israeli historiography, missing are names like Shaul Hazan, Rene Molho,[40] and Yaakov Gabbai[41] The Arditi mentioned by Kabeli as participating in the revolt also does not appear in the list published by Tomai.

Gun powder for the revolt was supplied from Auschwitz I by the young Salonikan Arbeitsdienst Jacko Maestro,[42] as well as by the well-known female inmates Rosa Robota, Ester Wajsblum, Ella Gartner, and Regina Safirsztain, who smuggled out the black powder from the munitions factory Union. The fifteen-year-old Jacko Maestro was born in Salonika, knew German through trading with German soldiers during the German occupation before being deported to Auschwitz on 15 March 1943, and became part of the Arbeitsdienst, coordinating the daily work placement for 16,000 primarily Jewish Auschwitz inmates, consequently having freedom to roam freely in Auschwitz and Birkenau. One occasion in Auschwitz, in the Strauenbau Kommando, he was given gun powder in a rag wrapped within napkins and papers, and brought it to the Shoekommando where it was passed on to Birkenau where it was used in the revolt.[43]

Rosa Robota and the three women, mentioned previously, who worked together in Union and smuggled out gunpowder to Yosef Baruch in Crematorium 2, were detected late in their period as prisoners in Auschwitz, were imprisoned in Bloc 11, and hung on 6 January 1945, several weeks before the general evacuation from the camp.[44] Rosa had made contact with some twenty women in Union who were willing to cooperate, including two Salonikan women, Matilda Haguel and Allegra Uziel.[45]

The Ashkenazi inmates in Crematorium 1 have a different narrative, and revolted some two months after the execution of Kapo Kaminski, the leader of the overall revolt committee, executed at the beginning of August 1944. Recently published memoirs by Zalman Gradowski,[46] an active participant and leader in the revolt, as well as his vivid depictions of the death process, add more details to the existing accounts of Ber

Mark, Bensoussan, and others. Gradowski noted that in April 1944, 180 Greek Jews were added to the Sonderkommando,[47] but does not mention them at all in regard to the revolt. He described smoke coming out of Crematorium 3, that in the Crematorium where he was, the prisoners started to revolt, some fled from Crematorium 4, but most were killed there, those in 2 were prevented from acting, and that 14 prisoners in Crematorium 1 were spared from being slaughtered by the Nazi guards.[48] He wrote nothing about the preparations in Crematorium 3, or what happened there during the revolt. This leaves the Greek narrative to fill in the events in Crematorium 3.

Kabeli noted that one-third of the Sonderkommando were Greek Jews (135 of 400 in his account); Ber Mark's *Scroll of Auschwitz* tried to correct Kabeli's account, while still acknowledging the Greek presence and their role in the revolt. Bowman noted the dissonance between the Greek account, where the Greek Jews overcame the Nazi guards in Crematoria 3 and 4, blew up the furnaces and smokestacks before they were finally killed, and in Crematorium 3 sang the Greek national anthem while they died, and the Ashkenazi Polish-Jewish versions, where the Greek Jews are not mentioned at all as being part of the revolt, in works by Josef Garlinski or Reuben Ainsztein.[49] At any rate, twenty German guards were killed, Crematorium 3 was totally destroyed and there was extensive damage to Crematorium 4. Two crematoria were put out of production and the death process in Birkenau slowed greatly.

After the liberation of Auschwitz, the Polish numbering system of the crematoria added one number value to each building, so while the Auschwitz Museum commemorates Crematorium 3 and 4, Greek survivors remember those buildings as 2 and 3. The Greek Jews, by setting fire to Crematorium 4, put it out of commission, and by blowing up the furnace in Crematorium 3, Yitzhak Baruch destroyed a great part of the building, and eliminated the possibility of future use of that crematorium. Hopefully, the role of the Greek Jews in the Sonderkommando Revolt will be remembered and commemorated more than at present where it is not mentioned in any Holocaust or Jewish museum in the world, not even in Greece, and will also appear on the walls of the two Holocaust museums in Los Angeles, in Washington, and New York City, at Yad Vashem, at the Imperial War Museum, in Holocaust museums in

Paris and Berlin, and other Holocaust museums as far away as Capetown, Sydney, Melbourne, and Buenos Aires.

Notes

1. Gideon Greif, *The Merciful Angel from Auschwitz, The Story of Jacob "Jakito" Maestro from Thessaloniki, Greece* (Tel Aviv: Am Zicharon Institute, 2014) 7. [Hebrew]

2. Yosef Ben, *Greek Jewry in the Holocaust and the Resistance 1941-1944* (Tel Aviv: The Institute for the Research of Salonikan Jewry, 1985) 148. [Hebrew]

3. Steven B. Bowman, *The Agony of Greek Jews 1940–1945* (Palo Alto, CA: Stanford University Press, 2009) 89.

4. Michael Molho and Joseph Nehama, *The Destruction of Greek Jewry, 1941-1944* (Jerusalem: Yad Vashem, 1965) 194-195.[Hebrew]

5. Hermann Langbein, People in Auschwitz (Chapel Hill, NC and London: University of North Carolina Press with United States Holocaust Memorial Museum, 2004) 100-101.

6. Langbein, 200.

7. Ben, 149.

8. Yitzchak Kerem, "Forgotten Heroes: Greek Jewry in the Holocaust," in Menachem Mor, ed., *Crisis & Reaction: The Hero in Jewish History* (Omaha, Nebraska: Creighton University Press, 1995) 229-238.

9. Steven Bowman, *Jewish Resistance in Wartime Greece* (London and Portland, OR: Vallentine Mitchell, 2006) 87.

10. Rae Dalven, *The Jews of Ioannina* (Philadelphia, PA: Cadmus Press, and Athens: Lycabettus Press, 1990) 42-43.

11. Bowman, *The Agony*, 96.

12. Ben, 147.

13. Bowman, *The Agony*, 97.

14. Yitzchak Kerem and Bracha Rivlin, "Saloniki" in Bracha Rivlin, Yitzchak Kerem, and Leah Matkovetski, *Pinkas Kehillot Yavan, Encyclopaedia of Jewish Communities from their foundation till after the Holocaust, Greece* (Jerusalem: Yad Vashem, 1998) 217-299.[Hebrew]

15. Photini Tomai, *Greeks in Auschwitz-Birkeanu* (Athens: Papazis Publishers and the Hellenic Ministry of Foreign Affairs, 2009) 159.

16. Albert Menasche, *Birkenau (Auschwitz II), (Memoirs of an eye-witness) How 72,000 Greek Jews Perished* (New York: Isaac Saltiel, 1947) 92-93.

17. Bowman, *The Agony,* 97-98.

18. Leon Cohen, *From Greece to Birkenau, The Crematoria Workers' Uprising* (Tel Aviv: The Salonika Jewry Research Center, 1996) 86.

19. Tomai, 162.

20. Marcel Natzari, *Chroniko 1941-1945* (Thessaloniki: Ets Achaim, 1991) 50.

21. Ibid., 60.

22. Ibid., 12.

23. Ibid., 21.

24. Ibid., 23.

25. Ben, 150.

26. Bowman, *The Agony,* 98.

27. Kerem and Rivlin, "Saloniki" 286.

28. Natzari, 85, 87.

29. Henry Levy, "The Jews of Salonica and the Holocaust: A Personal Memoir," in Haham Solomon Gaon and Mitchell Serels, eds. *Del Fuego, Sephardim and the Holocaust* (New York: Sepher-Hermon Press, 1995) 213-246.

30. Isaac Kabeli, "The Resistance of the Greek Jews," *YIVO Annual of Jewish Social Sciences,* Vol. III (New York: YIVO, 1953) 281-288.

31. Shlomo Venezia in collaboration with Beatrice Prasquier, *Inside the Gas Chambers, Eight Months in the Sonderkommando of Auschwitz* (Boston, MA: Polity in association with the United States Holocaust Memorial Museum, 2009) 116.

32. Gideon Greif, *We Wept Without Tears* (Jerusalem: Yad Vashem and Yediot Achronot, 1999) 343.[Hebrew].

33. Rebecca Camhi Fromer, *The Holocaust Odyssey of Daniel Bennahmias, Sonderkommando* (Tuscaloosa and London: The University of Alabama Press, 1993) 63-64.

34. Leon Cohen, *From Greece to Birkenau,* 83-89.

35. Bowman, *The Agony,* 98.

36. Tomai, 159.

37. Fromer, *The Holocaust Odyssey of Daniel Bennahmias, Sonderkommando,* 77.

38. Erikkos Sevillias, *Athens—Auschwitz* (Athens: Lycabettus Press, 1983) 52-54.

39. Tomai, 159.

40. Rene Molho with Rebecca Camhi Fromer, *They Say Diamonds Don't Burn: The Holocaust Experiences of Rene Molho of Salonika, Greece* (Berkeley, CA: Judah L.

Magnes Museum, 1994) 20-21.

41. Greif, 209-242, 290-320, and Shmuel Refael, ed., *Routes of Hell, Greek Jewry in the Holocaust, Testimonies* (Tel Aviv: The Center for the Research of Salonikan Jewry and The Organization of Greek Death Camp Survivors in Israel, 1988) 124-129. [Hebrew]

42. Yitzchak Kerem, "New Finds on Greek Jewish Heroism in the Holocaust," *Sephardic Horizons* 2:2 (Spring 2012) www.sephardichorizons.org.

43. Interview with Jacko Maestro, March 5, 2005, Bat Yam, Israel.

44. "Auschwitz Revolt," United States Holocaust Memorial Musuem website http://www.ushmm.org/research/center/lerman/medal_award/.

45. Henry Levy, 236.

46. Zalman Gradowsky, *In the Heart of Gehenna, A Diary of a Prisoner and a Leade of the Sonderkommando Revolt in Auschwitz* (Tel Aviv: Yedioth Ahronoth and Chemed Books, 2012) 280-291.[Hebrew]

47. Ibid., 283.

48. Ibid., 288-289.

49. Steven Bowman, "Jews in Wartime Greece," *Jewish Social Studies*, XLVIII: 1 (Winter 1986) 45-62.

CHAPTER 9

Seventy Years After: The Contribution of the Sonderkommando Research to the Understanding and Interpretation of the "Final Solution" in Auschwitz-Birkenau

GIDEON GREIF

It is a widely discussed question, how to deal with the understanding and interpretation of the "Final Solution." The historic facts connected with the Holocaust—especially the gassing of hundreds of thousands of Jews in the gas chambers of Auschwitz-Birkenau and the other Extermination Camps—seem to evade understanding. The established forms of perception and interpretation of historical events seem insufficient for this unique aspect of history

How can we understand the fact that millions of innocent Jews were murdered for a cause no other than pure annihilation, only because they were born Jewish? How can we deal with the numbers of those who were murdered? How can we understand what happened during the "Final Solution"?

Of course it is relatively easy to collect all the facts relevant for the "Final Solution." We can look at photographs or blueprints of the crematoria built in Auschwitz-Birkenau, we can count those who were murdered in the Extermination Camps and we can describe the technical methods of mass murder. But those aspects—as important as they are—can only give us a partial understanding of the "Final Solution." They will never enable us to gain a real and authentic insight in what meaning the "Final Solution" had for those forced into the gas chambers and left there as corpses. Numbers and facts cannot tell us what happened around the gas chambers, how the individual Jewish victim experienced the surroundings of death and how the "Death Factory" really worked. This problem has led to several discussions on the representation of the reality of the gas chambers. Philosophical, ethical and historical debates for example have raised the question whether pictures can give an appropriate insight to the reality of the "Death Factories."[1]

This aspect of the "Final Solution" can only be included in our understanding and interpretation of the "Final Solution" with the help of those few people who directly witnessed the events around the gas chambers. Those eyewitnesses who also made the photos Didi-Hubermann writes about. Of course, there are no witnesses of what happened inside the gas chamber after the SS-men on duty sealed the doors. What happened in there is simply beyond the possibility of understanding or interpretation. The only witnesses—besides the perpetrators—who can give us information about the gas chambers and crematoria, the criminal "heart" of the "Final Solution" in Auschwitz-Birkenau, are the members of the Sonderkommando. They are those who had to work at the crematoria and gas chambers through all stages of the "Assembly Line" of the death production and, being aware of each detail, they can supply the most precise information about the "Final Solution" as it unfolded in Auschwitz-Birkenau.

The German perpetrators did everything to destroy all evidence of their crimes. In summer 1942, the special unit 1005 ("Sonderaktion 1005"), under the command of Paul Blobel was ordered to exhume the corpses of the murdered in Auschwitz and burn them.[2] The murderers tried to destroy the traces of their crimes until the last moments. And they also were aware of the importance of the eye-witnesses, the "Sonderkommando."

One part of their attempt to leave no evidence was the plan to murder all members of the Sonderkommando after they completed their duty, leaving nobody alive. No one of those "Geheimnisträger" (bearers of secrets) should survive, and so no one could speak about the crimes perpetrated in the gas chambers and crematoria of Auschwitz-Birkenau. But, despite those attempts, several dozen prisoners from the "Sonderkommando" survived and could describe the events in the crematoria to posterity. Others, who did not survive, were able to bear clandestine witness while they were working in the "Sonderkommando" and managed to smuggle out information or bury their notes in the ground around the crematoria. A part of those notes were the photos Didi-Hubermann focuses on.

Those documents and testimonies of the "Sonderkommando" are essential to understand and reconstruct the history of the death camp. There are two methods of understanding and reconstructing the testimonies and reports, which lead to different perspectives on the historical events: at first, the testimonies and reports help us to reconstruct a detailed picture of the facts. The description of the work and life of the Sonderkommando enables us to get a deeper insight in the way the Germans conducted their crimes. On the other hand, the testimonies of the Sonderkommando enable us to understand how was it humanly possible to live and work in the center of death, sometimes for years. By this they enable us to get an insight to those aspects of the "Final Solution" that cannot be interpreted through the sheer knowledge of facts. This is ensured, if we understand the witnesses of the "Sonderkommando" as "human witnesses in a dehumanizing situation."[3] Their reports give us an insight in the technical, emotional and psychological aspects of the "Final Solution." They lead us closer to the understanding of something which is completely inconceivable for us today.

Without the testimonies of the survivors we could not reconstruct the conditions in the death camps. The German attempts to destroy all evidence left a documentary vacuum, which can only be filled by the memories of the survivors. Even one voice of one survivor can help us to reconstruct the history of the "Final Solution."[4] The crimes perpetrated in the death factories are so inconceivable, that we depend on these testimonies of the survivors: Only they can tell us about the last minutes in the lives of those who were sentenced to death. Only they can tell us, how they looked, what they said prior to their murder and which emotions they showed. The victims themselves cannot talk anymore and only the survivors of the Sonderkommando can speak in their name and become their echo and voice. In this sense the survivors of the Sonderkommando are the guardians of the legacy of the killed. Historical research cannot ignore this legacy but has to make it useful for its research. The reports of the survivors deliver an impressive picture of the reality of the prisoners and also inform us about the basic facts of the "Final Solution" as well as they draw a broad picture of the emotions of those who had to experience the terror. The oral history of the Sonderkommando is an essential source that historical research should not and cannot miss—especially for the understanding and interpretation of the "Final Solution."

Central for the understanding of the contribution of the Sonderkommando Research and the testimonies of the Sonderkommando is the fact that an eye-witness who reconstructs the historic events in a personal interview, not only aims at a correct description of those events but also tries to define his own identity.[5] Through this, the testimonies of the Sonderkommando deliver a different layer of history. Aspects like emotions, doubts, thoughts, restraints, the daily life in the crematoria, small or tiny details, and patterns of behavior of the SS—all that information cannot be found in official German documents—if such documents exist at all. Only the testimonies of the survivors, who had to experience everything on their own bodies, can enlighten those aspects. For this reason there is no substitute for oral history, especially when it comes to dealing with the "Final Solution." They can add the perspective of the "superstes," that Giorgio Agamben introduced in the discussion.[6] Only by including oral history into the research, will historians be able to reconstruct an authentic and full picture of the history of the "Final Solution."

Martin Sabrow describes the special perspective of the testimonies of eye-witnesses in his article "Die Zeitzeugen als Wanderer zwischen den Welten" as "a special perspective on the past from the inside as a bearer of experience and not from the outside as perceiving observer."[7] This special experience is what makes the testimonies of those, who survived the terror of the German National Socialist camps, so important to understand the essence of history. This is especially true in the case of Auschwitz-Birkenau and the "Final Solution." The memories, reminiscences, books, reports and interviews of the Sonderkommando-survivors are the expression of the personal motivation of the survivors to bear witness for the future and the attempt to talk about their human experiences, that sound inconceivable: the routine "work" the Sonderkommando had to do every day, surviving next to the gas chambers und cremation ovens and the fact that they were forced to be the servants inside the process of annihilation.[8]

The reports drastically document how, during extreme distress and danger, human beings dealt with moral conflicts and unprecedented moral and existential dilemmas. To be able to deal with the cruel work in the crematoria some of the Sonderkommando sealed themselves off against their surroundings and were able to survive because they functioned like robots or living machines.[9] The descriptions of the survivors enable us to gain an insight into the perverted and bizarre world of the concentration and extermination camp, which was a reality: an unbearable combination of life and death, richness and poverty, truth and lies, naïvete and subtletey, morality and brutality, sadism and humane feelings, coupled to the will to survive. The norms and ethical values of the world outside the Nazi camps were replaced by a new moral code, a distorted one, which contradicted each known moral norm from the times prior to National Socialism. The testimonies of the Sonderkomamndo survivors relate to this moral distortion and depict realistically the new anti-ethical code that prevailed in the camps.

A common critique against the use of oral reports in the framework of historical research raises the question of authenticity of oral memories, especially if the event in question happened a long time ago. However, after years of research on the field of the Sonderkommando and a profound experience in oral history, the author of this article has reached the firm conclusion that the memory of the Sonderkommando survivors in most points is extremely accurate, detailed and authentic. As we can see on different phases of interviews and many different publications, the various testimonies do not contradict each other in the central points and seem to have a high authenticity.

The reason for the accuracy and authenticity is certainly a result of the traumatic conditions under which the prisoners of the Sonderkommando had to act, surrounded with corpses, ashes, and death. Such conditions prevailed from the first shock treatment at the beginning until their last day at the Crematoria. Memories deriving from such a traumatic period, inside a death factory, in which the raw material is human beings and the final product human ashes, accompanied with terror and violence all day long,[10] are very often remembered to the very last detail. Historical research can now benefit from this fact.[11]

Using the method of oral history enriches our ability to delve into the unbelievable reality of the death factory Auschwitz, its scope, dimensions, insights and dilemmas. Historical research can only benefit from it. It gives us access to personal perspectives on several events in the camp, and to draw a broader picture of those murderous events at the killing sites, by connecting all individual perspectives into a comprehensive picture of the experience of different survivors and coming closer to understanding the events in the crematoria.

Taking into consideration the fact that the research on the Sonderkommand, supported by the method of oral history has such an impact on our understanding of the "Final Solution" in its making, we have to ask ourselves why it was not until several decades after the liberation of Auschwitz-Birkenau and the end of the gassings at the crematoria, that an intensive historical research focused on this aspect had begun. Why were the survivors of the Sonderkommando ignored and neglected? Why was no historian interested to save these precious historical sources?

In the first decades after the Holocaust, historical researches almost completely ignored the fact that there were dozens of survivors who witnessed the "Final Solution" from inside and were able to contribute precious information about the crimes perpetrated in Auschwitz. Similar to the artificial and distorted knowledge, the Sonderkommando was treated like the "Judenräte" and other Jewish functionaries in concentration and extermination camps, and was considered a group of traitors and collaborators. The issue was delicate, complicated, sensitive and explosive. Especially between 1945 and the mid-1980s, the Sonderkommando members were regularly accused in the literature of Auschwitz survivors and their testimonies of being collaborators, people who had become monsters and immoral during their work in the crematoria. No objective examination about the actual work and living conditions and the facts about the Sonderkommando was conducted.

Only in 1972 were parts of the "Secret Scrolls" published, enabling researchers and readers to gain a first insight into the real world of the Sonderkommando.[12] The "Secret Scrolls" were texts and reports, written clandestinely, by members of the Sonderkommando during their work in Auschwitz-Birkenau. The reports were buried in the grounds around the crematoria in order to preserve their information about the events in Auschwitz for the afterworld. The few parts of the documents which were found and discovered after the war are extremely important for research on the "Final Solution" and Auschwitz, since they were written directly during the events and give a detailed, authentic insight into the "Final Solution" in Auschwitz-Birkenau.

Zalman Gradowski, one of the authors of the "Secret Scrolls," describes the events at the crematoria in a vivid and emotional report. The writer informs the reader about the suffering and pain of the Jewish victims and tries to talk to the reader directly in order to prepare him for the description of the cruel events:

> Come to me, you happy citizen of the world, you, who is living in a land, where only happiness and fun might live, and I want to tell you how the modern and despised criminals changed the happiness of a complete nation to a disaster, their pleasure to eternal suffering, and the pleasing things of life in the eternity of destruction.[13]

After the first publication of memories of the Sonderkommando, the research slowly began to be aware of the existence and problematic of the Sonderkommando and researchers began carefully to investigate the accusations against the Sonderkommando, which were deepened by authors like Hannah Arendt and Primo Levi.[14] This new research on the Sonderkommando had the goal to gain an insight to the inner world of the Sonderkommando prisoners without prejudices and tried to focus on the real psyche and human conditions. The new focus of this research was no longer judging the Sonderkommando but to faithfully reconstruct the events, reality and atmosphere in the crematoria of Auschwitz-Birkenau. Nevertheless, interest in the Sonderkommando was still very limited. Only few historians, like Beer Mark, the Head of the Jewish History Institute in Poland, and Erich Kulka, who was an Auschwitz-survivor himself, researched the topic.[15] Only in the last twenty years has more and more research on the Sonderkommando been focused and published and the history of the Sonderkommando has been recognized as an essential aspect for the understanding of the "Final Solution."

What were the reasons for this years-long silence around the Sonderkommando? Why did it take so long, that the historical research tried to cope with the false accusations against the members of the Sonderkommando? One of the reasons might be that, for a very long time, it was unknown that members of the Sonderkommando still were alive. Those who were alive did not talk about their past and preferred to stay in the shadows. Because of the fact that public discourse condemned members of the Sonderkommando as collaborators or monsters, almost without exception, no survivor of the Sonderkommando wanted to be identified as such. For this reason, it was unknown for many years that members of the Sonderkommando had survived the camp, despite the desire of the SS to murder all members of the Sonderkommando after the destruction of the gas chambers. The fact that several members of the Sonderkommando were able to escape their murderers only became known when—after the discourse about the role of the Sonderkommando had been reevaluated—some of the survivors publicly admitted that they had been part of this controversial work squad.

Another reason why historical research did not deal with this aspect of the Shoah for so many years was that no historian wanted to become involved with this depressing topic in such a detailed way. Many researchers were content when they were able to deliver statistics of the murdered and abstractly describe the killing methods and the functional technique of the gas chambers. A closer look at the criminal events of the "Final Solution" was seen as too depressing and made historians reluctant to have a closer look at them.

Additionally, many people were certain that detailed research on the mass murder was a desecration of a holy place. They preferred that the last moments in the life of the murdered remain untouched and not be the object of a detailed historical research. Some even said that a more detailed research would renew the injustice against the dead and was comparable to a desecration of graves. Part of this position was the opinion that the focus on the spiritual fight of tormented, humiliated, and murdered Jews was more important than the detailed research on the events leading to their murder and the historical details on the process of the murder itself. All these reasons led to the fact that the topic of the Sonderkommando was an untouched area on the landscape of history for a very long time.

The more detailed research, which has taken place in the last twenty years, is based on the position that a focus on the Sonderkommando enables us to conduct a more profound historical research on the "Final Solution," its technical aspects, its concrete historical form and its emotional and spiritual aspects, and does not at all cause injustice to the victims of the "Final Solution." It is part of our obligation to honor the remembrance of the murdered. Historical research does not serve the honor of the victims, if it declares taboos and leaves unknown and undiscovered areas. If historical research is eager to deal with all aspects and areas of the "Final Solution," it honors the victims in a proper way.

There is another reason for the taboos and restrictions included on the research field of the "Final Solution." Many years after the Holocaust, people tried to deny that the crimes against European Jews had happened. The "Holocaust Deniers" tried to devaluate all historical research on the "Final Solution" and, in fact, they are the ones who desecrate the memory of the victims. Historical research has to make as its central objective to fight against any attempts of denial. Holocaust deniers morally continue the work of the National Socialists in their attempts to destroy all evidence and traces of the murder of millions of Jews. They make efforts to persuade others to forget the victims, murdered by the National Socialists in the Death Factories.

An historical research, which deals with the details of the "Final Solution" without any taboos and restrictions, can be an antidote to Holocaust denial. Any research, which declares some areas as taboo, arouses the suspicion that there is something to hide, and gives room for conspiracy theories. The testimonies of the Sonderkommando should stand in the center of each detailed research on the "Final Solution." Not only can they close the gaps that a research, solely based on documents, must leave open, but they also deliver a vivid and authentic insight to the events in the crematoria of Auschwitz-Birkenau, the biggest Concentration and Extermination Camp of the National Socialists. The testimonies of the Sonderkommando deliver this picture in such a detailed, complex, realistic and concrete way, that they are a useful weapon against all attempts at Holocaust denial.

The oral history of the Sonderkommando not only enables us to reconstruct the complex reality of the "Final Solution" in Auschwitz-Birkenau on the level of facts, dates and technical details, but also delivers a detailed insight into the human and emotional aspects of the "Final Solution." The memories of the Sonderkommando are the only documentation of the daily activities, routine and atmosphere in the area near the gas chambers; therefore, they are a central part of an historical research which tries to reconstruct the facts of the "Final Solution" or to understand its moral, emotional, spiritual, and philosophical implications. The Sonderkommando-survivors and their testimonies are the most basic documentation on the "Final Solution," and supply the closest insight in the world of the death factories.

Additionally, the testimonies of the Sonderkommando are especially important to gain an insight about the Holocaust from the perspective of the victims. National Socialist documents, which were not destroyed, and the testimonies of the perpetrators, like the memoirs of Rudolf Höss, only can deliver the perspective of the Germans, the perpetrators. Saul Friedländer emphasized the importance of the perspective of the victims, when he wrote: "Some of the best-known historical interpretations of these events [the Holocaust, GG] mainly concentrated on the persecution and death machinery of the Nazis and only gave small attention to the society in broader sense, in the sense of the general European and world-wide surroundings or in the sense of the changing fate of the victims."[16]

This perspective of the victims can be interpreted by oral history. In the case of the "Final Solution" in Auschwitz-Birkenau, it is the collection of testimonies of the Sonderkommando which can deliver the perspective of the victims in relation to the events of the "Final Solution." Since we are not able to fully know the events in the eyes of those who were murdered, we can only refer to the experience and the memories of the Sonderkommando to get a new dimension of millions of Jews who were forced to the gas chambers, who had to completely undress and who then were poisoned and burnt.

Notes

1. Cf. Didi-Hubermann, Georges, Images malgré tout, Paris 2003.

2. An extensive insight into the actions of is delivered by Hoffmann, Jens (ed.), Diese außerordentliche deutsche Bestialität. Wie die Nazis die Spuren ihrer Massenmorde in Osteuropa beseitigten. Augenzeugenberichte und Gespräche, Hamburg 2013.

3. Hartman, Geoffrey H., "Learning from Survivors. The Yale Testimony Project," *Holocaust Genocide Studies,* 9, 1995, p. 136.

4 Ginzburg, Carlo, "Just One Witness," in: Friedländer, Saul (ed.), *Probing the Limits of Representation,* Cambridge 1992, 82-96.

5. Pollack, Michael, Die Grenzen des Sagbaren. Lebensgeschichten von KZ-Überlebenden als. Augenzeugenberichte und als Identitätsarbeit, Frankfurt a.M. 1988, 109.

6. Agamben, Giorgio, *Was von Auschwitz bleibt,* Frankfurt am Main, 2003, 14f.

7. Sabrow, Der Zeitzeuge als Wanderer, *Die Geburt des Zeitzeugen,* 14.

8. At this point one could refer to uncounted memories, testimonies and literary texts. I want to concentrate only on a few book published by the men of the Sonderkommando. Cf.: Mordechai Ciechanower, *Der Dachdecker von Auschwitz,* Berlin 2007; Leon Cohen, *From Greece to Birkenau. The Crematoria Workers Uprising,* Tel Aviv 1996; or Filip Müller, *Sonderbehandlung,* München 1979.

9. "The man did not feel anything anymore. The corpses did not have any value in my eyes. After some time I did not have any human feelings for those corpses. Sometimes the corpses were covered with blood and excrements. One gets used to such things to a degree, that one sits on the corpses during a break or if you are hungry. We sat on the corpses and ate." Silberberg, Yaakov, Interview with GG on January 22, 1998 in Holon, from Private Archive GG.

10. Gideon Greif: Unique Testimonies: The World Wide Project of "Sonderkommando" testimonies, in: *International Journal on the Audio-Visual Testimony,* 2002, (nr.8), 33.

11. Cf. Ehlert, Martin/ Lorke, Beate, Zur Psychodynamik der traumatischen Reaktion, in: Psyche 42, 1988, 502- 532.

12. Wladyslaw Bartoszewksi, cit. after: Hefte von Auschwitz. Sonderheft I, Handschriften von Mitgliedern des Sonderkommandos, Oswiecim 1972, 305.

13. Gradowski, Zalman, 1944, Writings, in: Mark, Scrolls, 173.

14. Cf. Arendt, Hannah, Eichmann in *Jerusalem, Ein Bericht von der Banalität des Bösen,* München 1998, 215- 217 and Levi, Primo, *Die Untergegangen und die Geretteten,* München 1993, 48, 60.

15. Cf. for example Kulka, Erich, "Revolt of Jewish Prisoners in Auschwitz, based on new Testimonies," in: *The Voice of Auschwitz Survivors in Israel,* Nr. 28, 1984, S. 1-8 and Mark, Ber, The Scrolls of Auschwitz, Tel Aviv 1985.

16. Friedländer, *Das dritte Reich und die Juden,* 12.

Bibliography

Agamben, Giorgio, *Was von Auschwitz bleibt,* Frankfurt am Main, 2003.

Arendt, Hannah, *Eichmann in Jerusalem, Ein Bericht von der Banalität des Bösen,* München 1998, 215- 217.

Ciechanower, Mordechai, *Der Dachdecker von Auschwitz,* Berlin 2007.

Cohen, Leon, *From Greece to Birkenau. The Crematoria Workers Uprising,* Tel Aviv 1996.

Didi-Hubermann, *Georges, Images malgré tout,* Paris 2003.

Ehlert, Martin/ Lorke, Beate, "Zur Psychodynamik der traumatischen Reaktion," in: *Psyche* 42, 1988, pp. 502- 532.

Friedländer, Saul, *Das Dritte Reich und die Juden.* Gesamtausgabe, München 2008.

Ginzburg, Carlo, "Just One Witness," in: Friedländer, Saul (ed.), *Probing the Limits of Representation,* Cambridge 1992.

Greif, Gideon: "Unique Testimonies: The World Wide Project of 'Sonderkommando' Testimonies," in: *International Journal on the Audio-Visual Testimony,* 2002, (nr.8), pp.31-36.

Hartman, Geoffrey H, "Learning from Survivors." The Yale Testimony Project, *Holocaust Genocide Studies,* 9, 1995, pp. 192-207.

Hoffmann, Jens (ed.), *Diese außerordentliche deutsche Bestialität. Wie die Nazis die Spuren ihrer Massenmorde in Osteuropa beseitigten.* Augenzeugenberichte und Gespräche, Hamburg 2013.

Kulka, Erich, "Revolt of Jewish Prisoners in Auschwitz, based on new Testimonies," in: *The Voice of Auschwitz Survivors in Israel,* Nr. 28, 1984, pp. 1-8.

Levi, Primo, *Die Untergegangen und die Geretteten,* München 1993.

Mark, Ber, *The Scrolls of Auschwitz,* Tel Aviv 1985.

Müller, Filip, *Sonderbehandlung,* München 1979.

Pollack, Michael, *Die Grenzen des Sagbaren. Lebensgeschichten von KZ-Überlebenden als Augenzeugenberichte und als Identitätsarbeit,* Frankfurt a.M. 1988.

Sabrow, Martin, Bösch, Frank (Hrsg.), *Die Geburt des Zeitzeugen nach 1945,* Göttingen 2012.

Wladyslaw Bartoszewksi, cit. after: *Hefte von Auschwitz. Sonderheft I, Handschriften von Mitgliedern des Sonderkommandos,* Oswiecim 1972, pp. 275-279.

CHAPTER 10

Medics and Survivors: Emergency Care Administered by the Liberators

DIANE PLOTKIN

As they defeated their German enemies and marched into Europe, the Allied armies came upon an estimated 11,332,700 refugees and survivors of death and labor camps scattered throughout the continent.[1] Because there were so many concentration and labor camps, it was difficult to accurately ascertain the number of survivors. The number of prisoners counted by liberating forces in five camps alone—Dachau,[2] Mauthausen,[3] Belsen,[4] Buchenwald,[5] and Sandbostel[6]—totaled 159,000. Soviet troops came upon another 7,000 prisoners in the Auschwitz, Birkenau and Monowitz camps: 1,200 sick prisoners at Auschwitz, 5,800 at Birkenau, of whom 4,000 were women, and 600 sick prisoners at Monowitz.[7] Making it more difficult to determine the number of survivors was the fact that the dead and dying lay among the living, and the death rates increased constantly for at least the first few weeks. In addition, many who were physically able left the camps before they could be counted.

According to American army records 3,397,300 former prisoners were refugees within their own countries. These were defined by the liberating forces as persons within their own countries who were unable to return home without assistance, as opposed to displaced persons—those outside their countries due to the war and unable to return home without assistance. The army further delineated refugees and displaced persons into the following categories: evacuees; war or political fugitives, i.e. those who had fled the Nazi regime; political prisoners; forced or voluntary workers; *Todt* workers and members of other para-military organizations who were not members *per se* of German military forces; deportees; foreigners who had not been able to return home due to the war; persons placed in countries other than their own by force; civilian internees who had been incarcerated in labor camps; and stateless persons, i.e. those who had no homes to which they could return following the war.

According to one estimate, Allied troops came upon persons from at least twenty different countries—including Belgium, Denmark, France, Germany (excluding German refugees), Luxembourg, the Netherlands, and Norway, to name but a few. With so many persons scattered all over the European continent, Allied armies were forced to contend with refugees speaking at least twenty different languages. Because of this as well as the many illnesses the liberating troops encountered, care and disposition of these people presented technical as well as administrative difficulties. Proper feeding, medical care, and quarantine required nurses and physicians who were otherwise needed to care for the wounded soldiers, thus obstructing the smooth operation of military actions.[8]

American and British troops who liberated the camps did so at or near the cessation of hostilities. The Soviet troops who came upon the Auschwitz-Birkenau compound in January 1945, however, did so while the front line was only twenty-some kilometers from Oszweizim. In this area the Fourth Ukrainian Front was still engaged in battle with pockets of German troops. Because of the ongoing battles, many bridges had been destroyed, and roads were filled with Soviet transports and civilians making their way home, thereby impeding railroad transportation and adequate communication via any kind of effective postal service.[9]

Although the International Red Cross had attempted to aid the prisoners by sending parcels to those camps which were known to them, such as Dachau, Buchenwald, Sangerhausen, Sachsenhausen, Oranienburg, Flossenburg, Landsberg-am-Lech, Flöha, Ravensbrück, Hamburg-Neuengamme, Mauthausen, Theresienstadt, Auschwitz, Bergen-Belsen, camps near Vienna, as well as some in Central and Southern Germany, most prisoners, particularly the Jews, never received them. From January to June 1945, however, ICRC [International Committee of the Red Cross] delegates were admitted to the camps and administered what help they could.[10]

Disease was rampant in all the camps. Although typhus in the camps had been reported to U.S. Army troops prior to their invasion of Germany, once they actually entered the camps, liberating soldiers found survivors who suffered from a multiplicity of other illnesses and life-threatening conditions as well. Camps in East Germany were found to be more heavily infested, the infection thought to have been brought into the area from Russia and Poland, while in the newly liberated areas further west, it was believed to have been brought in by persons recently liberated from the camps. There were, however, relatively few cases among former prisoners of war.[11] Interestingly, some records of Soviet armies in Eastern Europe, particularly in the archives at Auschwitz, make no mention of typhus.

The first Russian soldier from a reconnaissance unit of the 100th Infantry of the 106th Corps entered Monowitz at approximately 9:00 A.M. on January 27, 1945. The entire division arrived half an hour later. Approximately 3:00 P.M. the same day, the Red Army arrived at Auschwitz and Birkenau. Thereafter, the site of the liberated camp was guarded by Soviet soldiers, who stood next to the crematorium in the main camp.[12] Miles away from the camps there was a horrific stench due to unwashed and decomposing bodies which lay in piles of excrement, waste and filth. In many camps the liberators found remains of partially burned bodies in crematory ovens. Captain Miszczenko, a Soviet military investigator, described the appearance of Auschwitz in a report from Brzezinka, dated February 4, 1945:

> Going in the direction of the crematoria, we found on the camp road and on the side of the road, along a stretch of 500 meters, 15 bodies of prisoners, men and women, who had been shot several days earlier by the Germans [the SS]... In another place, at a distance of 50 meters from the [ruins of the] crematorium 34 bodies of prisoners were found, both men and women, all victims of Nazi degeneration, among them the corpse of a 3-or-4-month-old baby. Judging from their appearance, these were bodies of people who had starved to death...
>
> [T]here was no garbage or waste disposal. All kinds of waste and trash were heaped directly by the walls of the barracks, and at their back doors. Heaps of rubbish mixed with excrement reach up to half the height of the building...
>
> In the Birkenau Camp, in the vicinity of the barracks marked 32 and 11, which had been the camp hospitals for men and women, over 400 dead bodies of prisoners were found—men, women and children, dead from exhaustion, victims of the German degeneration.[13]

Of the 850 sick prisoners who had been left behind during the deportation to Germany, 200 died. Disorders among the prisoners that are mentioned in the Soviet records include diarrhea, starvation, and tuberculosis. According to all records, however, in camp after camp the description of the prisoners by their liberators is the same: extremely ill, skeletal, exhausted, apathetic, and incontinent. Patients suffered from such diverse conditions as dysentery, extreme weakness, tremors, typhus, typhoid fever,[14] which was frequently followed by pleuritic (pulmonary) pain, tuberculosis, petechial rashes,[15] scabies,[16] erysipelas,[17] gangrene, particularly gangrene of the toes, scurvy,[18] polyneuritic[19] pains in the legs and other conditions secondary to starvation.

Perhaps a Soviet physician who examined the inmates gives the best description of their physical appearance. He found inmates sleepy and apathetic, complaining of a feeling of heaviness, inertia, and slowing of the thought process. They suffered from diarrhea, often bloody, and had a frequent need to urinate, especially at night. Often they were thirsty rather than hungry. Women had lost their menstrual periods and men were impotent. Their hair was thin, dull and soft. The skin was dry, rough, scaly and pigmented and could be squeezed into long-lasting folds. Patients suffered from deep bedsores and abscesses. There were no layers of fat, and the muscles were atrophied and flaccid. The pulse was slow, sometimes as low as 35 beats per minute (normal is 80), and there was free fluid in the chest. There was visible edema (secondary to lack of protein) on the legs, arms and face, and the abdomen and genitals were visibly swollen. Reflexes were poor, and sensation in the skin, especially in edematous areas, was almost absent. They also suffered from severe anemia and had little gastric acid. They did not, however, complain of any loss of vision or hearing.[20]

The first organized medical care for the patients came from the Soviet army physicians. One of the first things they did was arrange for the inmates to receive easily digestible food, as opposed to the more unsuitable food that had been given them by the local population and soldiers who had originally come into the camp. The inmates were then taken to the two field hospitals of the 60th Army of the First Ukrainian Front. The commander of the first—hospital 2197—located in former main camp in blocks 9 -11, 16—21, and 28, was physician Major Wejkow. The commander of the second, in blocks 12–14 and 22–24, was physician Major Mieaj. Prisoners from Brzezinka and Monowitz were moved to the main camp in February. Thereafter the two hospitals merged, under the command of physician Major Zylinskaja, who ran the hospital until June.

There were up to twenty personnel per Soviet field hospital, composed of doctors, nurses, orderlies, lab assistants, and administration officials. They were aided by physicians and nurses recruited from among the former prisoners as well as members of the Polish Red Cross (PCK) from Kraków, Ozsweizim and Brzeszinka. On February 6-7, 1945, Soviet military personnel placed the ill survivors who had been in the BIIe and BIIf sections of Birkenau (approximately 2,200 people) under the care of the Red Cross (PCK) team that had come from Kraków. In addition to several doctors and other personnel, twelve nurses were sent to Brzezinka, a ratio of twelve nurses to two hundred patients. Because there were so few nurses caring for so many patients, they often worked from twelve to twenty hours a day, and sometimes two or three days without a break.[21] According to nurse Joanna Zawislak's daily report, dated February 12, 1945, twelve nurses and seventeen orderlies of the PCK team cared for 2,200 patients in Brzezinka, blocks 2, 6, 8, 12, 20, 22, 24, 28, and 30. In addition to caring for the patients, they buried the dead, scrubbed floors, carried buckets of excrement, and brought food and fuel to the barracks.[22]

One major problem the Polish Red Cross nurses and Soviet Army physicians encountered was a shortage of medications, particularly an insufficient supply of heart medication, analgesics, and bandages.[23] Nor was there enough medical equipment. Nurses and orderlies who combed the camp for these and other supplies found large quantities in the former SS Revier and pharmacy, which was located in the attic of block 28. There was also a large supply of bandages, although they had no way to sterilize them.

Because of the continued fighting, health care for the inmates was limited, as camp hospitals could not be fully operative until the war ended in the spring. Furthermore, because supplies were limited, only minor surgery was performed in the camp Red Cross hospital, while major cases as well as seriously ill patients were transported "to the Clinic of Surgical Illnesses of Jagiellonian University... St. Lazarus Hospital...

the Municipal Sanitary Institution in Kraków and to the sanatorium in Prudnik, (a district of Kraków)."[24]

In February and March the nurses who came into the barracks in the morning had to climb into the bunk beds in order to check whether or not patients were still alive. Nurses, orderlies, and patients who were strong enough then removed any corpses and took them to the morgue. Following their first morning duties, nurses then bathed the patients and changed their linen, administered medications and meals and performed other tasks, the completion of which required ten to twenty hours per day.[25]

Nurses devoted much of their time to feeding the most seriously ill patients such foods as strained potato soup in small doses—one tablespoon three times a day—"as if it were medicine." Patients feared baths and intramuscular and intravenous injections, as it made them think they were going to the gas chamber or being killed by injections of phenol.[26] Medical personnel found that what was most beneficial to patients suffering from the effects of starvation was the administration of large amounts of animal protein, such as cheese, rather than large quantities of vitamins. Issuing warm clothing also helped to raise the body temperature of starving patients who still suffered from hypothermia as a result of forced heavy labor in insufficient clothing, under conditions of poor physical health.

Within three to four months after liberation, however, most patients were able to leave the PCK camp hospital and Soviet field hospitals, although some remained in them until the summer of 1945, at which time they were taken to the PCK camp hospital. Some of the former inmates set out on their own, while others were taken in transports organized by the military authorities. Many were transported by Red Cross volunteers as well as delegations from various countries who had come to the camp to witness the horrors.

The PCK camp hospital was closed on October 1, 1945.[27] Some of the children were sent to orphanages and children's homes, others to various centers in Kraków. Thirty-one Polish children were taken to the Institute for Children, and the chronically ill to Warsaw-Opiece. Among these were children who had been deported during and after the Warsaw uprising.[28] In many cases the children, still emaciated and louse-infested, required up to three more months of continuous care before their health began to improve.[29]

Contrary to the reports of the Soviet medical personnel, most testimonies and memoirs of physicians and nurses in former American and British liberating forces emphasize the typhus epidemics they encountered in the camps. In fact, because there was so much typhus in Germany and in the camps, Allied personnel took immediate measures to prevent its further spread westward. For this reason, after they had established the first bridgehead across the Rhine at Remagen on March 7, 1945, the First Army, in consensus with the Ninth Army, established what was to be called a *Cordon Sanitaire*, i.e. the establishment of a "Sanitary Border to Control Typhus"[30] along the French-Swiss-German border, from the east side of the Rhine River to the Weal River, and alongside the Weal to the North Sea. In an effort to control the disease, all civilians and returning POWs were to be dusted with DDT powder. This was followed by an order from ETOUSA [European Theater of Operations United States Army] dated April 12, 1945. Guard stations were to be placed at specific ports of entry; delousing stations were to be placed at all ports of entry; transportation by rivers and canals was to be suspended; and all civilians traveling by rail were to undergo dusting with DDT powder.

Liberated concentration camp prisoners in Western Europe were cared for by physicians and nurses in the Army Evacuation units and British medical personnel. From April through June 1945, the greatest problem encountered by the nurses in the Army Nurse Corps was the care of displaced persons. In addition to caring for the wounded soldiers, it was their responsibility to visit the camps, make suggestions regarding sanitation, check on communicable diseases, establish dispensaries, arrange for hospitalization in German hospitals, and assist with planning and supplementing food supplies in the camps. Beginning in June, they began to work with German public health officials in order to help them become functional and self-sufficient.[31] Despite their best efforts, however, many former inmates were beyond help.

Buchenwald was liberated by the Third U.S. Army on April 10, 1945. At the time, approximately 25,000 men from almost every country in Europe were imprisoned there. When the First Army arrived on April 15, they found 21,000 inmates, 3,950 of whom were hospitalized. The majority suffered from malnutrition, dehydration and diarrhea, much of which responded well to sulfaguandine. There were 320 cases of tuberculosis, which had been brought in by patients from other camps. According to Army records, there were 52 cases of typhus on the day of liberation, resulting in a 25 percent mortality rate. The disease had spread in epidemic proportions in the winter of 1945 due to the unsanitary living conditions and close quarters. The liberating Army personnel who assumed command began an intensive care program, and all patients with typhus were hospitalized and quarantined.[32]

On April 16, Army personnel set up a hospital in the former German Army barracks, which were cleaned and deloused prior to being taken over for use as hospital wards.[33] Nurses were sent to care for the patients, who received blood transfusions, intravenous fluids, and plasma. Diets were administered as tolerated. According to the record of an American nurse with the 120th Evacuation Hospital, the number of patients hospitalized between April 19 and 22 rose from 3,250 to 5,492. There were 130 deaths.[34] By June 1, the number of patients had dropped to 1,200, most of whom suffered from gastro-enteritis. In an effort to control the further spread of typhus, the Army medical corps organized twenty dusting teams, and the entire personnel of the camp was dusted with DDT powder. All bedding and clothing was cleaned and deloused, and the entire hospital staff of about 150 doctors and attendants was given typhus vaccine. After two weeks, the medical and nursing staff of the 120th Evacuation Hospital was relieved of its assignment and replaced by another hospital unit.

Typhus had not occurred in Flossenberg until September 1944, when a number of workers sent from Cologne became ill shortly after their arrival.[35] By October 15, there were 82 cases of typhus, although prior to the liberation of the camp the SS doctor had not isolated the patients and insisted the term "typhus" euphemistically be called "the grippe." An assembly center for Messerschmidt aircraft, Flossenberg had housed as many as 15,000 workers, mainly Poles, Rumanians, Czechs, Yugoslavs, French, and Bulgarians. Before the Germans evacuated the camp, all but 1,600 sick and wounded prisoners were forced to relocate to Dachau. About 6,000 of them reached Cham, about sixty kilometers away, but many became sick and died along the way, presumably of typhus. Most fled, scattering into surrounding areas and spreading typhus into nearby German communities, resulting in one of the most serious problems the Allied armies were to encounter. The camp itself was freed by the Third U.S. Army in late April 1945.

A Russian POW had apparently brought typhus into Mauthausen in 1942. Following that there had been typhus epidemics every winter. According to one study there had been as many as 600 cases of typhus at one time. A Third Army Finding Team had been sent to the camp to make arrangements and set up control measures prior to its liberation on May 5, 1945. Of the 28,000 inmates, of whom 3,000 were women, there were 246 cases of typhus, 134 among the men, and 112 among the women. Living quarters, as in other camps, were crowded, filthy and louse infested.

After the typhus control program was set up, medical personnel hospitalized and quarantined patients with active disease as well as anyone who was suspected to be incubating it. Army and prisoner personnel organized delousing teams, and the entire camp was deloused within a week. Their efforts were so effective that the incidence of typhus decreased rapidly. By June 1, 1945 only 70 typhus patients remained in the hospital.[36]

Dr. William V. McDermott[37] writes about the conditions in Ebensee. According to his report, the first Americans came into the camp on May 10, 1945. They found that although prisoners had been receiving six ounces of bread per day, when they were sent to the so-called "hospital," patients were put on half rations in order to hasten their deaths. Although the American doctors, having seen thousands of injuries and deaths throughout the war, had become somewhat inured to illness, they were overcome and physically ill by what they saw. In Ebensee, Dr. McDermott comments that medical personnel in his platoon were faced with an impossibility. He writes of prisoners who fell dead as they stood awaiting their food. The doctors, needing to improve sanitation, living conditions, and food before they could begin medical treatment, felt helpless. Faced with chores almost beyond their control, they ordered Austrians living nearby to work in the camp, cleaning filth, scrubbing barracks, washing patients, and transporting the dead to the outskirts of town to individual graves in a plot marked "German Atrocity Cemetery."

The three small, specialized surgical units in Dr. McDermott's platoon, working constantly, were overcome with difficulties. In addition to setting up their own tents, they had to find a way to run water into the camp in order to set up outdoor showers, delousing stations, latrines, and dressing stations. They also had to scour the surrounding area for clean clothing. Once that was completed, they had to set up a system of categorizing patients according to their medical diagnoses and isolating those who had come down with typhus, tuberculosis, and other infectious diseases.

All the Americans were not only horrified at what they saw but deeply touched by the reactions of the prisoners to the "miracle of liberation." One incident in particular bears repeating. In Dr. McDermott's words: "When I walked into one of the frightfully crowded barracks on the first night, there were three pitifully weak cheers for the American Army. A few who were apparently ex-soldiers struggled to their feet in an attempt to salute and someone tried to sing 'Over There.' I broke down completely."[38] He was relieved when a larger Evacuation Hospital soon moved into the area.

Smaller camps included Vught, where there were four cases of typhoid fever reported, rather than typhus;[39] Sandbostel, where out of 22,000 inmates, there were 400 cases of typhus; and Neustadt, to which about 7,000 prisoners, who had been transported by sea from other German concentration camps, suffered from malnourishment and typhus. In addition there were a few cases among DPs returning to Denmark, but in all these cases effective measures soon had the situation under control.

Perhaps the worst typhus epidemic was in Bergen-Belsen. Although the Army had knowledge of it by April 9, it wasn't until April 15, when the camp was liberated by the British, that the situation could be assessed and appropriate measures taken. Camp 1, called "the horror camp," was riddled with patients suffering from tuberculosis, pneumonia, sore throats and fevers, streptoccal infections, scabies from infested blankets, and every other condition imaginable. Major William A. Davis, MG. AUS, of the U.S.A. Typhus Commission in Cairo, reported that when the camp was liberated an estimated 45,000 internees were suffering from malnutrition and other diseases.[40] Approximately 500 persons had been dying per day, mainly due to the effects of starvation, typhus, tuberculosis, and dysentery. In addition, prior to liberation SS guards had been constantly killing more.[41] Conditions were so deplorable, in fact, that Camp 1 was to be burned and the hospital established in Camp 2. Because there was a shortage of medical personnel, they used as few barracks as possible. Short of sufficient staff to deal with the countless difficulties they faced, Army physicians requested whatever help they could get. For this reason, a group of one hundred senior medical students, under the direction of Commander Meiklejohn of the U.N.R.R.A. [United Nations Relief and Rehabilitation Administration] was sent from Britain to Belsen to help. Their efforts were so effective that soon after they began to care for the survivors the daily death rate fell from 300 per day to approximately 60. In addition a contingent of the British Red Cross also arrived and did anything and everything asked of them.[42]

The primary duty of those sent to care for the patients was preventive. Few of the physicians at Belsen had ever seen typhus and were unaware of the research being done on the disease by the U.S.A.Typhus Commission in Cairo. For this reason Major Davis spoke to the students and other caregivers about diagnosis and treatment. In an attempt to protect key personnel working in Camp 1, they were administered the Cox virus vaccine. Despite these measures, however, several people working with the survivors contracted the disease.

Former medical students describe huts, particularly in the female section of the camp, that were filled with dead, dying, and live women, the dead lying among the living. Floors were covered with about an inch of feces which, added to the odor of the decomposing bodies, created an unbearable stench. For this reason, their first task was to clean the barracks as well as possible. Each day, before they entered the camp and upon their return, everyone was dusted with DDT powder, although this did not always prevent lice from spreading from the prisoners to the personnel. In addition, physicians and nurses operated what was called a "human laundry," in which the inmates were washed, dusted with DDT, and issued clean clothing by the British Red Cross.[43] Before entering the hospital in Camp 2, 11,890 former inmates underwent this procedure.[44] The general delousing of the entire camp was completed between April 22 and 30.

Anyone who was able to walk was considered "well." Anyone who could not was taken to the hospital. The larger portion of Camp 2 consisted of the main hospital in which there were 11, 200 patients.

> It [was] divided into squares of five houses, each square accommodating approximately 700 patients. Each square [was] under the control of one medical officer from the R.A.M.C. [Royal Army Medical Corps]. Each house of 150 patients [had] one Swiss internee or German doctor in charge, one or two British trained nurses, the rest being internee nurses or German nurses.[45]

> Emphasis was laid upon nursing care, hydration, and as high a vitamin, caloric, and protein diet as each patient could tolerate. Because of the high incidence of typhus, clinical observations per se were of little value. Most patients suffered from prostration and various other conditions secondary to the disease. The patients, however, were terrified of any German personnel.

Dr. W.R.F. Collis wrote an article entitled "Belsen Camp: A Preliminary Report," which was published in the *British Medical Journal* in June 1945. By that time more than 20,000 internees had been buried. Approximately 30,000 remained, of whom 11,200 were in the main hospital area. It is with good reason that he completes his report as follows:

> This is a brief preliminary report of the Belsen Camp to give the medical profession in Britain some idea of the medical problems involved. It is a complete understatement. No words can describe the stench of decaying feces, rotting bodies, and burning rags, which in the first weeks one could smell miles from the camp, and it can be left to the imagination of the medical men who read this article to appreciate what doctors and nurses and medical students at Belsen have endured and accomplished.[46]

There is a significant amount of source material regarding the number and physical state of inmates in Dachau as well as detailed information and statistical material regarding diseases and medical care.[47] Dachau, with a camp population of 67,566, was liberated by the 45th Division of the U.S. Seventh Army on April 29, 1945. The following is a graphic description of its appearance:

> Barracks greatly overcrowded. A few had no bunks at all and inmates slept on the floor on dirty bedsacks with a little straw. Those with

> "bunks" were all three decks high, and in the worse barracks men slept 3 to 5 in a single bunk of about 30" width. Some sleeping was done in shifts. Some barracks were simply equipped with "shelves" across the end or along the side of the room [sic] where men slept on "edge" like sardines packed in a can. If an inmate died during the night, those closer to the wall had to crawl out over the body. There were approximately 300 women in the camp in a separately enclosed area within the general compound. Women's barracks were just about as crowded as the men's. Saw forty plus women housed in a room approximately 20 feet square, all sleeping on the floor. Men were clamoring at the gates to the women's enclosure trying to get to the women. Camp doctors said this was the public house for the SS troops on duty there, and that they selected the best looking foreign girls of proper age—Polish, Russian, French, etc.—for the prostitution activities of the SS troops on duty. Saw what looked like women of almost all nationalities, including Hindus and Chinese. (Saw no one I could classify as an Arab.) One room in the women's compound had seven babies in it, none over a month old.
>
> The entire compound looks smaller than the area outlined as that of the Civil War Prisoner of War Enclosure at Andersonville, Georgia.[48]
>
> Shortly after liberation the entire camp was placed under quarantine for typhus, an epidemic which had begun in December 1944 and peaked in April 1945.[49] Several prisoners had managed to escape before these measures could be put into effect, however, thereby spreading the disease to people in the surrounding areas. Despite the number of prisoners suffering from typhus and the emphasis placed upon its care and treatment, the greatest medical problem at Dachau was tuberculosis, approximately 35% of the patients being afflicted with the disease.[50]

The greatest number of prisoners were Poles, Russians, Hungarians, Germans, and French, although between April 26 and 29, convoys from Buchenwald had brought an estimated 10,000 people. (The army records do not mention the fact that the survivors were Jews from these countries). Also during this time, 8,000 persons had been marched out of the camp by the SS for unknown reasons. Most were believed to have been killed.

Inside the camp there were as many as 1,700 persons in most blocks. One block housed 1,900 men. The overcrowding and unhygienic conditions contributed to the incidence of typhus. Other epidemics, which had infested the camp previously, included scabies, in January and February 1941, and typhoid fever, from December 1942 to February 1943, which had killed approximately 270 persons. The greatest number of patients, however, suffered from tuberculosis.[51] As in other camps, however, it was impossible to know the exact number of deaths, as these figures only include medical deaths, not men who had been gassed, shot, or killed by other means. In addition, in many cases, when men had reported to the hospital, they were given reduced rations; as a result, many died from starvation.

On May 15, 1945, Brig. General Leon A. Fox, Field Director, U.S.A. Typhus Commission, Col. John E. Gordon, Chief of Medicine, OCS, ETOUSA, and four other officers arrived at the camp to meet and develop a plan of treatment. A ward of 64 beds in the 116th Evacuation Hospital was set aside for the Commission. On May 16, 1945, six nurses from the 59th Evacuation Hospital arrived in order to work with the Typhus Commission. During the next few days, patients were admitted for treatment as rapidly as possible, the last being admitted on May 30. The Commission stayed until June 11.

Dusting with DDT powder was immediately put into effect. All prisoners of Dachau and Allach received dusting between May 3 and May 8. In addition everyone, including camp guards, attendants and visitors on official business were dusted upon leaving the inner camp. If they had not already been vaccinated for the disease, they were also administered 1 cc. of Cox vaccine.

Approximately 13,000, of a census of 30,000, prisoners were vaccinated on May 9 and 10, while a second dose of the vaccine was administered to 18,400 prisoners on May 15 and 16. Unfortunately, some prisoners received two doses, while others received none. Personnel also administered 7,000 injections at the Allach Camp on May 7 and 14.

During the first few days of May 1945, the 116th and 127th Evacuation Hospitals were set up in the former SS barracks in the outer camp, after first removing the contents of the buildings and tearing out the partitions. They began to receive patients at the rate of 200 per hospital per day. The hospital personnel attempted to admit male typhus patients to the 116th Evacuation Hospital and females to the 127th.

In another effort to control the disease, groups of prisoners of the same nationality were moved together from the overcrowded barracks in the inner camp to cleaned barracks in the outer camp.

Contrary to what physicians and nurses had encountered at other camps, symptoms of typhus at Dachau were relatively mild. Fewer patients had full-blown rashes, and there seemed to be less prostration and delirium, as well as a shorter convalescence. Perhaps vaccination played a part in this, although the vaccine was shown to be ineffective in persons already incubating the disease.

During May 1945, the 116th Evacuation Hospital admitted a total of 2,057 patients, of whom 1,755 either had or were suspected of having typhus, although the exact number typhus patients is unknown. Other patients were diagnosed as having tuberculosis or pneumonia. One hundred ninety patients died during the month, 140 of them from typhus.

Treatment consisted of administration of hyper-immune anti-typhus rabbit serum, which was ineffective in shortening the length of fever, and sodium para amino benzoic acid [PABA], which was continued until temperature levels returned to normal. The average duration of fever for patients receiving PABA was 12.7 days, as opposed to 16.2 days for those who did not. The drug, however, was not without dangerous side effects, as patients suffered from nausea and vomiting, secondary fever, lowered white blood cell counts [leukopenia], blood in the urine [hematuria], and nitrogen retention [azotemia]. Administration of PABA was thought to be sufficiently effective, however, despite the danger of these side effects. Of the three deaths among 79 typhus patients treated with PABA, one died of tuberculosis and the other two of severe myocarditis [inflammation of the heart muscle].

By the time the patients in Dachau had begun to recuperate, there had been 71 U.S., 62 German, and 31 Polish doctors caring for them. A French Vatican Mission provided sufficient medical personnel to care for 110 more. The French Red Cross also sent four people, although their personnel did not work in the camp itself.[52]

Gradually the epidemic was brought under control, the living under treatment, the dead buried, and those well enough able to return home.

As Drs. Graham A. Cosmas and Albert E. Cowdry note:

> Cheering groups of prisoners began to depart for home. Allied soldiers who had liberated the camp and Army medics who had worked there were left to record in official reports, private letters, and diaries their recollections of a situation that is fortunately without an exact parallel in recent or perhaps any history...
>
> The compassionate treatment of the camp survivors marked the restoration of moral order amid the worst scenes that Nazi tyranny had been able to devise.[53]

Following the war, relief, rehabilitation, retraining and relocation of the survivors in the liberated camps was undertaken by voluntary relief agencies, which, under the sponsorship of the President's War Relief Council and recognition of the UNRRA,[54] organized themselves into the American Council of Voluntary Agencies for Foreign Service. It included the following agencies: The Hebrew Sheltering and Immigrant Aid Society (HIAS), The American Jewish Joint Distribution Committee (A.J.D.C.), The American ORT Foundation,[55] and Hadassah. This was augmented by relief and rehabilitation agencies from Great Britain, set up under the Council of British Societies for Relief Abroad at the suggestion of the Allied Post-War Requirements Bureau.

Emergency medical care administered by the many physicians and nurses who encountered the living skeletons in the newly liberated camps had brought immediate relief and restored the physical health of untold numbers of survivors. This, however, was only the first step in attempting to rebuild the millions of shattered lives.

Notes

1. Records of the Office of the Surgeon General (Army) WWII, Administrative Records 1940-1949, 15th Evacuation Hospital ETO thru 129th Evacuation Hospital, 1945, Record Group 112, Box 498, NWCH, HM 1999, National Archives, College Park, Maryland.

2. Records of the Surgeon General (Army) Army Group U.S.A. Typhus Commission, 1942-1946, General Records of the Paris Office, 1944-45, Record Group 112, Entry 343A, Box 70, National Archives, College Park, Maryland. Subsequently noted as U.S.A. Typhus Commission, 1942-1946.

3. Allied Operational Headquarters, World War II, Supreme Headquarters Allied Expeditionary Forces (SHAEF), Medical Division Decimal Files January 1944-July 1945, 000.75-211, Record Group 331, Entry 65, Box 1, National Archives, College Park, Maryland. Subsequently noted as Medical Division Decimal Files January 1944-July 1945, Record Group 331, Entry 65, Box 70.

4. U.S.A. Typhus Commission, 1942-1946.

5. Allied Operational and Occupation Headquarters, World War II, Supreme Headquarters Allied Expeditionary Forces, (SHAEF) Record Group 331, Entry 65, Box 1, National Archives, College Park, Maryland.

6. U.S.A. Typhus Commission, 1942-1946, Entry 343A, Box 70.

7. Danuta Czech, *Auschwitz Chronicle 1939-1945: From the Archives of the Auschwitz Memorial and the German Federal Archives*, (New York: Henry Holt & Co., 1990), 803-805.

8. Ibid.

9. Andrez Strzelecki, *Wyzwolenie KL Auschwitz* (The Liberation of Auschwitz, *Zeszyty* Ozsweimsky, Numer Specjalny (Special Issue) [III], 1974, 41-42, trans. Zygmunt Mazur, Auschwitz Archives.

10. XVII International Red Cross Conference, Stockholm, August 1948, *Report of the International Committee of the Red Cross on its Activities during the Second World War* (September 1, 1939—June 30, 1947), Volume III, Relief Activities, (Geneva, May 1948), 83.

11. Allied Operational Headquarters, World War II, Supreme Headquarters Allied Expeditionary Forces (SHAEF), Medical Division, Decimal File Jan. 1944-July 1945, File 383.63 to 560.5, Record Group 331, Entry 65, Box 4, National Archives, College Park, Maryland.

12. Czech, 803-805.

13. Photocopy of the protocol of the inspection of Brzezinka, dated 4 February 1945. Files of the Soviet Commission. APMO [The Archive of the State Museum in

Ozsweizim]—Varia, IZ-1/5, 2-3 in *Wyzwolenie KL Auschwitz*, 42-43.

14. Although the symptoms are similar, typhus is caused by rickettsia, which are borne by lice and other insects, while typhoid fever is spread by contaminated water and food. Symptoms are high fever, macular or papular rash appearing from the third to the seventh day, malaise, and severe headache. *Dorland's Pocket Medical Dictionary*, Twenty-third edition, (Philadelphia, London, Toronto: W.B. Saunders Co., 1982), 701

15. Minute red spots due to the escape of small amounts of blood. (*Dorland's*, 533).

16. A contagious skin disease due to the itch mite. (Ibid. 608).

17. Contagious disease of the skin and subcutaneous tissue due to infection. (Ibid. 252).

18. Disease due to deficiency of Vitamin C, marked by anemia, spongy gums, mucocutaneous hemorrhages, and induration of the calf muscles. (Ibid., 554).

19. Pain due to simultaneous inflammation of many nerves, probably due to Vitamin B12 deficiency. (Ibid. 554).

20 The first observations made by Dr. Bolesw Urbalski on the diseases found in the PCK Camp Hospital were published as a note in *Przeglad Lekarski*, Krakow:, 2:1946, nr 4-6, p. 18, in *Wyzwolenie KL Auschwitz*, 83-87.

21. Among other sources: Account of former prisoner Anna Chomicz (APMO, Collection of Testimonies, vol.75, pp. 16-17); accounts of former PCK team members, Genoefa Przbysz and Wilhelm Wazdrag (ibid. vol. 75, pp. 245-246; H. Kodl pp. 108-112; J. Bellert: Praca. pp. 669. In *Wyzwolenie KL Auschwitz*, 64.

22. H. Kodl p. 111 in *Wyzwolenie KL Auschwitz*, 64-65.

23. The accounts of former PCK members, Joanna Jakobi, Lidia Polonska, Genoefa Przbysz. (APMO Collection of Testimonies, vol. 75, p. 254; vol. 77, p. 147-148; vol. 78, p. 45); H. Kodï, p. 109. In *Wyzwolenie KL Auschwitz*, 74.

24. *Wyzwolenie KL Auschwitz*, 93.

25. Ibid. 79.

26. *Wyzwolenie KL Auschwitz*, 79.

27. J. Bellert: Praca. p. 69, In *Wyzwolenie KL Auschwitz*, 115.

28. Annotation about the children Waclaw and Andrzej Donten being sent to Krakow, the register of former prisoners of KL Auschwitz treated at Soviet field hospitals (APMO. The PCK Collection, file IV, PCK/11, p. 4; account of former prisoners Zofia Lutomska-Kucharska and Helena Bunsch-Konopka (APMO. Collection of Testimonies, vol. 30, pp. 22-23; 74. P. 236). The first group of children sent to Kraków at the end of January 1945. *Wyzwolenie KL Auschwitz*, 100-101.

29. Account of a former employee of the orphanage in Harbutowice, Helena

Bunsch-Konopka (APMO. Collection of Testimonies, vol. 30, pp. 23-24). In *Wyzwolenie KL Auschwitz*, 101-102.

30. "U.S.A. Typhus Commission, 1942-1946." Record Group331, Entry 65, Box 1, 28-29.

31. Records of the Office of the Surgeon General (Army) WWII Administrative Records 1940-1949 with Annual Reports, Administrative Division thru Medical Records Division DIV-ETO File 6668-9 Record Group112, Entry 54A, Box 317. "Report of Activities—Army Nurse Corps—Jan 1945-June 1945," National Archives, College Park, Maryland.

32. U.S.A. Typhus Commission, 1942-1945.Record Group 331, Entry 65, Box 1.

33. Records of the Office of the Surgeon General (Army) World War II, Administrative Reports, 1940-1949, 15th Evacuation Hospital ETO thru 129th Evacuation Hospital 1945, Section 319.1-2 120th Evacuation Hospital, ETO, Record Group 112, Box 408 NWCH HM 1999, Entry 54A. National Archives, College Park, Maryland.

34. Ibid. 120th Evacuation Hospital SM.

35. Information about typhus in Flossenberg from U.S.A. Typhus Commission 1942-1946, Record Group 331, Entry 65, Box 1, p. 25.

36. Ibid, 12, 26.

37. William V. McDermott, M.D. *A Surgeon in Combat: European Theatre—World War II: Omaha Beach to Ebensee*, (Dublin, New Hampshire: William L. Bauhan, 1997), 260-263.

38. Ibid., 262.

39. Typhus is a rickettsial disease borne by lice and other insects; typhoid fever, although the symptoms are similar, is spread by salmonella in contaminated food and water. (*Dorland's),* 701.

40. Records of the Surgeon General (Army) Office of the USA Typhus Commission, 942-46. General Records of the Paris Office1944-45, Record Group 112, Entry 343A, Box 70, National Archives, College Park, Maryland.

41. W.R.F. Collis, M.D. F.R.C.P., F.R.C.P.I., D.P.H., "Belsen Camp: A Preliminary Report," *British Medical Journal*, June 9, 1945, 814-816.

42. Ibid. 814.

43 A. Dosseter, M.D. Interview, Sound Archive 8902/2. Imperial War Museum, Lambeth Road, London.

44. U.S.A. Typhus Commission,1942-46, Record Group 112, Entry 343A, Box 70, p. 16.

45. Collis, 815.

46. Ibid.

47. Information in this section obtained from HD 383.6 ETO (Dachau) Source Materials—M.P. Rudolph, Colonel M.E. Office of the Surgeon General of the Army, WWII Administrative Records ETO 370.5-383.6, Record Group 112, Entry 31, Box 31, National Archives, College Park, Maryland.

48. Notes on Concentration Camp at Dachau, in ETO (Dachau) Source Materials.

49. Dr. David Clements, Interview, by Laurel Block and Harvey Rubin, April 14, 1980. Oral History T- 44, Fortunoff Library, Yale University.

50. U.S.A. Typhus Commission, 1942-1946, Record Group 331, Entry 65, Box 1.

51. Ibid.

52. Ibid.

53. Graham A. Cosmas and Albert E. Cowdry, *United States Army in World War II,Technical Services, The Medical Department: Medical Service in the European Theater of Operations,* (Washington, D.C.: Center of Military History United States Army, 1992), 578.

54. Zorach Warhaftig, *From War to Peace [No.1] Relief and Rehabilitation: Implications of the UNRRA Program for Jewish Needs,* (New York: Institute of Jewish Affairs of the American Jewish Congress and World Jewish Congress, 1944), 34.

55. *Obschevsto remeslenovo i zemledekcheskovo trouda* (The Society for Trades and Agricultural Labor).

Part IV

The Aftermath

Chapter 11

The Origin and Reception of Martin Niemöller's Quotation, "First they came for the communists ..."

Harold Marcuse

Since 1993, visitors to the US Holocaust Memorial Museum in Washington, D.C. have read the following inscription on a wall in the Hall of Witness, a memorial space on the ground floor:

> First they came for the Socialists, and I did not speak out—
>   Because I was not a Socialist.
> Then they came for the Trade Unionists, and I did not speak out—
>   Because I was not a Trade Unionist.
> Then they came for the Jews, and I did not speak out—
>   Because I was not a Jew.
> Then they came for me—and there was no one left to speak for me.

The quotation is attributed to "Martin Niemöller (1892-1984), Lutheran Minister and early Nazi supporter who was later imprisoned for opposing Hitler's regime."[1] The Museum's online Holocaust Encyclopedia contains an entry for "Martin Niemöller: 'First they came for the socialists...,'" which offers the following discussion of the quotation and the groups it lists:[2]

The quotation stems from Niemöller's lectures during the early postwar period. Different versions of the quotation exist. These can be attributed to the fact that Niemöller spoke extemporaneously and in a number of settings. Much controversy surrounds the content of the poem as it has been printed in varying forms, referring to diverse groups such as Catholics, Jehovah's Witnesses, Jews, Trade Unionists, or Communists depending upon the version. Nonetheless his point was that Germans—in particular, he believed, the leaders of the Protestant churches—had been complicit through their silence in the Nazi imprisonment, persecution, and murder of millions of people.

Indeed, there are numerous versions of this quotation in circulation today, some of them set in stone, with varying claims of legitimacy. For example, visitors to the New England Holocaust Memorial on Boston's Freedom Trail find this version, inscribed in 1995:[3]

> They came first for the Communists,
>   But I didn't speak up because I wasn't a Communist.
> Then they came for the Jews,
>   and I didn't speak up because I wasn't a Jew.
> Then they came for the trade unionists,
>   and I didn't speak up because I wasn't a trade unionist.
> Then they came for the Catholics,
>   and I didn't speak up because I was a Protestant.
> Then they came for me,
>   and by that time no one was left to speak up.

This version substitutes Communists for Socialists, moves Jews up before Trade Unionists, and adds Catholics as a persecuted group. Although various historical arguments can be made for the ordering of the groups, as we will see, the selection of groups generally relates to the person or organization employing the quotation. In this case it might be expected that predominantly Irish-Catholic Boston would use a version including Catholics, while in the Communist-phobic United States capital only a few years after the end of the Cold War, one might similarly expect that including Communists would have been awkward. We find a further common variation in Germany, from which Jews are excluded. For example, the Martin Niemöller Foundation's website gives an "official" version (my translation):[4]

> When the Nazis came for the Communists, I kept silent;
>   I was after all not a Communist.
> When they locked up the Social Democrats, I kept silent;
>   I was after all not a Social Democrat.
> When they came for the trade unionists, I kept silent,
>   I was after all not a trade unionist.
> When they came for me, there was no one left who could protest.

While such variations may be attributed to the respective context and speaker invoking Niemöller's words, they do raise the question, which groups Niemöller himself included. If he did exclude Jews, for example, would he have included Catholics? What about other groups persecuted by the Nazis, such as Roma, homosexuals, or the disabled? Since the 1990s scholars have debated these questions. In 1994 Ruth Zerner published an essay citing several witnesses who claimed Niemöller had never included Catholics.[5] In a 1997 article one of her witnesses, Franklin Littell, claimed that Niemöller himself did not include Catholics and would never have included gays, although he certainly included Jews, just not as the first group.[6] Recent internet searches indicate that the version excluding Communists at the US Holocaust Memorial Museum—which I will show is definitely historically incorrect, and indeed distorts both Niemöller's politics and original meaning—is becoming the most prevalent in English, and should be modified.[7]

So what did Niemöller himself say? It turns out that we cannot yet answer this question definitively. My research into the published interviews, sermons and speeches Niemöller delivered in the early postwar years 1945-1947 indicates that in January 1946 Niemöller began using a narrative version naming several groups—foremost among them Communists—but those texts do not converge into the rhythmically repeating "poetic" version, which he may have begun to employ during his speaking tour in the United States in early 1947. A short biographical overview shows why and with what meaning Niemöller began invoking this anecdote.[8]

Niemöller, a decorated naval officer in World War I, was a conservative German nationalist. He turned to theology in the early 1920s after the German navy had been disbanded under the terms of the Versailles treaty. He was the pastor of St. Ann's church in the wealthy Berlin district Dahlem from 1931 until his arrest in 1937. He welcomed Hitler's accession to power in 1933, objecting only to state encroachment on Church policy, in particular the exclusion of Christians with Jewish ancestry from serving as officers of the Church. In September 1933, in protest against the official German Protestant Church's willingness to accept Nazi interference in church affairs, he formed the Pastor's Emergency League, which became the Confessing Church in October 1934. Niemöller's continued outspokenness against some Nazi rules finally led to his arrest in July 1937 and trial in February 1938. Although his 7-month sentence was less than the 8 months he had served in Moabit prison, so that he should have been released, Hitler personally had him sent to the Sachsenhausen concentration camp for "preventative detention."

It is important to understand that, except for Nazi decrees regarding Church policy, Niemöller was an avid Hitler supporter. As he later readily admitted, he sent Hitler a personal telegram of congratulations after Germany's withdrawal from the League of Nations in October 1933. Witnesses say that Niemöller greeted his Dahlem congregation with the Hitler salute, and at his 1938 trial he boasted about his patriotic unwillingness to turn over his submarine to the British after the November 1918 armistice, about his leadership of a *Freikorps* battalion in putting down a left-wing insurgency in 1920, and that he had voted Nazi since 1924.[9] He also testified in his defense that he found Jews "disagreeable and alien," which was typical of an "officer in the Kaiser's navy" from a "Westphalian family of peasants and clerics." However, ancestry was changed by baptism: one had to accept the "embarrassing and serious offence" that "God had revealed Himself through the Jew Jesus of Nazareth."

A year and a half later when World War II began, Niemöller did something else that came back to haunt him after the war. In September 1939 Niemöller, then 47, wrote to Admiral Raeder offering his services to the navy, a request that was turned down two months later. Although this would also have offered a way out of Sachsenhausen, we may believe the explanation Niemöller offered in interviews in the summer and fall of 1945, namely that he saw this as a way of supporting his country while being in a position to work to dislodge the Nazi government.

Niemöller was transferred to Dachau in July 1941, where he remained until the end of the war. As the US Army closed in on Dachau he was evacuated to Austria, where he was liberated in early May 1945. In an interview soon thereafter he said some importune things that made Allied observers critical of his hitherto spotless reputation as an anti-Nazi hero. For example, he denied the principle of German national guilt and defended those who fought in Hitler's armies as having merely obeyed the call of patriotism, for which, as we will see, he was roundly criticized in the US press.[10]

That criticism, and his exposure to international public opinion, led Niemöller to recognize that denying responsibility would likely backfire and bring harsher policies down on Germany. In August he laid the groundwork for a meeting of international church leaders in Germany in October. At that meeting he was instrumental in the formulation of what is known as the Stuttgart Declaration of Guilt.[11] In fact, he insisted upon its most famous (and controversial) sentence: "We did fight for long years in the name of Jesus Christ against the mentality that found its awful expression in the National Socialist regime of violence, but we accuse ourselves for not standing to our beliefs more courageously, for not praying more faithfully, for not believing more joyously, and for not loving more ardently."

This profession of responsibility was limited to the Church as an institution, stopping short of taking on personal meaning, but it still elicited strong criticism from Germans reeling from the devastation of "total war." Shortly thereafter, in early November 1945, a key experience closely linked to the formulation of the insight in the quotation occurred when Niemöller visited the former Dachau concentration camp to show his wife where he had been imprisoned. He related the anecdote in several of his 1946 and 1947 speeches. A July 3, 1946 speech in Stuttgart, published under the title "The Path to Freedom," is a good example, also typical in that it is a transcript of his extemporaneous oral style (my translation):[12]

> When I returned from prison a year ago, I played along with this game [of passing along the packet of responsibility to someone else]. I came home, actually after all of the dangers of the previous weeks and the many disappointments, loaded with a lot of good conscience. I had in my pocket a certificate that I had been deprived of my liberty from July 1, 1937 to June 24, 1945 as a political prisoner and personal prisoner of the Führer. Who is going to demonstrate to me that the guilt that is now being claimed of my people, has anything to do with me? Already I was standing in line and passed the packet on. I did that for quite a while, not a pleasant game, but a necessary game. Because if one holds on to the packet, it won't burn only one's fingers! And then one day something happened to me. One day I drove by near Dachau in my car. My wife was with me and said, "Couldn't I see your cell, where

you were imprisoned for the past four years?" I said, "I'll see what can be done." And drove there and was allowed to enter the cell block and show my wife the cell. Then something happened. When we came out the American officer accompanying us led us along a wall. I had often walked along it. There was a large gate in it. I had never seen it open. This time it was open. I knew what was behind it, but entered anyway. I stood with my wife in front of the crematorium in Dachau, and on a tree in front of this building there was a white-painted board with black lettering. [...] There one could read: "Here in the years 1933-1945 238,756 people[13] were cremated." While I read it, not aloud, I noticed that my wife fainted and sank trembling into my arms. I had to support her and noticed how at that moment a cold shudder ran down my spine. I think my wife fainted when she read the quarter-million number. That hadn't moved me. Because it didn't tell me anything new. What ran through me hot and cold at that moment was something else. That was the other two numbers: "1933-1945." I groped for my alibi and knew that the two numbers were the wanted poster of the living God for Pastor Niemöller. My alibi reached from July 1, 1937 to mid-1945. There stood: "1933-1945." Adam, where are you? Mensch, where were you? Yes, I know, from mid-1937 until the end you have an alibi. Here you're being asked: "Where were you from 1933 until July 1, 1937?" And I couldn't avoid this question any longer. In 1933 I was a free man. 1933—at that moment in the crematorium yard it occurred to me—yes 1933, that's right: Hermann Göring boasted publicly that he had gotten rid of the Communist danger. Since all Communists who were not under lock and key because of their crimes were now sitting behind the barbed wire of the newly established concentration camps. Adam, where are you? Hey, Martin Niemöller, where were you then? asked God with those two numbers. And then it occurred to me: this whole thing had made no impression on me; somewhere in a corner of my heart I may have thought, at least later I did think: this is a cheap way to actually be rid of the danger of godlessness. But that these people, with no law, no criminal charges, no investigation, no sentence, no enforceable sentence, simply had their profession, their family, their lives taken from them, were deprived of their freedom, that they were God's question put to me, to which I in God's eyes should have

> answered, that did not occur to me. Back then I was a free man. Back then I had already given myself over to my true responsibility. And now the wanted poster was there, and I couldn't avoid this wanted poster any longer. And on that day, when we got home, I read the chapter Matthew 25 with new meaning: "I was hungry and you gave me nothing to eat; I was thirsty and you gave me nothing to drink; I was sick and in prison and you did not come to me." As a Christian I could have known and should have known in 1933 that in each of these human brothers—may they be called Communists or whatever—God in Jesus Christ was asking me whether I wouldn't want to serve him.

In this case Niemöller did not follow the Dachau anecdote with a list of groups, but mentioned only Communists. He then went into detail about the meaning of the Stuttgart Declaration, about which, he said, there was so much misinformed talk in the press. He said that it was being absurdly distorted, for instance that the Protestant Church was admitting that Germany had sole responsibility [*Alleinschuld*] for the war.[14] He then quoted from memory what he called the key sentence of the Declaration, with "we" meaning the postwar German Protestant Church: "We know that we are one with our German Volk not only in a great community of suffering, but also in the solidary of responsibility [*Schuld*]!" He argued that no one could deny that, invoking "the six million murdered Jews" to explain why Protestant Christians could not pass on the "packet of guilt." Again invoking Matthew 25, Niemöller limited the scope of the Stuttgart Declaration, saying that it meant that "the Protestant Church, at least in its leadership, again proclaims itself responsible: We are not avoiding our guilt; we recognize the responsibility that we neglected, and we recognize thereby at the same time the responsibility that we again desire to become just."

Let us go back to the earliest traceable texts from January 1946 to see how Niemöller invoked the Dachau anecdote, and its relationship to what was to become the poetic quotation. On January 6, 1946 he told an audience of representatives of the Confessing Church in Frankfurt, which one can assume was much more open to their own leader's message than other audiences may have been (my translation, emphasis added):[15]

> When Pastor Niemöller was put in a concentration camp we wrote the year 1937; when the concentration camp was opened we wrote the year 1933, and the people who were put in the camps then were **Communists**. Who bothered with them? We knew it, it was printed in the newspapers. Who raised their voice, maybe the Confessing Church? We thought: Communists, those opponents of religion, those enemies of Christians—"should I be my brother's keeper?" Then they did away with the **sick**, the **so-called incurables** [*Kranke, sogenannte Unheilbare*].—I remember a conversation I had with a person who claimed to be a Christian. He said: Perhaps it's right, these incurably sick people just cost the state money, they are just a burden to themselves and to others. Isn't it best all-around if they are taken out of the middle [of society]? —Only then did it start affecting the Church as such [*an die Kirche als solche herangekommen*].[16] Then we started making noise, until our public voices again fell silent. Can we say, we aren't guilty/responsible? The persecution of the **Jews**, the way we treated the occupied countries, or the things in **Greece, in Poland, in Czechoslovakia or in Holland**, which were even written in the newspapers....
>
> We preferred to **keep silent**. We are certainly not without guilt, and I ask myself over and over again what would have happened if we had in 1933 or 1934—it must have been a possibility—14,000 Protestant pastors and all Protestant congregations in Germany, if we had defended the truth with our lives. If we had **said** back then, it is not right when Hermann Göring simply puts 100,000 Communists in concentration camps, to let them die. I can imagine that then perhaps 30,000 to 40,000 Protestant Christians would have been made a head shorter, but can also imagine that we would have saved the lives of 30-40 million people, which is what it costs us now.

In this earliest known public delivery of the anecdote Niemöller names several groups: Communists, "so-called incurables," Jews, and those in several of the countries occupied by Germany. This particular speech also happens to be the most widely published of all of Niemöller's sermons from 1946. After its German publication, it was published in French and Danish as well, and in English in February 1947, under the title *Of Guilt and Hope*, in New York shortly after Niemöller's speaking engagements there.[17]

On January 17, 1946 Niemöller gave a similar speech to students in Göttingen, in which he began the Dachau anecdote, then after a longer argumentative digression on the advisability of Germans under occupation admitting guilt, continued in the same vein, with Göring and the Communists, then "lives unworthy of life" [*lebensunwertes Leben*], and Jews. This time he was much more personal, using the pronoun "I" instead of "we:"[18]

> Hermann Goring wrote in the newspapers that on his command all active Communists were sent to the KZ in 1933. I knew that, I also knew about the killing of lives unworthy of life, I saw how the Jews were being persecuted on a grand scale [*im grossen Stil*] for the first time—and I kept silent [*habe geschwiegen*]. I only began to speak out [*reden*] when it was about the Church. I know I'm guilty.

This version, by the way, refutes a recent explanation or justification I have heard from defenders of versions that do not include Jews, namely because Niemöller was already imprisoned by the time the Nazi persecution of Jews became violent. Here Niemöller clearly acknowledges that the persecution was sufficient in 1933 that he should have spoken out. In the following months student audiences heckled him in Erlangen, Marburg, and Siegen, and his argumentation became more targeted and concise.[19] In a May 4, 1946 speech at Marburg University he expressed the argument in the pithiest form I have found before the poetic form emerged (emphasis added):[20]

> Here is the basis of our Christian recognition of guilt in consideration of what happened. We did not recognize the Lord Christ when he came into our lives in the form of a suffering brother. I didn't recognize him when he was put in the camp as a **Communist**, nor did I recognize him when he was murdered as an **incurably ill person**, nor did I recognize him when he was gassed and burned as the poor **victims of his own people** [an allusion to the fact that Christ was Jewish]. Here I incurred guilt in my very personal responsibility and I cannot excuse myself, neither before God, nor before humanity.

In this case Niemöller set the anecdote in the context of Matthew 25:31f, in which Christ reproaches the self-righteous for not having recognized him in the lowly and needy of society. The groups are Communists, incurably ill, and Jews (with no mention of the Church), and the action is to recognize, parallel to the biblical passage.

Of the other texts from this period, there is one more that I would like to quote; the publication is titled *The Renewal of Our Church*, and the date and venue are not given. It is noteworthy because Niemöller names Jehovah's Witnesses among the persecuted as well:[21]

> God didn't ask me where I was from 1937 to 1945, he asked me where I was from 1933 to 1937. From 1933 to 1937 I didn't have an answer. Should I perhaps have said: I was a brave pastor of the Confessing Church in those years, I risked speaking out [*ein Wort riskiert*] and thus risked freedom and my life? But God didn't ask me about all that. God asked: Where were you from 1933 to 1937, when human beings were being burned here? Those weren't my Christian brothers, who were burned there, those were **Communists, Jehovah's Witnesses, etc.** *[ernste Bibelforscher usw.]*. That's why I didn't care *[mich nicht gekümmert]*.

To summarize: from January into the fall of 1946 Niemöller presented various narrative versions of what was to become his famous quotation. They were part of his argument trying to convince Germans why they should repent and accept personal responsibility, in particular why the Protestant Church's Stuttgart Declaration of Guilt was only a prerequisite, a necessary first step in the restoration of German autonomy after its unconditional surrender. In the context of hostile receptions by some audiences Niemöller honed and personalized his argument, using the Dachau anecdote to show why even the Church's Stuttgart Declaration did not go far enough.

However, the meaning of the quotation as we know it does not fit into that context. The litany of groups used in Germany in 1946 was a personal profession of Niemöller's own guilt, used to argue why members of his audiences should not reject their own responsibility. In this context culminating with his own arrest in 1937 ("when they came for me") would have been irrelevant and even weakened his argument. In contrast, the message of the poetic version of the quotation is an exhortation not to stand by when others are being persecuted, thus not to incur guilt in the first place, as opposed to accepting responsibility afterwards. For this reason, although I have not been able to find texts to document it, I believe Niemöller may have begun using the anecdote to convey this new, additional meaning during his speaking tour in the United States from December 1946 to April 1947.

At the end of November 1946 Niemöller was allowed to accept an invitation from the US Federal Council of Churches to go to the United States, where his speaking tour would begin in Seattle on December 4.[22] The agenda of his extensive tour included pleading with foreign Christians to send food aid to Germany. His opening speech in Seattle focused on the Church's *mea culpa* in the Stuttgart Declaration, mentioning the "planned murder of millions of Jews," but no other persecuted groups. Niemöller cleverly wove his plea for aid into his conclusion:[23]

> Now I'm at the end. I thought it better not to offer you a wealth of details, but just to outline the important strands of development of the present-day life of our Church....
>
> I intentionally did not speak about the material misery in Europe. We know that you know about that. You know yourselves that many of us would have died of starvation months ago, if not for your hands-on help and regular support. Believe me, we thank you for that from our hearts. But in spite of all human efforts hunger, cold and homelessness are continually increasing. No one can see the end....

However, his extended tour met with strong criticism from influential figures, which did not abate. Eleanor Roosevelt, after noting that Niemöller had said he did not disagree with Nazi politics except with regard to the Church, and that he had offered his services for submarine work in the Navy, wrote in her syndicated newspaper column on December 4: "I am sure he is a good man according to his lights but his lights are not those of the people of the United States who did not like the Hitler political doctrines."

The Federal Council of Churches, a chaplain who had interviewed Niemöller in Italy in May 1945, and the influential Chicago serial *Christian Century* all published articles in Niemöller's defense, which

Eleanor Roosevelt rejected in a later column. Niemöller spoke in 52 cities, with thousands sometimes coming to hear him speak, but press coverage of what he said was scant. In none of the reports did I find any mention of anything resembling the famous quotation. However, a German bi-weekly newspaper obtained and printed a translation of the speech he gave in New York on January 25, 1947.[24] I do not have the full transcript of the speech, but a substantial excerpt published a few months later contains the anecdote about Dachau, with the key sentences reading (retranslated):

> I couldn't say: I was a brave pastor of the Confessing Church and opened my mouth wide, that wasn't what was going on from 1933 to 1937, those weren't the churchmen who were incinerated there, those were Communists and other people who were bothersome to those in power back then.

After a few remarks paraphrasing Matthew 23, Niemöller made his key argument—no longer that he now saw that he (and all Germans) had to repent and recognize his responsibility, as he had said so often in Germany—but that he realized that only if Christian teaching were true could he receive reconciliation and be rescued from damnation:

> Yes, you see, dear friends, from that moment on the question of guilt was for me no longer a theoretical one, to whom guilt belongs; from that moment I knew either it is true, what was preached to me since my childhood, that there is a savior for sinners, or I am already in hell, without having died.

With a clever rhetorical pivot Niemöller said the gospel must of course be true, and appealed to his US-American listeners:

> Dear friends and brothers and sisters, what then... counts is a Lord Jesus of Nazareth... who is so close that he holds one firmly when the earth trembles and one is about to sink into hell, then what is important is that he is so close as imaginable, namely so close that he grasps one and holds on.

I read this as Niemöller telling his American listeners that as Christians they should reach out and help their German brethren in spite of their past sins. Without other texts from this speaking tour we cannot document conclusively that Niemöller wrote or said the poetic version of the quotation during that trip in the United States.[25] I reiterate, however, that he did shift the meaning of the longer anecdote to fit the new context and agenda: instead of calling on his listeners to recognize their own responsibility for atrocities, he was calling on them to reach out to Germans in spite of their responsibility for those horrific crimes.

When Niemöller returned to Germany in May—after having had a last appeal for Americans to send CARE packages into the Congressional Record—he faced strong criticism in the media for not having shown solidarity by defending his countryfolk.[26] Given the topics about which he spoke after that, namely against denazification and for clemency for convicted German war criminals, it is unlikely that he had occasion to preach his message of recognizing one's own guilt again for some time.

In fact, the next mentions of Niemöller's statement that I could find are invocations by others in English that were published in 1955, by which time the familiar "poetic" version had already emerged. These publications indicate that a more narrative version was still familiar in the early 1950s, but also that the version with the poetic refrain was already in circulation. As we have seen, Niemöller himself had included different groups at different times, perhaps intuiting the prejudices of his audiences. In Germany he would have wanted to strengthen his argument by using groups that he—and his listeners—would understandably not have supported. In the US, in contrast, his call for support might have been strengthened by naming groups with whom his listeners might sympathize. In any case, these earliest documented invocations of the quotation by others contain a selection of groups related to the identity of the speaker, not the audience.

Milton Sanford Mayer (1908-1986) was a Chicago-based Jewish journalist who spent time at the Frankfurt Institute for Social Research in 1950-51, where he conducted what he called a "small experiment": interviewing ten "average" Germans about their feelings towards Nazism.[27] He summarized his findings in a 1953 article series in *Harper's Magazine*, and published them in book form in 1955 under the title *They Thought They Were Free*. Not in the article series but in the book, he included an invocation of Niemöller by the interlocutor he calls "the teacher," the only non-antisemite of the ten:[28]

> Pastor Niemöller spoke for thousands and thousands of men like me when he spoke (too modestly of himself) and said that, when the Nazis attacked the Communists, he was a little uneasy, but, after all, he was not a Communist, and so he did nothing; and then they attacked the Socialists, and he was a little uneasier, but, still, he was not a Socialist, and he did nothing; and then the schools, the press, the Jews, and so on, and he was always uneasier, but still he did nothing. And then they attacked the Church, and he was a Churchman, and he did something—but then it was too late.

We note the order: Communists, Socialists, schools and press, Jews; and the key verbs: the Nazis attack, he was uneasy, but did nothing. Although Mayer did not publish this until 1955, we can use the date of his interviews, 1950-51, as a date before which Niemöller used the poetic form, since the paraphrase is pithy enough that it implies a paraphrase based on a repeating structure. That passage was quoted in July 1955 in an article in the *Annals of the American Association of Political and Social Science*, which was in turn quoted in a 1959 book.[29]

The other published invocation I found was printed that same year, in a March 1955 speech by African-American Communist activist Claude Lightfoot (1910-1991). Lightfoot, who had been convicted under the Smith Act for being a member of the Communist party, told his Los Angeles audience:[30]

> It was under the smokescreen of "anti-Communism" that Hitler led the German people and the rest of the world to the brink of disaster. What proof do we still need in America before we learn the lesson of Pastor Niemoller?—"When Communists were jailed, it was all right—we weren't Communists," said Niemoller. "When Jews were hounded, we didn't care. When the union leaders were arrested, we preferred to keep quiet .... When I was jailed—it was too late."

Here the groups are Communists, Jews, and union leaders, and the actions are more varied, namely jailed/hounded/arrested, and all right/didn't care/keep quiet. This not only indicates that Lightfoot had heard or read this from a different source than the teacher interviewed by Mayer, but also that he had a model with very precise actions. Interestingly, in a related pamphlet published about Lightfoot that same year, the poetic version is rendered in bold and block form as a direct quotation of Niemöller:[31]

> For those who still feel that what happens to the Communists won't affect them, let them think over the words of Pastor Martin Niemöller, world famous German Protestant and leader of the World Council of Churches:
>
> "When the Communists were jailed, it was all right, we weren't Communists.
>
> "When the Jews were hounded, we didn't care.
>
> "When the union leaders were arrested—we preferred to keep quiet; we were not union members.
>
> "When I was jailed—it was too late to do anything."

This pamphlet about Lightfoot, with its quotation marks and exact list of key actions (jailed, hounded, arrested; all right, didn't care, keep quiet) indicates that it was based on a yet-undiscovered published source, or that it was a rendition of Lightfoot's words as a direct quotation.

The next print appearance of the quotation I found was from 1958, in the script for a school play based on *The Diary of Anne Frank*. Its version, added at the end of the second edition as one of seven "Further Activities," is again in the full poetic form:[32]

> First they came for the Jews
> and I did not speak out —
> because I was not a Jew
> Then they came for the communists
> and I did not speak out —
> because I was not a communist
> Then they came for the trade unionists
> and I did not speak out
> because I was not a trade unionist
> Then they came for me
> and there was no one left to speak for me
> (Pastor Niemoeller, Victim of the Nazis in Germany)

Now the groups are: Jews, communists, trade unionists, me; and the actions are the repeated "come for" and "not speak out" (as opposed to the varying "was uneasy," "didn't care," or "kept silent"). The verbs in this version are the blueprint for most later versions, and the "poetic" form again indicates that there was a concise and probably published version that the authors used as a guide. Moving Communists from first to second position can be seen as the editors' concession to anticommunist sentiment in the US in the 1950s. This order and the verb choice indicate that neither the narrative version from Germany published by Mayer, nor the "poetic" one used by Lightfoot, were the source for this invocation, but an additional, yet undiscovered, text.

The next time I found that Niemöller told the Dachau anecdote, and presumably used the narrative form of the quotation as well, was in 1962, in a script for an interview with the BBC.[33] In that interview Niemöller mentioned only Communists. Two years later, in a 1964 commemorative speech honoring the July 20, 1944 conspiracy against Hitler, Niemöller did not invoke the Dachau anecdote, nor did he use the narrative version of the quotation, but he did list three groups persecuted under Nazism. "Communists, Jews, and Jehovah's Witnesses," he said, "were all people whose suffering and dying rose up again [*wieder aufstand*] and came alive in the conscience of the men of July 20."[34] It is unlikely that this speech was noted in the Anglophone world, but it does confirm that both Communists and Jews were among the groups Niemöller considered the primary victims of Nazism. This belies both the US Holocaust Memorial Museum's and the Niemöller Foundation's justifications for their omissions.

The next documented invocation of the quotation, in 1965, already contains the Catholics as a persecuted group. In an article in the journal *Social Education* about teaching values in a current events curriculum, the authors name "an American Civil Liberties Union newsletter" as the source of the following version:[35]

> In Germany they first came for the Communists, and I didn't speak up because I wasn't a Communist. Then they came for the Jews, and I didn't speak up because I wasn't a Jew. Then they came for the trade unionists, and I didn't speak up because I wasn't a trade unionist. Then they came for the Catholics, and I didn't speak up because I was a Protestant. Then they came for me—and by that time no one was left to speak up.
>
> —Pastor Martin Niemöller

This version including Catholics became the most widely invoked one from the 1970s through about 1990. One can find scattered printings of it in books published in the late 1960s and early 1970s, but once it was printed by Abigail van Buren in her "Dear Abby" column in 1977 it reached the widest readership, and was regularly requested by readers and reprinted every few years until 1993.[36]

I cannot say definitively whether or not Niemöller himself might have included Catholics as one of the groups in the poetic version. If, as I presume, he first coined it during his US speaking tour under the auspices of the US Federal Council of Churches, an ecumenical organization, he might well have added Catholics in some of his many talks. We also know that he was imprisoned with prominent Catholic resisters in Dachau whom he respected and with whom he celebrated mass. In a letter written two days after his November 1945 return visit to Dachau, responding to a friend who had apparently written that the (Protestant) Church had indeed protested against Nazism, Niemöller asked rhetorically, "Why were there in Dachau for example only 45 Protestant pastors but 450 Catholic German priests?"[37] On the other hand Ruth Zerner cites people close to Niemöller who claim that the pastor himself would not have and did not include Catholics. Littell writes that "when we asked him years ago," Niemöller responded, "I never said it. They can take care of themselves."

The question whether Niemöller included Jews as one of the persecuted groups is made more confusing by statements Niemöller himself made in the 1970s. The justification for this exclusion, found as far as I know solely in Germany, is given on the website of the Martin-Niemöller Foundation, which cites—and as I will argue misinterprets and takes out of context—Niemöller's response in a 1976 interview.[38] That year Niemöller was interviewed by Dietmar Schmidt, who had already published a biography of him in 1959. The interview was published a decade later in a 1986 book made to publicize a documentary film about Niemöller's life. Schmidt asked Niemöller about the origin of the poetic version of the quotation. Here is my translation of that dialog (emphasis added):[39]

> [Q:] When did this poem originate with the saying: When they came for the Communists we kept silent ...?

[A:] That wasn't a poem, no. Once I gave a sermon in Oeffler's congregation, when the general bishop of the Lutheran-Slovakian church was there in the church in Siegelbach near Kaiserslautern. Afterwards we had a discussion with the congregation in a meeting room right next to the church. There the people asked their questions and spoke their minds. And then they asked **me** whether **we** weren't woken up after Kristallnacht 1938. And I say, for heaven's sake, don't ask me about after '38, in '37 **I** came into imprisonment and was always in a solitary cell and otherwise, you know, when they began **locking up** the **Communists** and maybe **we** heard about that right away, I don't know anymore, but **we** didn't protest, since **we** lived for the Church and in the Church, and the Communists were no friends of the Church, but on the contrary its declared enemies and that's why **we** kept silent then. And then came the **trade unions**, and the trade unions weren't any friends of the Church, and we had little or nothing to do with them anymore and said well let them contend with their own problems. There was no transcript or copy of what I said and it can certainly be that I expressed it differently. But the idea was certainly: The **Communists**, we just calmly let that happen; and the **trade unions**, we also just let that happen; and the **Social Democrats** we let happen too. That wasn't our business. **The Church** didn't yet have anything to do with politics back then, and one shouldn't have anything to do with them. **We in the Confessing Church** basically didn't want to resist politically, we rather wanted to confirm for the Church that that isn't right and cannot be legal in the Church, that's why we, in '33, when we established the Pastor's Emergency League, put the 4th point in it: if a united stand is made against the pastors and they're simply forced out as pastors because they are **of Jewish descent** or something like that, then we as a Church could only say: No. And that became the fourth point in the commitment and that was probably the first anti-antisemitic statement by the Protestant Church. That is all that I can say to this history of the: 'When they locked up the **Communists**, **no one** said anything, **we** weren't Communists and were ok with having those opponents off our backs.' But **we** didn't see ourselves obligated to say anything for people outside the Church, that wasn't fashionable then, and **we** hadn't come far enough yet that **we** understood that **we** were responsible for our [entire German] people.

There are two important things to note here. First, in paraphrasing the dialog from a couple of years earlier, Niemöller spoke of the Church, using "we" and "no one" speaking out, as opposed to the "I" of the 1940s texts and widely known poetic versions of the quotation. This indicates that Niemöller either forgot his original invocations of the anecdote and quotation, or that he was adapting it to the 1970s context and responding to a young audience's question about why the Church collectively, but not he personally, had not protested sooner. In his paraphrase of the incident he says "they asked *me* whether *we* weren't woken up," transitioning seamlessly from the self to the collective and remaining there.

Second, Niemöller gives a historically correct progression in this list of persecuted groups, naming the trade unions (outlawed May 1, 1933) before the Social Democrats (prohibited June 22, 1933), and twice putting trade unions right after Communists (arrests Feb. 28, 1933). Additionally, he does put people "of Jewish descent" after the Social Democrats (the Emergency League was formed in September 1933), implicitly including their persecution long before Kristallnacht in 1938.

The book also contains a rendition of the poetic version, inserted by the authors as an image on the next page, using a version common in Germany from that time until today, with only Communists, Social Democrats and Trade Unionists—in that order, and the key verbs "came for" (but lock up for the Social Democrats) and "kept silent," ending with "could protest." On that same page the book authors reprint a longer quotation from Niemöller's 1946 speech "On the Current Situation of Evangelical Christendom," in which he invoked Matthew 25 to make the point that the Protestant pastors hadn't realized that in the Jewish persecution of 1938 and thereafter, that Christ himself was already being persecuted and beaten and killed in the "lowest of our human brothers." Thus both Niemöller and the book authors understood the quotation in the context of the persecution of Jews, and based on this evidence alone one would not be justified in leaving them out of an "official" version of the quotation, discarding decades of invocations.[40] The book authors, in their choice of a version to print, ignored the order of groups Niemöller had used in the interview, so we may conclude that they were merely using recent invocations with which they were familiar, not his words as spoken in the interview. This conclusion is made more likely because in the book's version Social Democrats are (ahistorically) the only group that was "locked up," while the interview used that action only in relation to Communists.

This raises the question of when Jews were dropped from the German version. As with Catholics in the English version, I have not yet been able to answer this unequivocally. To confuse matters, in an article published in 1979 Niemöller himself, quoting his own quotation, omits them. In a text for a political monthly initiating a series of prominent commentators reflecting on "30 Years of West Germany, "Niemöller reproduces almost verbatim the Dachau anecdote as it was published in *The Path to Freedom* in 1946 (the version cited and reproduced above, see note 12). He begins the next paragraph by—incorrectly—placing the Dachau anecdote prior to the German Protestant Church's collective profession of guilt at Stuttgart:[41]

> It was experiences such as this that stand behind the Stuttgart "Declaration of Guilt." It was the remembering of an experience that couldn't be relegated to forgetting any more [*nicht mehr vergessen zu machend*]: the common ground of Christians and atheists, of Communists and Social Democrats in Hitler's concentration camps, in their common affliction, in their common opposition against Nazi barbarism.

Within this new context of shared repression and solidarity forged in the camps Niemöller then quotes himself:

> I once formulated this experience as follows (and I have often been quoted with it): When the Nazis came for the Communists, I kept silent; after all [*ja*] I wasn't a Communist. —When they locked up the Social Democrats, I kept silent; after all, I wasn't a Social Democrat. —When they came for the trade unionists, I didn't protest; after all I wasn't a trade unionist. —When they came for me, there wasn't anyone left who protested...

From this re-invocation Niemöller concludes—in 1979—that such solidarity is still important in the present day. This is a wholly new meaning compared to 1946, when he was trying to convince his countryfolk to recognize their own responsibility for the murder of millions of Jews, as well as compared to 1974, when he was trying to explain how a lack of solidarity enabled the pogroms against Jewish Germans in 1938. Interestingly, in this case Niemöller himself quotes the commonly circulating version with "came for," but "lock up" for the Social Democrats, who again ahistorically precede the trade unionists. He also switches from "kept silent" to " not protest," which is also common in other German texts from the 1970s, adding his own ellipses, which may implicitly allow for the inclusion of other groups, such as Jews.[42]

I think the 1976 interview and 1979 article indicate that by this time Niemöller no longer remembered or cared about the original 1940s contexts in which he developed the quotation, but rather began to employ it with new meanings, similar to how it was being invoked by others for their own purposes. In light of the evidence from 1945-47 presented above, in the "original" context of its emergence, Niemöller's famous quotation was first invoked to move beyond the institutional declaration of guilt in the Stuttgart Declaration, to a personal profession of responsibility in his 1946 German speeches, and then back to an admission of collective German failure (now in the first person) on his US speaking tour in 1947. In all contexts, except the final one from 1979, Jews were always part of the context of the invocations. Only in the "solidarity" context of that last self-invocation did Niemöller explicitly omit Jews, and it thus does not provide justification for omitting from an "official" version of the quotation this best-known and universally recognized group of persecuted people in Nazi Germany.

In conclusion, what can we say about the "original" groups and their order? I would argue that we can ignore the 1970s statements by Niemöller, as they are corrupted by loose paraphrasing, poor memory, and new contexts. Based on the documents from 1946-47 and 1962-64, Niemöller *always* mentioned Communists, and with one exception Jews as well, although never as the first group. From the 1951/1955 Mayer and 1955 Lightfoot versions we can infer with some confidence that in the yet undocumented earliest poetic version(s), whether spoken by Niemöller himself or not, Communists came first, then Socialists/Social Democrats/trade unionists or Jews, perhaps depending on which language and which venue. As for the inclusion of Catholics, until new documentary sources are found, we cannot definitively state whether, when, or by whom they came to be included in the quotation. Is it proper to include other groups? In some narrative versions Niemöller did name others, in particular incurably ill and Jehovah's Witnesses, but we have no evidence that he named them in any of his poetic versions. As a final point: Niemöller's original argument was premised on naming groups he and his audience would instinctively not care about. When his poem is invoked today it is usually to add one's own group to the list of persecuted. That was not a meaning that Niemöller ever wished to convey. The omission of Communists in Washington, and of Jews in Germany, distorts that meaning and should be corrected.

Notes

1. The museum's FAQ offers the following more detailed information: "Source: Attributed to Pastor Martin Niemöller, as stated in Franklin H. Littell's foreword to *Exile in the Fatherland: Martin Niemöller's Letters from Moabit Prison*, edited by Hubert G. Locke (Grand Rapids, Michigan: William B. Eerdman's Publishing Company, 1986), p. viii."

2. United States Holocaust Memorial Museum. Martin Niemöller: "First they came for the socialists..." Holocaust Encyclopedia. http://www.ushmm.org/wlc/en/article.php?ModuleId=10007392. Accessed on June 15, 2014.

3. The accompanying explanation reads: "Martin Niemoeller / Lutheran Pastor. This statement, attributed to Pastor Niemoeller, has become a legendary expression of the lesson of the Holocaust. Ironically Niemoeller had delivered anti-Semitic sermons early in the Nazi regime. He later opposed Hitler and was sent to a concentration camp." A photo of the inscription is available in the Wikimedia commons: http://commons.wikimedia.org/wiki/Category:New_England_Holocaust_Memorial

4. See Martin-Niemöller-Stiftung, "Als die Nazis die Kommunisten holten..." Sept. 22, 2005 http://www.martin-niemoeller-stiftung.de/search/a31.

The original German reads:

Als die Nazis die Kommunisten holten, habe ich geschwiegen; ich war ja kein Kommunist.

Als sie die Sozialdemokraten einsperrten, habe ich geschwiegen; ich war ja kein Sozialdemokrat.

Als sie die Gewerkschafter holten, habe ich geschwiegen, ich war ja kein Gewerkschafter.

Als sie mich holten, gab es keinen mehr, der protestieren konnte.

The selection of groups is explained on the page: "Was sagte Niemöller wirklich?" Sept. 16, 2007, http://www.martin-niemoeller-stiftung.de/search/a46. This version was again used in an October 2011 article by Martin Stöhr on the Foundation's website; see: http://www.martin-niemoeller-stiftung.de/4/zumnachlesen/a100.

5. Ruth Zerner, "Martin Niemoeller, Activist as Bystander: The Oft-Quoted Reflection," in: Marvin Perry and Frederick Schweitzer (eds.), Jewish-Christian Encounters over the Centuries: Symbiosis, Prejudice, Holocaust, Dialogue (New York: Peter Lang, 1994), 327-340. Zerner cites conversations with Franklin Littell, who had been the Protestant adviser on denazification to the US High Commissioner in occupied Germany and had heard Niemöller speak in the US in 1946-47, Niemöller's daughter Brigitte Johannesson (born 1920), and his second wife Sibylle Niemöller-von Sell (married 1971).

6. Franklin Littell, "First they came for the Communists..." in: *Christian Ethics Today*, vol. 3, no. 1 (February 1997). A version of this article, updated in 2001, is available at the Internet Archive. As an aside on how different authors vary the groups, note that the title words in the URL indicate Jews as the "first" group, not Communists, in contrast to the article title: http://web.archive.org/web/*/http://christianethictoday.com/Issue/009/First%20They%20Came%20for%20the%20Jews%20By%20Franklin%20H%20Littell_009_29_.htm. Note further that Littell's 1986 publication cited by the USHMM (see note 1 above) does not name the Communists at all.

7. The frequent use of this version is attributable to the prestige of the US Holocaust Memorial Museum and the google PageRank of its website. An example of the recent use of the USHMM version (Socialists, Trade Unionists, Jews, me) is: Laura Glenn, "The Reality of Modern anti-Semitism," *The Intelligencer*, June 6, 2014. http://www.theintell.com/life-style/reality/the-reality-of-modern-anti-semitism/article_5cef2290-c461-5241-a8d5-8021db9d22c0.html. The Holocaust Memorial Park in Brooklyn, New York's Sheepshead Bay is another example; an image is available at: http://www.flickr.com/photos/wallyg/1318026494/.

8. The best short overview of Niemöller's entire biography I have found is: Matthias Schreiber, *Martin Niemöller* (Reinbek: Rowohlt, 1997). Unless otherwise noted, the information below is taken from that work. In English, the USHMM's Encyclopedia of the Holocaust entry on Niemöller is a reliable source: http://www.ushmm.org/wlc/en/article.php?ModuleId=10007391. Hubert Locke's historical introduction to his 1986 edition of Niemöller's letters from Moabit prison (cited in note 1, pp. 1-10) offers a more detailed summary of key events from 1933 to 1938 in English.

9. See the document published in: Hans Buchheim, "Ein NS-Funktionär zum Niemöller-Prozess," in: *Vierteljahrshefte für Zeitgeschichte*, 4:3(July 1956), pp. 307-315, p. 312. The following remark about Jews is found on p. 313.

10. Clarissa Start, *God's Man: The Story of Pastor Niemoeller.* (New York: I.

Washburn, 1959; reprint 1979), chap. 18, "The Unfortunate Press Conference," pp. 145-151, recounts the May 1945 press conference at which Niemöller made his first public statements since he was imprisoned after his 1938 trial.

11. The text of that declaration is available at: http://www.ekd.de/glauben/bekenntnisse/stuttgarter_schulderklaerung.html.

12. Martin Niemöller, *Der Weg ins Freie* (Stuttgart: F. Mittelbach, 1946), p. 17-20.

13. I would like to note that this number from 1945 has long since proven to be incorrect. About 200,000 inmates were registered in Dachau; ca. 42,000 of them died during their imprisonment. The number cremated in the camp is probably around 15,000-20,000. See Harold Marcuse, "Dachau," in: John Merriman & Jay Winter (eds.), *Encyclopedia of the Age of War and Reconstruction*, vol. 2 (New York: Scribners, 2006), 763-766.

14. The following passages are found on Niemöller, *Der Weg*, pp. 22-23.

15. Martin Niemöller, *Über die deutsche Schuld, Not und Hoffnung* (Zollikon-Zürich: Evangelischer Verlag, 1946), p. 5ff. This is my translation, which is closer to the German original than the 1947 published English translation, which also contains additional biblical references and thus may have been slightly reworked by Niemöller himself. See Martin Niemöller, *Of Guilt and Hope*, trans. Renee Spodheim (New York: Philosophical Library, 1947), p. 32.

16. The published English translation of this sentence, which may have been modified by Niemöller himself, reads: "And only after that did the attack on the Church itself begin. Then we did have our say, and did so until officially silenced too." It renders the German *herankommen an*, literally "come to," as "attack." It also makes the German "*in der Öffentlichkeit wieder verstummt*" more actively as "officially silenced" than the passive literal translation "fall silent."

17. See *De la culpabilité allemande* (Neuchatel: Delachaux & Niestlé, 1946), and *Tysklands Skyld, Tysklands Nød og Tysklands Haab* (Copenhagen: De Unges Forlag 1946). The English publication was announced in "Books Published Today," *New York Times*, Feb. 28, 1947, p. 21. According to a short announcement in the *New York Times* on Aug. 5, 1947, this translation was withdrawn from circulation by the Philosophical Society after it became known that Niemöller supported the Nazis as early as 1924.

18. Pfarrer Niemöller D.D. an die Göttinger Studenten. Rede, gehalten auf Einladung der evangelischen Studentengemeinde am 17. Januar 1946 zu St. Jacobi in Göttingen.

19. See Drew Middleton, "Pan-Germanism, Militarism Goals of Ex-Soldier Students at Erlangen," *New York Times* (Feb. 18, 1946), p. 1, 3. Start, *God's Man*, p. 176 writes that students threw stones at him when he left the venue in Siegen, a bomb shelter in a mountain tunnel. The Erlangen text was published as *Ansprache in der Neustädter*

Kirche in Erlangen am 22. Januar 1946 (Dortmund, 1946). The Erlangen incident is also discussed in one of Niemoller's biographies: Dietmar Schmidt, *Pastor Niemöller.* (London: Odhams Press, 1959), p. 148.

20. Martin Niemöller, *Die politische Verantwortung des Christen im akademischen Stand: Vortrag gehalten auf Einladung der evangelischen Studentengemeinde vor Studierenden der Philipps-Universität zu Marburg an der Lahn am 4. Mai 1946* (Giessen: W. Schmitz, 1946).

21. Martin Niemöller, *Die Erneuerung unserer Kirche* (Munich, 1946); reprinted in: *Reden* 1945-1954, p. 19.

22. Start, *God's Man: The Story of Pastor Niemoeller.*, chapter 23 contains the most detailed description of this tour I have found. Unless otherwise noted, my description is taken from Start's.

23. "Was Niemöller in Amerika wirklich sagte. Eröffnungsansprache auf der Tagung des Federal Council of Churches am 4. Dezember 1946 in Seattle" (Flugblätter der Bekennenden Kirche Nr. 7), Stuttgart 1947. I could not find an English publication of this speech; this is my retranslation into English.

24. "Der Fall Niemöller," *VVN-Nachrichten*, Aug. 17, 1947, p. 1 includes a long excerpt from the Jan. 25, 1947 speech, which it says was published in full in the June 21, 1947 issue under the title "Pastor Niemöller: Amerikanische Predigt."

25. We do, however, have Franklin Littell's presumably firsthand testimony that Niemöller "concluded many of his addresses [in the US in 1946-47] with the now famous statement." See Martin Niemöller, *Exile in the Fatherland: Martin Niemöller's Letters from Moabit Prison*, ed. Hubert G. Locke (Grand Rapids, Mich.: W.B. Eerdmans Pub. Co., 1986), p. vii.

26. These events are well documented in "Martin Niemöller antwortet seinen Freunden," in: *Amtsblatt der Bekennenden Kirche Nassau-Hessen* 1:3(Sept. 20, 1947), pp. 17-20. See also the article cited in note 32.

27. Milton Mayer, "The Germans, Their Cause and Cure: My Ten Nazis" in: *Harper's Magazine* (Dec. 1953), 23-31; (Jan. 1954), 70-77; (Feb. 1954), 82-90.

28. Milton Mayer, *They Thought They Were Free: The Germans, 1933-45* (Chicago: Univ. of Chicago Press, 1955, 2nd ed. 1966), p. 168f.

29. Robert M. Hutchins, "The Meaning and Significance of Academic Freedom," in: *Annals of the American Academy of Political and Social Science*, v. 300 (July 1955), 72-78, p. 75. Hutchins refers to Mayer's book as "forthcoming." The passage in this review was later quoted in: Sidney Hook, *Political Power and Personal Freedom: Critical Studies in Democracy, Communism, and Civil Rights* (New York: Criterion, 1959), 281f.

30. Claude Lightfoot, *"Not Guilty!": The Case of Claude Lightfoot* (New York: New Century, 1955), p. 4.

31. Lightfoot Defense Committee (ed.), *The Case of Claude Lightfoot* (New York: Lightfoot Defense Committee, 1955), p. 15.

32. Frances Goodrich, Albert Hackett, and Anne Frank, *The Play of the Diary of Anne Frank* (New York: Heinemann, 1958), p. 150. The quotation in the concluding instructional materials was not in the previous edition of this book, previous edition: New York: Random House, 1956.

33. I have not seen this document myself, but it is paraphrased in: James Bentley, *Martin Niemöller* (Oxford; New York: Oxford University Press, 1984), p. 164f. Bentley references a handwritten script preserved with Niemöller's papers at the Zentralarchiv der Evangelischen Kirche Hessen-Nassau, 62 Vol. 396/2442c. It is unclear from Bentley's text to what extent the Dachau anecdote is taken from the Sept. 23, 1946 Rendsburg church version he paraphrases and quotes on p. 164, as he seamlessly transitions to the 1962 manuscript, embedding the whole in a discussion of Niemöller's antisemitism. In the early 1990s, Niemöller's oldest child Brigitte Johannesson, told Ruth Zerner that she thought Niemöller might have started using the quotation in the early 1960s. This might be the origin of that speculation. See Zerner, "Martin Niemoeller, Activist as Bystander" (note 5, above), 327-340.

34. KNA [Katholische Nachrichten-Agentur], "Kirchenpräsident D. Niemöller über den deutschen Widerstand," in: *Politische Studien* 27(Sept./Oct. 1964), p. 581.

35. Phyllis Lieberman and Sidney B. Simon, "Current Events and Values," in: *Social Education* 29(Dec. 1965), pp. 532-533. This article was reprinted in: William Gardner and Fred Johnson, *Social Studies in the Secondary Schools: A Book of Readings* (Boston: Allyn and Bacon, 1970), pp. 298-300. Simon again used the quotation in: Sidney B. Simon and Howard Kirschenbaum. *Readings in Values Clarification* (Minneapolis: Winston Press, 1973), p. 128. I have not yet been able to locate the ACLU newsletter in question.

36. The first publication I found was in the week of Sept. 16, 1977, when a reader responded to Abby's request for an attribution of the "recently published" quotation. Abby published again in response to readers' requests on Dec. 19, 1980; Jan. 23, 1984; Feb. 25, 1986 (with mention of Indians, Jews and Negroes by the requesting reader); Feb. 11, 1987; Feb. 1, 1990, and Apr. 29, 1993. In the 1984 column Abby writes that she has "kept it for nearly 30 years," thus dating her discovery of it to about 1955.

37. Wilhelm Niemöller et al., *Neuanfang 1945: Zur Biographie Martin Niemöllers nach seinen Tagebuchaufzeichnungen aus dem Jahre 1945.* (Frankfurt: Stimme-Verlag, 1967), 69.

38. See note 4, above.

39. Hannes Karnick and Wolfgang Richter, Martin Niemöller, *Was würde Jesus dazu sagen? Eine Reise durch ein protestantisches Leben. Ein Film Bilder-Lesebuch* (Frankfurt: Röderberg, 1986), p. 69f.

40. Admittedly most of these invocations, except for Mayer's teacher in 1950/51, were in English. I have not made as detailed a search in German as I have in English.

41. Martin Niemöller, "30 Jahre Bundesrepublik: Erlebnisse und Gedanken," in: *Blätter für Deutsche und Internationale Politik* 24:1(1979), 13-16, p. 16. Oddly, the Niemöller Foundation does not cite this publication.

42. The earliest of these other texts that I have found so far is: Erasmus Schöfer, and Werkkreis Literatur der Arbeitswelt, *Die Kinder des roten Grossvaters erzählen: Berichte zur Vor- und Frühgeschichte d. Bundesrepublik Deutschland* (Frankfurt am Main: Fischer Taschenbuch Verlag, 1975), 163. Interestingly, this version includes Catholics.

CHAPTER 12

Against Forgetting: Another Look at Böll's *Billiards at Half-Past Nine*

JOAN PETERSON

Since its publication in 1959, German writer Heinrich Böll's *Billiards at Half-Past Nine* has been alternately celebrated, criticized, and misunderstood—depending on the political mood of the time, the country of the reviewer, the theoretical stance of the critic, and the disposition of the reader. There are several reasons why *Billiards at Half-Past Nine* should be re-introduced to today's reader of the Holocaust. Though this novel is famous for breaking open the silence that pervaded Germany about the war, it did so in an ambiguous manner that at once mirrored the society of the time but also reached far beyond what members of that society were thinking at the time. Though this novel takes a fierce stance about an unspeakable past, it does not (perhaps cannot) look at, grieve for, or discuss the Jewish victims of the war except by way of very enigmatic and buried enclosures—something missed by previous readings but revealing in its very secretiveness. As such, this novel has much to teach about post-war West Germany, and about Böll himself, in relation to the Holocaust. I find references to victims of the Holocaust—both Jews and Jehovah's Witnesses. The way those references are sometimes blurred with Christian symbolism suggests that Böll couldn't write directly about victims who were not German; instead, Jews and Jehovah's Witnesses are hidden in the background of the novel. What readers bring to a text is always new, due to one's own history as well as the time in which one reads. I draw on Reader-Response theory—especially the idea that part of the meaning of a text resides within the text itself and part with the reader who brings him or herself to the text. In addition, I believe that *Billiards at Half-Past Nine* must be read in relation to the Germany of 1959, a time that shapes the story, and gives readers necessary historical perspective.

Billiards at Half-Past Nine is a difficult and complex work, told from the perspective of eight different characters. A deep tone of sadness pervades the novel—manifested by stream of consciousness style, disruptions in time, modernist language that employs symbols, metaphors, repetitions, and allusions to 60 years of history. A German refusal to be reconciled to the past, accompanied by state-wide amnesia, result in rage and psychological disorder in the story of the Faehmel family.

The Nazi period in the novel is only designated by dates and the reader fills in occurrences that match the context of what one knows of a given time. The 1930s are mentioned much more often than the war years. Most importantly, the words "Nazi," "Holocaust," and "Hitler" are never used. Allusions to the Holocaust, to Jews, and to Jehovah's Witnesses, are buried, mysterious, and sometimes confusing. Böll endeavors to dig up the roots of the Nazi past by focusing on Hindenburg—either because he cannot discuss Hitler or Nazism directly—or because he thinks that Hindenburg holds the key to understanding what transpired after his governance. It may also be that, in 1959, Germans were fixated on the *causes* of WW II and Böll was reflecting that fixation; however, the Holocaust lurks in the background in coded references.

In her important work *The Language of Silence*, written in 1999, Ernestine Schlant chastised the novels of Böll for avoiding any mention of The Holocaust, for using simplified metaphors of good and evil, and for his clichéd references to the few Jews found in his stories. Though she does not specifically discuss *Billiards at Half-Past Nine*, she concludes that Böll could not discuss Jews due to a deeply ingrained and unconscious prejudice. Other critics, including Theodor Adorno and Jean Amery, highlighted Böll's strong moral conscience, and the attention he paid to victims and underdogs. He was called the man who "represents our conscience," throughout Germany. Still others have written extensively on how the suffering incurred by Germans who did not follow Hitler was a critical element in all his works. Commonly known, long explicated by scholars, and still of consequence, Böll demonstrates in his work and in *Billiards* the failure of Christianity, German culture, and language, as he warns against a poisonous future.

Winner of the Noble Prize for Literature in 1972, Böll established the

"German Judaica" section of the Cologne City Library, dedicated to the history of the Jews in Germany, the same year he wrote *Billiards*. In 1967 he received Germany's highest literary prize—the Georg Buchner Prize of the German Academy for Language and Literature, and in 1970 he was elected President of PEN. Eight works of Böll's[11], including *Billiards,* were recently released after having been out of print for some time. Böll was a member of Group 47, German writers who banded together and included Grass, Siegfried Lenz, Wolf, Thomas Mann, and also the dramatists Hochhuth, Weiss, Dorst, and others born between 1920 and 1930. They made *Vergangenheitsbewaltigung,* or "coming to terms with the Nazi past," part of their literary program and the basis of their political commitment to a democratic future. Considered the second wave of anti-fascist literature, works from Group 47 were literature by intellectuals for intellectuals, since "the population and the popular press derogated these efforts as *Nesbeschmutzung* (dirtying one's own nest).[2] Having no shared platform, they debated whether literature in Germany after "zero hour"[3] should be stark and transparent like Hemingway's, or metaphorical and complex like Faulkner's. What they shared was an anti-fascist consensus and a desire to understand how the German past would affect the new present. A writer of war stories that often depicted German soldiers disenfranchised and beaten down by the war, Böll was also known as a writer of "literature of the rubble."

Before Group 47, and except for Wolfgang Koeppen's *Death in Rome*,[4] the Nazi past accompanied by the Holocaust was seldom treated in German literature and in fact, there were no noteworthy novels written. 1959, however, was a watershed year. Both Böll's *Billiards at Half-Past Nine* and *The Tin Drum* by Günter Grass, were published to rave reviews in West Germany and in the United States. Judith Ryan saw these two novels, along with Uwe Johnson's *Speculations About Jacob,* as "reaching a new level of mastery" and "able to attack the large questions about the Nazi past with greater energy and more analytic subtlety."[5] She found common themes around the suppression of memory and a concern for how the Nazi past connected with the post-war present. Group 47 acknowledged that German literature would henceforward have a political cast, but the Jewish victims of WW II were essentially absent in the literature that emerged.

In *Billiards*, the paralysis in which characters find themselves is also symptomatic of an inability on the part of the writer to discuss the Holocaust—yet Böll manages to insert references to Jews and to Jehovah's Witnesses that show he is thinking, perhaps even worrying about, the problematic silence that encompassed Germany over the Holocaust. Of the many issues cited that attempt to explain this suppression throughout Germany, the enormity of the crimes committed against Jews, Jehovah's Witnesses, Roma and Sinti, and other peoples, makes the very fact of silence difficult to comprehend. Scholars note that immediately after the war, Germany was in ruins and under an allied-imposed denazification policy that had limited results and was despised by many Germans. In a few short years, the Cold War, the division of Berlin, the "economic miracle," the rapid rebuilding of cities, the normalization of relations with Israel, the materialistic and capitalistic society that took hold, de-militarization, German victimhood, reparations to victims, the need for distance, and the few Jews who lived in Germany, all served to make the Holocaust a peripheral concern—if it was a concern at all.

Eva Hoffman is taut and clear in her assessment:

> In the immediate aftermath of atrocity, in the generation of direct participants, the gulf—moral, political, affective—between the victims and the perpetrator is nearly absolute. The gulf is created in the first place by the perpetrator's utter failure to recognize the humanity of the victim; it is reinforced by the injustice of the deed itself; and it is sealed, most often, by the failure of most perpetrators to feel remorse for the deeds they have performed.[6]

Alexander and Margarete Mitscherlichs' *The Inability to Mourn*, published in 1967, attempted to understand the psychology of German avoidance by pointing out that it was easier for Germans to dismiss the Nazi era and to lay blame on Hitler and his hierarchy than accept blame and guilt themselves. Hannah Arendt, visiting Germany in 1950, noted:

> But nowhere is this nightmare of destruction and horror less felt and less talked about than in Germany itself.... And the indifference with which they walk through the rubble has its exact counterpart in the absence of mourning for the dead, or in the apathy with which they react, or rather fail to react, to the fate of refugees in their midst....

> The average German looks for the causes that lead to the expulsion of Adam and Eve from paradise. Such an escape from reality is also, of course, an escape from responsibility.[7]

It is not until the late 1960s that Germans *begin* to "come to terms with the past" even though *Billiards at Half-Past Nine* preceded *Vergangenheitsbewaltigung* by at least ten years. It is also during this time that German-Jewish voices are first heard. But when Böll wrote *Billiards*, his voice was largely a lone one, publically stating that Germany must cross a difficult, even anguished, threshold, by acknowledging, remembering, and mourning the crimes. Robert E. Sackett writes that, "The kind of German that he wants to see does not hate Germany, but is full of the emotion of loss, including both personal loss and the immense losses caused by German aggression."[8] Into this combination of sociological, political, and psychological hindrances, is the fact that Böll served in the German military as a young man, and was conscripted and saw combat on the Eastern front. He was wounded four times, deserted, and was a POW after surrendering to American soldiers. How those experiences shaped his work, and particularly *Billiards at Half-Past Nine,* has not been addressed in English. In the novel, the mother Johanna does say of her son Robert, "I only wish I knew just what he did in the war."(149) Publisher Dennis Loy Johnson noted, "He did survive the war, and he did write about having been a conscripted Nazi soldier very quickly after the war—he didn't obscure the fact for decades, the way Gunter Grass did. He did, very bravely, place himself squarely in the ranks of those who must atone, who took part in the horror."[99] Much of Böll's oeuvre, however, is much concerned with how former Nazis became part of the new coalition government and nested in that concern is the government's argument for amnesty of Nazi war criminals.

The novel takes place over a 24-hour period—Sept. 6, 1958—the day of Heinrich Faehmel's 80th birthday. Robert, the main character, lives a strictly ordered, colorless life where the high spot of his day is a morning billiards game where he tells the stories of his past to the hotel bell hop Hugo. There are 14 characters in total and each of 13 chapters is devoted to various parts of each. Some of the characters serve as confidants to major characters and others let the reader "in on" what's really true of a character. Because much of the novel is written in stream of consciousness, one character can morph into another and one time period can meld into a different time period, thus asking for vigilance on the part of the reader.

Two events are central to the story: the first concerns the exile of Robert Faehmel (son of Heinrich) and the concurrent death of Robert's friends who opposed and fought against the Brown Shirts in 1935. All the major characters grieve for these losses. The second is the destruction of St. Anthony's Abbey—bombed in the last days of the war by main character Robert. His father Heinrich, also an architect, built the abbey and Robert's son Joseph is supposed to reconstruct the Abbey. All the major characters secretly applaud the annihilation of the Abbey and despise the lack of moral opposition displayed by the Monks during the Nazi period. The following quotation encapsulates both events:

> . . . he had waited through five years of war for that moment, the moment when the Abbey would be his booty, lying there like a gift of God. He had wanted to erect a monument of dust and rubble for those who had not been historical monuments and whom no one had thought to spare. Edith, killed by a piece of shrapnel; Ferdi, would-be assassin condemned by process of law; the boy who had pushed the tiny slips of paper with his messages into the letter box; Schrella's father, who had disappeared; Schrella himself, who had to live so far away from the land where Hölderlin had lived; Groll, the waiter in The Anchor; and the many others who had gone marching off, singing *How weary, weary these old bones* . . . No one could be called to account for them . . . . *(156)*

Robert, in the German Air Force as an engineer, bombs the Abbey in the last days of the war in retribution for the silence of the Monks during the Nazi years. It is impossible to not read this action as heavily symbolic, knowing what we do now, about the Catholic Church's lack of public response to the Holocaust. Robert's act carries more weight than it did in 1959. The second part of the quotation refers to 1935, when Robert and his friends tried to defy and fight against the Brown Shirts. Böll appears to be authenticating that actors and resisters against Nazis resulted in deaths among them. He is establishing that there were good, young Germans, who risked their lives (like those of the White Rose) who must be acknowledged and remembered. The young Germans in the story attempted to assassinate a reprehensible Nazi who had been a bully when all the friends were in school. The assassination failed and instead, Ferdi, who had the bomb, was murdered; Robert, who obtained the gun powder for Ferdi, was tortured and went into exile along with his close friend Schrella; the mysterious boy (also referred to as "the carpenter's apprentice") who secreted letters to Robert's parents was killed, along with Groll, a waiter who tried to intervene for the family; and Schrella's father, who hid Ferdi, disappeared along with other Germans.

The story is fraught with the tragedies of family, friends, and acquaintances of the Faehmels' during the war: Robert's wife, Edith, (also sister to Schrella) is killed during the bombing of Cologne; Robert's mother, Johanna, is institutionalized in an asylum at war's end; Johanna and Heinrich's son Otto becomes a virulent Nazi to the horror and bereavement of the whole family. Otto dies at Kiev—a city that echoes now, more than when the book was published, with the infamous murders of Babi Yar. Böll chose his place names well.

Oblique, well-hidden allusions bring the Holocaust into the novel. When Heinrich, the father, remembers the terrible times, he thinks of all the young people killed and how "even an uncalled-for glance, certain kind of hair, certain shape of the nose were enough . . . .The father's or grandmother's birth certificate was enough." (163) Jochen, an old waiter at the hotel who disturbs the novel as a truth-teller, remembers one of the Brown Shirts and says, "If I knew all the things he's done, no doubt I'd be sick to my stomach . . . . He's the type that has the gold teeth ripped out of corpses, that orders kids' heads shaved. . . . murder in the air." (24) Though neither the words "Nazi" nor "Holocaust" are ever used, one overt and several significantly veiled references to the Jewish Holocaust are associated with two characters: Johanna and Hugo. In addition, there are hints that Schrella and his sister Edith are Jehovah's Witnesses, a group also persecuted by the Nazis. The following examines each of these four characters.

Johanna

Johanna, according to Jochen, was a fine woman who lost three of her children and who, during the war, gave away most of her rations to those in need—even at the expense of starving her own family. Early in the story she "went down to the freight yard and tried to go along in the cars with the Jews." (21) Never again is this incident referred to and there are only two other mentions of the words "Jew" or "Jews" in the novel. Her mantra, the words she murmurs over and over throughout the novel, are "whywhywhywhy." Though she has spent her life in an asylum since 1945, it is made clear by all characters in the story that she is saner than most Germans. Her granddaughter, Ruth, says "Her craziness is a lie, grief behind thick walls, I know it, I get drunk on it sometimes myself and swim away in a lie." (232) Why did Böll cause Johanna to try to join the Jews on the train? I can only speculate that since he casts Johanna as the truest socialist and truest humanitarian in the novel, in retrospect, in 1959, she is the one who must shoulder what the great majority of Germans did not do—she must symbolize what could have been—or what should have been. Johanna's attempt to unite with the Jews on the train positions her as the opposite of a bystander; her role as a woman and a mother limits what she could do during the war. But in 1959, she tries to complete the assassination that Ferdi could not by shooting at "M," one of many former Nazis back in power campaigning as Minister: "I'm ready with death in my handbag to return to life." (240) That former Nazis were indeed welcomed back by the Adenauer administration was anathema to Böll, who publically wrote and spoke about this sinister turn of events. His vehemence can be sensed when Johanna says, watching a parade of the Fighting Veterans' League, that these faces frighten her and make her wish she were back among "poor old harmless lunatics." These people she says, "will kill you all for less than a gesture, for less than a sandwich. You needn't even be dark-haired or blond any more, or show your grandmother's birth certificate. They'd kill you if they just didn't like your faces." (251) Johanna's attempt at retroactive justice is most probably meant by Böll to underscore both how a "good" German could be turned into a murderer when confronted by newly empowered Nazis, and a pointed reference to the many war criminals who escaped justice in Germany after the war. Johanna, who feels herself a stranger among Germans, also gives voice to the lack of compassion and responsibility for the war and the war dead all around her: "Maybe I do need time, but even centuries wouldn't be enough to get me used to their faces.

Respectable, respectable, without a trace of grief. What's a human being without grief?" (251)

Johanna's earlier effort to join the Jews on the train, however, passed over by critics and buried in thick text, can be viewed now as Böll's small attempt to justify revenge for the Holocaust in one character. Her repetitious questioning of "why" is a reverberation voiced by characters in literature about the Holocaust through decades and certainly by anyone who is initiated into that history. Her whys just sound louder today. Finally, that she shoots and misses is arresting. She mimics Ferdi's botched assassination attempt and the message seems to be that though violence begets violence, the good people must find other ways to contain evil. Böll was a Catholic pacifist,[10] thus, presumably, he could not have this character actually commit a murder. Perhaps to Böll, this sane, raging character living in an insane world, would lose the lucidity with which she viewed Germany at that time had she succeeded, though thinking of the bombing of the Abbey, Johanna says she would have "blown every abbey in the world sky-high" to have all the dead back.... to be able to learn who Otto really was. *Killed at Kiev.* It sounds so stupid and smells of history." (241)

Hugo

The character of Hugo is a strange and more complicated invention. At the end of the novel, Robert adopts Hugo. I want to suggest that Hugo is actually Jewish and that his Jewishness is so deeply buried that even Böll himself couldn't admit to it—whether personally, or whether publically in the writing of this novel, is not clear. Every morning Robert plays billiards in the Prince Heinrich Hotel in Cologne where his only attendant and confidant is Hugo—a young bell hop. The Germans outside the hotel are menacing: "Respectable matronly faces took on a depraved look. Frock-coated waiters with knowing eyes looked like so many bellzebubs, emissaries from Asmodeus, ...now they seemed to be concealing cloven hooves inside cleverly constructed orthopedic shoes." (32)

From half-past nine to eleven, while billiard balls roll in an oasis of calm, Hugo listens to Robert's anguished stories of the Brown Shirts who made the lives of the Faehmel family and friends hell. Hugo is passive and attentive and slowly shares his own tale of being bullied by similar types in more recent time. Of the neo-Nazis, Robert thinks, "These were the people who tormented Hugo—perhaps one of them was even Ferdi's hangman." (166) Hugo is an innocent but he is different from the other innocents in the novel. Beaten and tortured by thugs as a child, like Robert's friend Schrella, Hugo was also taunted as *lamby boy* and *God's little lamb*. Like Schrella, he is able to share his story only with Robert. If Hugo is Jewish and Schrella is a Jehovah's Witness, it is Robert who rails against the injustice rendered to both of these characters by old and new Nazis. Significantly, Robert can tell the stories of his own tortured past, a past that involved Schrella's secret, cult-like religious group, only to Hugo—perhaps because as a Jew, Hugo is the only one, in Germany in 1959, who can hear those stories.

Hugo longs to stay in the billiard room where time stands still, where time made his head spin—decades, half-centuries—"yet it was all there, hidden far back in time." (44) As a bellhop, all the guests in the hotel want to be served by Hugo, explained by the fact that he's very good looking. In fact, in a most bizarre episode, a woman in the hotel called the sheep-lady, whose parents said of her "*A thing like that should never have been born.*" (46) stalks Hugo. She exudes an odor of excrement, knits all day, holds court with a group of disciples, opens boxes of sheep dung for all to sniff, looks as if she drinks gall for breakfast, and "left a trail of dread behind her, the breath of disaster" wherever she goes. She tries to get Hugo to become "the Lamb of God in my new religion." She will make him rich and famous and asks him "Haven't you been around long enough to know that only a new religion can cure their boredom?" Presumably she is one who pulls the wool over the eyes of many Germans who still follow like sheep. Perhaps Böll was thinking of Matthew 7:15 when Jesus says "Beware of false prophets, who come to you in sheep's clothing but inwardly are ravenous wolves."[1111] That she knits all day is suggestive of the mythological three fates who spin, measure, and cut the thread of a person's life as well as of Conrad's two women in black who knit black wool in *Heart of Darkness* or even Madame Defarge from Dicken's *A Tale of Two Cities*. It is Hugo that she most wants. Her portrayal is repugnant and her fawning over Hugo strange and aberrant. Hugo fears her. She is contrasted to the cruelty of former and new Nazis in this reader's mind and she evokes aversion. Her rendering is the closest we get to the dreadfulness of the Holocaust—that she attaches herself to Hugo creates an image of vileness and depravity.

The most striking intimation that Hugo is Jewish is shown through his separation of himself from other Christians. He alludes to the fact that "they" have been lying in wait for him for five or six hundred years:

> . . . why did Christ die, anyway? What good did it ever do me? What do I care if they pray every morning, take Communion every Sunday and hang a big crucifix in the kitchen . . . . Nothing, that's how much I care. What's it all amount to, if they lie in wait every day and beat me up? It's been going on like this for five or six hundred years. Yet they're always shooting off about how old their church is . . . . You know what they used to holler at me when they were beating me up? *God's little lamb.* That was my nickname." (59)

Böll was cognizant of theological anti-Semitism and anti-Judaism. Though one could argue that Hugo is simply not a Christian, rather than Jewish, he is called, by the bullies—or neo-Nazis—"a devil" an attack that harkens back to Christian condemnations against Jews in the Middle Ages. Thrashed and cynically called, "God's little lamb. Feed my lambs," also suggests the real Jesus—the Jesus who was a Jew. Hugo is well aware of his status as "other." He sees that throughout modern history, harassment of Jews continued: "I was one lamb they didn't feed, if I ever was His to begin with. No use, Doctor. The wind blows, the snow falls, the trees turn green, the leaves fall—they go right on eating potatoes and gravy, ham and cabbage." (60)

Hugo tells Robert how he ended up in a children's shelter after repeatedly running away from home. He did this in part because his mother, who drank, went out on "expeditions," and screamed *whywhywhy* over and over—the same mantra that Johanna cried. He is laughed at in the shelter because he doesn't know what breakfast is—similar to Edith who wasn't familiar with cutlery. Whether this is a reference to poverty, or to Jews, or to Jehovah's Witnesses, is mysterious as Edith's background is also blurred. Hugo doesn't know anything about the war—he hadn't been born and wants to know from Robert what it was like. A Jewish boy who doesn't know about the war seems impossible—unless German silence about the Holocaust is read into his ignorance—along with a mother who, unlike Johanna, became genuinely insane.

At the end of the novel, when the whole family is reunited for Heinrich's birthday party, where Johanna's assassination attempt takes place, Hugo is there. Robert wants Hugo—says he needs him, calls him son, publically adopts him, and hopes Hugo needs them as much as they need him. He tells Hugo that he has Edith's smile and Ferdi's spirit, combining one who was a Jehovah's Witness with one who suffered and died fighting against Nazis. Heinrich accepts the adoption and says he's acquired a grandson but admits that some voice or feeling prevents him from calling Hugo "grandson." Heinrich, of all the older Faehmels, has been the least courageous over the years, and visibly lacks his wife and son's hostility towards old and new Nazis. The voice that prevents him from not calling Hugo "grandson" may come from some far-off anti-Semitic German compulsion—though Heinrich redeems himself in the eyes of the reader as the story progresses. Ironically, before learning about the adoption of Hugo, Johanna thinks about the various neo-Nazi's she might kill and thinks, "My grandson's murderer is sitting nearby on the balcony, can you see him in his dark suit, respectable, oh so respectable.... Death will bring the great wonder back into his face." (254) Johanna did not have a grandson who was murdered—unless she is thinking of Hugo—in a strange backwards-in-time way—and thinking about what might have happened to him, as a Jew, if he had been deported as a child during the war.

In a disturbing twist at the end of the novel, the sheep-lady tries to entice Hugo to come with her:

> You're the one they're waiting for Hugo.... You'll see the whole world and they'll lie at your feet. . . . You won't need to say anything, you'll only need to be there.... It was just despair made me do it—come now, Hugo for their sake—they're waiting for you, you're our lamb...." (277)

What "despair" made her do what? Does she want Hugo in order to redeem herself—Germany—to the world? Hugo leaves with his new "father" Robert: "He could hear her sobbing on his way down the service stairs." (278)

Schrella

Schrella, struck hard in the face by a ball again and again by Brown Shirt bullies, is saved by Robert, who stops the persecution by miraculously hitting a ball out of the ballpark, during a game of rounders. Robert learns the tormenters trip Schrella, beat him with barbed-wire whips, push him down steps, and break his arm. Alluding perhaps to centuries of Jewish men who hid circumcisions, Robert notes in the locker room that Schrella "never took a shower after a game, never took off his jersey in front of the rest." (38) Apprehensive, Robert trembles in fear over the possibility that Schrella might be Jewish:

> ... for now I had to ask him, and if once I did, I would be involved, there would be no turning back. It must have been a terrible secret.... Now it was almost dead still, and that gave a great weight to my impending question. It burdened it with eternity, you might say... I was saying goodbye to St. Severin's dark tower,... to my parents' house.... (41)

Böll appears to be suggesting that to become involved with a Jew meant life as Robert knew it would end. There is a long litany of places and people he will miss—including his religion and his future plans before he finally asks, "Are you Jewish?" The dread with which he asks the question is important because the reader knows that Robert will soon escape with Schrella. The passage suggests that neither Böll nor his friends knew Jews during the war—or were afraid to know them. Schrella answers that he is not Jewish but that he's a Lamb—one "sworn never to put the *Host of the Beast* to our lips." (42) Robert says he can't be a Lamb (presumably because he is of another religion) but Schrella tells him he can be a shepherd—and there begins Robert's initiation into a clandestine group that resists the Brown Shirts.

I believe that Schrella (and his sister Edith who Robert marries) are members of the Jehovah's Witness church. Only Schrella and Edith are called Lambs. During the 30s, Brown Shirts broke up Witness Bible study meetings and beat up school children. Witnesses refused to fight in WWI, refused to pledge loyalty to Hitler, or to fight, in WW II. Witnesses do not bear arms. Banned in Bavaria in 1937, they lost jobs and social welfare and pension benefits throughout Germany. Then, thousands were sent to concentration camps. Most importantly to the novel, Witnesses met covertly in Germany during the war and became "an island of spiritual resistance to the Nazi demand for absolute German commitment to the state." Nazis linked Witnesses to "international Jewry" by pointing out a reliance on certain Old Testament texts.[12] The 144,000 who are among the "anointed" are referred to as "lambs" and the remaining "great crowd," are "the other sheep." Allusions to lambs from both the Old and New Testaments abound in church literature. Witnesses believe in the end of the world. Schrella's mother, so undone by the poverty all around her in the early 30s, gave away food, like Johanna, to hungry children. She starved herself, whispering "*Lord, Lord*," while reading a prayer book that "foretold the end of the world." (212)

Robert joins Schrella's late night meetings though the words "Jehovah's Witness" are never used in the text. Witnesses are pacifists, and several times the novel makes clear that Schrella was not involved in the bomb plot even though he escapes with Robert after the assassination attempt.

Only anointed Witnesses partake of unleavened bread and wine, but in turning Christian symbolism on its head, Schrella's group refuses to "partake of the host of the beast" which is clearly National Socialism. "Wine was not wine, bread not bread, both aglow like ingredients of some secret vice." (32) Robert, though a shepherd, not a lamb, also refuses this "host." Böll blurs Christian, Judaic, and Witness allusions. It's almost as if he can't bring himself to write about Jews, perhaps doesn't have the right. On the other hand, his inability to directly bind good Germans with Jews could come from motives, conscious or unconscious, that are deeper and more problematic. Jesus' injunction in John 21:15 to "feed my lambs" is uttered over and over by group members. Hugo, at one point, is referred to as "that nice little young one who looks like an altar boy." (19) There are intentional inclusions of Old Testament names. Johanna thinks of Heinrich as her "David," as "Daniel," and also as "Abraham." Robert names his children "Joseph" and "Ruth." Schrella is thought of as a "dark angel" and "God's deputy sheriff" by Heinrich, come to take Robert away from his family. When Schrella returns to Germany after a 14-year absence, this "much-mocked student of Hölderlin wonders if anyone will recognize "his spectacles or his walk, or the close set of his eyes...his foreign overcoat...." (217)

Schrella underscores the state of affairs of 1959 and the return of unrepentant Nazis—with their principles of order, obedience, and hypocrisy. He cannot stay in Germany—he's afraid of houses where life goes on—where one gets used to anything in time. Cologne should seem a strange and changed place but instead he sees old Nazis returned to positions of power and the dead lost to memory—not even "remembered in the Jewish memorial services, since they weren't Jews." (269) He even states that to have children is precarious—they could become Nazis. He tells Robert, "I couldn't have stood it if my children had grown as alien to me as Otto became to your parents." (270)

Edith

Edith, Schrella's sister and Robert's wife, is left alone and pregnant when Robert must disappear after the failed assassination attempt. It is Edith who tells Robert to kill the Brown Shirt who had tortured her brother, Schrella. Johanna takes her into her house though admitting she never liked "mystics," and notes that all the other lambs had been scattered—only Edith remained—another allusion to disappeared Jehovah's Witnesses. In order to save her, (in all probability from the Nazis) Johanna had Edith certified insane. She is portrayed as separate from the other Faehmels and different. She refers often to "The Lord," and when she dies after a bomb hits the house, there are "no martyrs or cardinals, hermits, knights or saints standing around in adoration." Witnesses do not have ordained clergy and, though Christians, do not see themselves as Protestants, and do not accept the symbol of the cross. Several times in the novel, Edith is connected to blood. (Witnesses refuse blood transfusions.) Johanna says, "I wrote 'Edith, Edith' in the layer of dust, with my fingers. I loved you more than if our blood had been the same. Where did you come from, Edith, tell me?" (244) On the other hand, Edith's strong bond with the family suggests that true relationships are bound by behavior, rather than blood—something Robert confirms when he adopts Hugo and something that flies in the face of Hitler's doctrine on the purity of German blood. Schrella, too, tells Robert that one can't be a father but only become a father—hence his adoption of Hugo is correct:

"That feeling in the blood is false, the other feeling alone is true."

Calling her an "emissary of the Lord," Heinrich loves Edith more than he could a daughter and wonders if the message she brought was "revenge for the lambs." (162) Mixing Christian symbolism with that of Witnesses, Heinrich says, "Edith lay there as if our family coat-of-arms had come alive, a lamb with the blood flowing out of her breast . . . ." (122-3) When Heinrich hears of the destruction of a twelfth-century crucifixion panel he thinks he would give up all the crucifixions throughout the centuries in order to see Edith's smile again: "What did the Lord's pictures mean to me, compared to His emissary's real smile"? (164) Edith is a stranger and Christ-like—or sometimes—Jewish-like. Her daughter Ruth, who only knew her to the age of three, says ." . . when I think of her, I think of seventeen or of two thousand years." (232) The blurring of religious symbols and peoples could suggest that in Böll's own mind, all victims—German, Jewish, Jehovah's Witness—were grouped together. Such a view would have to be seen as a failure to grasp the truth of what occurred. It's also possible, however, that the only course Böll believed he could take, given the silence and refusal of Germans to look at the horrors perpetuated by their country during the 1950s, was through the concealment and creation of victims who were indistinct. Today's reader can uncover some of that former obscurity.

The characterizations of Edith, Schrella, Hugo, Johanna and the Faehmel family carry havoc within them. They are an amalgamation of damage, fear, and tragedy. Scattered throughout the novel are vestiges of a buried, implied Holocaust. The tone of *Billiards* is urgent and somber. A rush of words and symbols tell of dreams flattened and lives lost. Death hovers around the edges of a terrible past. There are those who show compassion, those who are lambs, and one who is a shepherd. There is a palpable disdain for the failure of Christianity and a small hope for the promise that it contains. The future is one to be greatly feared as monsters of the past take over a new Germany. In 1959, the Holocaust is positioned in the background—boundless—and only faintly visible. The event is never grappled with—only alluded to—but it is not silent. Instead, remnants of the Holocaust are found prominently in the perpetrators returned to power, and incompletely, as through a glass darkly, in the ambiguous characterizations of Johanna, Hugo, Schrella and Edith.

Notes

1. Eight works of Böll's, including a single volume edition of his short stories, were reissued in 2011 by Melville House. The total effort was called "The Essential Heinrich Böll."

2. Ursula Mahlendorf, "Confronting the Fascist Past and Coming to Terms with It." *World Literature Today, Entering the Eighties: The Mosaic of German Literature* Vol. 55, No. 4 (1981): 554.

3. Zero Hour is the term for the end of the German war and is referred to as midnight, May 8, 1945. It is thought of as a complete break with the Nazi past and a look towards a new future.

4. *Death in Rome* was Wolfgang Koeppen's third novel of a trilogy. It is a disturbing and angst-ridden portrait of unrepentant Nazis. Published in 1954, it was derided and then ignored by the German reading public.

5. Judith Ryan, "Postoccupation Literary Movements and Developments in West Germany." In *Legacies and Ambiguities: Postwar Fiction and Culture in West Germany and Japan*, edited by Ernestine Schlant and J. Thomas Rimer, 189-206. Baltimore, Maryland: The Johns Hopkins U Press, 1991 .

6. Eva Hoffman, *After Such Knowledge: Memory, History and the Legacy of the Holocaust.* (New York: Public Affairs, 2004.)

7. Hannah Arendt, "The Aftermath of Nazi Rule. Report from Germany." *Commentary* 10 (Oct. 1950): 342.

8. Robert E. Sackett. "Germans, Guilt, and the Second Threshold of Heinrich Böll: A Study of Three Non-Fictional Works." *The Modern Language Review*, Vol. 97, No. 2 (2002): 339.

9. Dennis Loy Johnson, December 2010, interview with Jessa Crispin on "Heinrich Böll and the Literature of Aftermath: A Correspondence." Johnson is the editor of the newly released editions of Böll's works: www.bookslut.com/features/2010_12_016948.php

10. Böll later left the Catholic Church. He remained a pacifist.

11. Matthew 7:15. (The Access Bible. New Revised Standard Version with the Apocryphal/Deuterocanonical Books).

12. United States Holocaust Memorial Museum. "Jehovah's Witnesses: Article." Holocaust Encyclopedia. http://www.ushmm.org/wlc/en/article.php?ModuleId=10006187. Accessed on 5/28/14.

Bibliography

Arendt, Hannah. "The Aftermath of Nazi Rule. Report from Germany." *Commentary* 10. Oct. 1950.

Böll, Heinrich. *Billiards at Half-Past Nine*. Translated by Patrick Bowles. New York: Penguin Books, 1994.

Hoffman, Eva. *After Such Knowledge: Memory, History and the Legacy of the Holocaust.* New York: Public Affairs, 2004.

Johnson, Dennis Loy. Interview with Jessa Crispin, December 2010: "Heinrich Böll and the Literature of Aftermath: A Correspondence." www.bookslut.com/features/2010_12_016948.php.

Koeppen, Wolfgang. *Death in Rome*. Translated by Michael Hofmann. New York: W.W. Norton & Company, 1992.

Mahlendorf, Ursula. "Confronting the Fascist Past and Coming to Terms with It." *World Literature Today, Entering the Eighties: The Mosaic of German Literature* Vol. 55, No. 4, 1981.

Mitscherlich, Alexander and Margarete Mitscherlich. *The Inability to Mourn*. Translated by Beverley R. Placzek. New York: Grove Press, 1975.

Sackett, Robert E. "Germans, Guilt, and the Second Threshold of Heinrich Böll: A Study of Three Non-Fictional Works." *The Modern Language Review*, Vol. 97, No. 2, 2002.

Schlant, Ernestine. *The Language of Silence: West German Literature and the Holocaust.* New York: Routledge, 1999.

Schlant, Ernestine and J. Thomas Rimer. *Legacies and Ambiguities: Postwar Fiction and Culture in West Germany and Japan*. Baltimore: The John Hopkins U Press, 1991.

United States Holocaust Memorial Museum. Holocaust Encyclopedia. http://www.ushmm.org.

CHAPTER 13

Business as Usual: SNCF, Money, and Morality

HARRIET TAMEN, ESQ.

Harriet Tamen has provided an update on the legal efforts to hold the French National Railroad (SCNF) responsible for its activities during the Shoah. Ms. Tamen, a New York-based attorney, is a lead legal expert pursuing the efforts against the SCNF. She first reported on the case involving SCNF at the 2010 Annual Scholars' Conference: "Legal Ethics After Auschwitz." That original report was published in the Journal of Ecumenical Studies, *volume 46, Number 4, pp. 510-514.*

There is no anti-semitism in France today. Or so I have been told by French friends. Of course, no one making those statements is Jewish, although some said their Jewish friends have assured them there is no discrimination. I spoke to another friend about holding the French rail company, Société national *de chemins de fer français,* (SNCF) accountable for its wartime deportations. She was furious. She wanted to know what I was doing for the rail workers who helped the Jews.

The truth is, there is anti-semitism in France today; the truth is, rail-workers did not help the Jews. That willful blindness, that insistence on rewriting history, the refusal to accept responsibility, are among the reasons we have spent more than 14 years trying to hold SNCF accountable.

For those unfamiliar with the history, SNCF deported more than 75,000 Jews to Nazi concentration camps. The first convoy left Paris for Auschwitz on March 27, 1942. The last one left France on August 17, 1944, one week before the liberation of Paris. Fewer than 3% of those deported survived.

SNCF was paid, per head, per kilometer, for the deportations at the normal rate of .04 RM per kilometer, children under 4 rode for free. This was business as usual. Like any good business, SNCF billed quarterly; like any good business, SNCF charged interest for late payments. Language on the bills reminded the recipient that payments more than thirty days late accrued interest of 1.5 percent. Indeed, SNCF sent its last bill to DeGaulle after the liberation of Paris. Business as usual.

Although the deportations were priced at the normal rate for third class tickets, the cars used were not normal third class cars. They were cattle cars. A bucket in the corner served as the bathroom. There was no food or water—a decision made by SNCF management, not the Nazis. In fact, senior management complained when the Red Cross tried to provide water to the deportation rains in transit because that slowed the schedule—and that was bad for business.

In 1946, SNCF scored a public relations coup with the release of the very popular French movie "La Bataille du Rail"—the Battle of the Rails. A story of railroad workers sabotaging troop trains, the unwavering contention of the movie is that all relations with the German authorities during the Occupation were forced, and if not forced, were resistant. The concept of collaboration did not exist. The film quickly entered into collective French memory as evidence of strong railroad resistence to the Nazis. But the movie is fiction. It is true that certain railroad workers committed extraordinarily brave acts of resistence, but they acted as individuals, and often against SNCF. Trains carrying works of art or troop trains were sabotaged; no action was ever taken against a deportation train. SNCF management worked too comfortably with the Germans, and accepted money for the deportation trains—business as usual.

SNCF has never been held accountable; it has never paid one penny to its victims. Legal proceedings have been ultimately unsuccessful in France and so far in the U.S.

In 2006, suit was brought against SNCF and the French government in administrative court by the Lipietz family; in that administrative court, for the first time, SNCF was found liable. The court found that SNCF had not been under duress and had not been forced to treat the deportees so abominably. SNCF appealed, arguing that it was a private company providing private service when it carried out the deportations, and therefore, the administrative court had no jurisdiction; it won the appeal, and the victims were again without legal redress.

We tried in U.S. courts as well—equally unsuccessfully. Under current U.S. law, the Foreign Sovereign Immunity Act, SNCF has sovereign immunity since its shares are owned by the French government. We are currently trying to get the law changed. To that end, Senator Schumer in the Senate, and Congresswomen Carolyn Maloney and Ileana Ros-Lethinen in the House, have introduced legislation (S.1393 and H.R. 1505) that would preclude SNCF from raising a defense of sovereign immunity. That legislation has been introduced in the last few Congresses. And, by the way, neither California Senator has signed on, so if anyone here can help convince them to support us, that would be great. The U.S. Department of State has informed us that they will not oppose the legislation, a first for them, as the Department of State has always opposed amendments to the FSIA.

SNCF is now buying support to fight against paying reparations. It is all business. SNCF made a contribution to the Museum of the Shoah in Paris of hundreds of thousands of dollars, and both organizations talked about a "partnership." SNCF is also spending money in Washington—more than $1,000,000 a year to lobby Congress against us.

And it is because of money that SNCF and the French government are discussing reparations, not because SNCF feels any moral obligation to its victims. Specifically it is because of what is happening in Maryland, where a project to expand the Washington D.C. metro system is under consideration. SNCF, through Keolis, an American subsidiary, is actively pursuing that contract, worth billions of dollars. It is only because SNCF believes that it may not be able to bid on that contract that discussions are taking place. Business as usual.

But, Maryland has an active community of survivors, a supportive governor, and a sympathetic legislature. Many find it obscene that taxpayer money will be paid to an entity that has refused to pay reparations, particularly since SNCF was paid to deport some of those same taxpayers.

State Senator Joan Carter Conway, an African-American woman from Baltimore, has introduced legislation that would require companies connected to the deportation of people to Nazi death camps to pay reparations before they can obtain publically funded contracts. A companion bill has been introduced in the Maryland Assembly. Hearings on the bill begin tomorrow.

At the same time, with our help, Leo Bretholz, a Baltimore resident and survivor posted a petition online on change.org, urging that Keolis not be awarded the contract until reparations are paid. As of today, we have more than 150,000 signatures. Another e-mail has been sent to those signatories asking them to tweet their support for the Maryland legislation to Governor O'Malley and the chairs of the relevant committees.

And SNCF continues to try to rewrite history. It now says that the terms of the 1940 Armistice Agreement forced it to obey the commands of the Nazis, or that SNCF was "conscripted" by the Germans. There is no truth in either argument. SNCF cites Article 13 of the Agreement as proof that it was put at the disposal of the Nazis and under duress. As Christian Bachelier pointed out in his report, under the Armistice Agreement, SNCF would retain ownership and would operate the railway network as usual, and the Germans would supervise. The Germans would not interfere with the company's operations so as not to hamper it in any way.

Nor was SNCF conscripted. SNCF remained independent during the war, and from the very first meeting between the Germans and SNCF, it was agreed that SNCF would retain the control and responsibility for the trains. A note from a senior official of SNCF (and in the National Archives of France) reminded the Germans that while SNCF remained responsible for running the railroad, SNCF could not be disrupted without grave consequences.

The court in the Lipietz case pointed out that SNCF provided no evidence that demonstrated any duress whatsoever. The success of the German approach to the final solution in France was dependent upon the good collaboration of SNCF; for SNCF, those trains were an ordinary business venture. Business as usual.

The Bachelier Report found that SNCF was at great pains to assure that it was paid for its services. Even Serge Klarsfeld said that although SNCF didn't ask to transport the Jews, it did make money. He pointed out that "SNCF should have and could have shown its opposition to the role it played by, at a minimum, refusing to be paid for the transports with which SNCF supported the commission of the crimes. We note the absolute indifference of the management that would not miss an opportunity to get paid, and didn't seem to realize that in accepting payment of the bills, SNCF became morally complicit in the commission of the crimes that were being carried out."

SNCF is now saying that the French government has paid billions to French Holocaust survivors. That number is so silly it isn't worth discussing.

The programs touted by the French government are limited and largely focus on compensation for lost property or funding for organizations like the Foundation for the Memory of the Shoah. Those specifically related to the deportations are inadequate and contain discouraging restrictions and qualification requirements.

Where are the claimed billions? And where are the reparations to those on the trains and their heirs? And more importantly, where is anything from SNCF. Six thousand German companies have paid reparations; SNCF has paid nothing.

SNCF argues that it is an arm of the government, and therefore covered by government programs. Yet, in the Lipietz case, SNCF argued that it was a legal entity under private law and was not providing a public service when it deported people. And as we have seen, existing programs provide no compensation to the majority of SNCF victims and their heirs.

Business controls. SNCF wants to bid on rail contracts in the United States, so the French government is prepared to negotiate with the US government. We do not know where those negotiations will lead. They may not be successful. We hope they are; but what the French offer may not be acceptable to the victims.

And SNCF is annoyed. Who are we, the victims, to interfere with providing high speed rail to Americans? We know only that after almost 70 years, money has finally gotten SNCF to the negotiating table. Business as usual.

Afterword

Contrary to recent American and French government announcements, nothing new has transpired and recent statements about the December 2014 settlement are misleading.

That settlement between the U.S. and French governments is very limited. SNCF is not a party and is paying nothing to its victims. The French government will pay only those who were actually on the trains, or their surviving spouses—those few still alive. In certain instances, payments may also be made to their heirs, if one parent survived until 1948. Those who lost both parents, or who lost siblings or who lost entire families in the camps, do not qualify, leading some to ask: "Where is the justice?"

Part V

Personal Experiences and Education

CHAPTER 14

Acknowledging the "Other" in Suffering: Reconciliation in Jewish-Muslim Relations?

MEHNAZ M. AFRIDI

I am a Muslim woman who teaches the Holocaust, Genocide and Islam. To understand how and why I got to this calling requires that I share my journey through the following memories I have of growing up.

The first time I heard about the Holocaust was in Geneva, Switzerland, where I attended the International School of Geneva for three years. I recall the black and white photographs embedded amongst the World War II history pages and the words: *Holocaust...6 million Jews murdered...*

The first time I was referred to as one of those "sand-n*ggers" was when I was in a van going home from school in Geneva.

The first time I saw the Dome of the Rock in Jerusalem was when my Swiss godmother went to Israel and sent me a postcard. It read: "My Dear little M, this is a magical place and I am so happy to be close to God. Love, Aunt Irma."

The first time I celebrated Hanukkah was in London (1979) at my Orthodox Jewish girlfriend's house down the street from our apartment in Kensington during the season of Christmas, and we lit candles and pulled on cracker-jacks, laughing, and eating kosher cookies.

The first time I experienced anti-Semitism was in Dubai, U.A.E., at the International School of *Choueifat* when the teachers blotted out the words; "Israel" and "Jew" in our history textbooks with their black markers in hand.

The first time I experienced anti-Muslim sentiment in the United States was when I was kicked in the chin during a soccer practice at Scarsdale High School for being a Muslim.

These poignant memories have been part of the experiential journey that has carried me to my academic and personal work on the *Shoah* and Islam. Memory is how we fragment our life's perceptions and retain the ones that are reaffirmed through our adulthood. Memory is also the means by which we sort through our history and the way in which we remember other people's history. Elie Wiesel's famous words "Never shall I forget" in *Night*, his memoir about his life in the camps, articulate a cruel memory, but one that requires courage and confrontation with the evil or horror created by human beings. The juxtaposed memories that I have laid out in the beginning of this essay are those that have carved my work and role as a human being—for these memories remind me of the lasting marks of prejudice and omission of the "other."

I am a Muslim woman who teaches the Holocaust, Genocide, World Religions and Islam; many questions are raised about my work and identity. Some scholars and community members view the two areas of study, Holocaust and Islam, in contradiction—they seem puzzled and at times, accuse me of being "divided." They ask me: "How can you teach two unrelated fields? How can a Muslim teach the Holocaust? What kind of a scholar are you?" I am amused by these questions as I think of how much esoteric knowledge rests on dusty shelves, for I believe there is an important connection between my two areas of research. My work has steered me to confront my own Muslim community on the suffering of "others," which I argue can become a bridge of mutual understanding and interreligious dialogue. How can we create interreligious dialogue and confront the sufferings of one another at different historical moments? How can we discuss and sustain dialogue, which by its very nature also risks dehumanizing the "other"? What aspects about Islam and about the Holocaust might connect both Muslims and Jews? And in a greater sense, what does my work offer students, communities, and academia? These and other questions haunt me every day, knocking on my faith, my study of Holocaust memoirs, my study of new research on Muslims and Jews during the Holocaust and colonialism.

Interreligious education about genocide is essential to my own work and the classes that I teach on genocides, from the Armenian to Darfur. I examine how religion has worn many garments, and how at different times it can play both a protecting and an instigating force in matters of genocide. The charge that religion is the existential motivation for genocide is based upon myths, false assumptions and historical inaccuracies. Religion should be at the forefront of these discussions and there should be a deeper understanding of religion's role in suffering and genocide:

> Certainly, specific religious traditions and concepts have no intrinsic power to influence either genocidal behavior or the responses of rescuers and victims. Muslims were (and are) victims of Orthodox Christians in Bosnia, while in the Ottoman Empire, Muslims drowned Armenian Christian babies and forcibly converted women and children. Indeed, perpetrators of genocide define religious groups in racial and cultural terms, not in terms of ideas or beliefs of individual perpetrators or victims. People were murdered because they were Jews or Armenians or Bosnian Muslims, regardless of whether or not they (or their killers) actually believed in Jewish, Christian, or Muslim precepts.[1]

Thus, as a teacher of Islam, I am searching for new meanings and ways through which religious beliefs and perceptions can be discussed. Whether it is through literature, memoirs or sacred texts, I am always more inclined to see how religion manifests itself in dialogue and issues in the social world. In other words, religious narrative is what one creates at a historical moment amidst pressing social and political concerns. Dialogues and interactions between Muslims and non-Muslims create new ways of experiencing religious difference and questions about ethics and life for both parties. As Abdullah Zain writes:

> Islam is not an orthodoxy (based on correct doctrine) but it is more of an orthopraxy (based on correct practice), which means it pays less attention to theology (kalam) and about God. Yet even when it comes to ritual practice, of more than six thousand verses of the Qur'an, Islam's holy scripture, only eighty deal directly with law, while most focus more on existential questions about the meaning of life, faith, and ethical concerns about poverty and achieving justice. If doctrine is not a central feature of the Islamic tradition, and the Qur'an is essentially not a book of law, where do we go for a conversation about what being Muslim means? Perhaps our focus should be on actual conversations among Muslims themselves, their overarching discourse, to examine some of the key ideas that shape their reality.[2]

As I listen to the conversations between Muslims all over the world about Jews, Israel, and the Holocaust (including in Pakistan where I was born), the perspective Zain describes shapes "their overarching discourse," and it is here that I believe we must listen and "examine some of the key ideas that shape their reality," as well as the realities that shape the Jewish understanding of the Holocaust.

Some of the factors that shape Muslim understandings of the Holocaust are:

- Interpretations of their own experience under colonialism, which has led them to see and understand the Holocaust primarily through that lens
- The ongoing Middle East conflict and tensions with Israel
- Contemporary experiences of Islamophobia
- Fears of terrorism

In many of the conversations I have experienced, these are the aspects that shape Jewish understandings of the Holocaust:

- The still-immediate experience of the genocide; many survivors are still alive
- The ongoing Middle East conflict and concerns about terrorism and security in Israel
- Contemporary experiences of ongoing anti-semitism, including examples from the Arab world
- Fears of terrorism

Some of these factors have fed misperceptions of one another, and then there are misperceptions that stem simply from ignorance of each other's religious traditions. But as these aspects show, many of these understandings and misunderstandings are connected in profound ways; they "mirror" one another, offering an opportunity not just for disagreement but for dialogue.

Is there a way for interreligious dialogue to make them shared concerns, or at least common conversations? In response to these different understandings and sometimes competing interpretations, a growing number of interfaith alliances, documentaries and scholars have attempted to bridge the gaps, especially by looking at the history of

Muslims during the Holocaust. They have documented how Albanians (mostly Muslim) rescued Jews; how the grand Mosque of Paris issued certificates and provided shelter to the persecuted minority; how Tunisians, Moroccans, and Algerians protected both French and North African Jews from Occupation forces.[3] These stories are important to both Jews and Muslims. The stories of rescue come both as a welcome surprise and a shock for both groups. Jews welcome the examples of Muslim heroes who willfully risked their lives in the name of Islam and justice—the Islamic principles come across strongly and paint a different image of Muslims for Jews. For example, in the many stories of *Besa* (Albanian promise), the Muslim rescuers discuss the Qur'an and its message of justice for all and the acceptance of the Jewish belief. One of these examples is from two rescuers, the brothers Hamid and Xhemal Veseli, who state:

> We never took money from our Jewish guests. *Besa* exists in every Albanian soul. Our parents were devout Muslims and believed, as we do, that 'every knock on the door is a blessed welcome from God.[4]

These courageous stories open up broader questions of coexistence and dialogue that can illustrate the positive aspect of how religious people act during times of turmoil, especially in light of the Muslim rescue of Jews. In 2012, the Holocaust, Genocide and Interfaith Education Center at Manhattan College hosted *Besa*, an exhibition of photographs of the Albanian rescuers. I invited Jews, Christians and Muslims to the opening reception. There were speeches by leaders of all three faiths that showed mutual respect and recognition for these Muslim and Christian Albanian heroes. The local Jewish community had never heard of these stories and they spent many hours scrutinizing the photographs and asking questions. This event turned into a powerful interreligious dialogue that was initiated by the mutual recognition of courage and suffering.

It also uncovers aspects of Holocaust history that are new for many people. Many Jews and Muslims have no knowledge of concentration camps in Arab countries; the memory of the Holocaust lies in Europe. The Holocaust was an event that reached places that were unknown, even to many survivors and Muslims living in Morocco, Tunisia, Libya and Algeria. This helps explain why this aspect of the history is sometimes a shock for Muslims that creates a tension with their interpretation of the

Holocaust as an example of colonialism. Muslims who had been under colonial rule for hundreds of years conflate the reconstructed memory of the suffering under colonial governments, the Vichy regime and Nazi era, into a broader history of suffering that does not differentiate between the actions of the Nazis and the actions of colonial regimes,

Thus, although Muslims welcome the positive portrayal of rescue as an illustration of core Islamic values, their shock about stories of rescue is connected to several factors: the historical omission of Holocaust studies and the lack of awareness that any Muslims or Arab populations were involved in the Holocaust, juxtaposed with the issues that arose in the aftermath of the Holocaust and colonialism. To most Muslims, the Holocaust was a European crime against Jews, and Jewish-Muslim relations disintegrated after the establishment of the state of Israel. Shaped by the colonial oppression experienced under the British, French, Dutch, Italians, and then Americans, many Muslims viewed the new state of Israel through that lens, and interpreted the Holocaust from that perspective. Popular and academic post-colonial writers such as Edward Said, David Carroll, and Frantz Fanon addressed the pain and suffering of Muslims under colonial rule and the memory of European oppression, linking it to the memory of primarily European Jewish immigration to Palestine since the 1920s. In 1995 former Arab Knesset member Azmi Bishara wrote a controversial article on "The Arabs and the Holocaust" which said in part:

> The scene of the disaster was Europe, and the perpetrators of the extermination acts were Europeans, but the reparations were paid first and foremost in the Middle East by the Palestinians. This is probably the reason that the discussion of the Holocaust in the Arab context always revolves around its political implications, and circumvents the event itself. The basic Arab anti-Zionist stance determined their [Arabs'/Muslims'] attitude toward the Holocaust, as towards anti-Semitism in general. This stance is not the cause of the Arab-Israeli conflict, but its outcome. Anti-Jewish texts were engaged in the justification of the Holocaust and with its denial as a Zionist hoax—a rhetoric which, among other things, was an attempt to deal with the Zionist instrumentalization of the Holocaust.[6]

Two recent examples demonstrate the silence and the deep psychological pain in accepting even heroic acts of Muslims during the Holocaust because of the tensions with Israel. The first example was of the Egyptian doctor, Dr. Helmy, who was the first Arab recognized by Yad Vashem in Israel. It was discovered that when the Nazis began deporting Jews, Dr. Helmy hid 21-year-old Anna Boros, a family friend, at a cabin on the outskirts of the city and provided her relatives with medical care. After Boros' relatives admitted to Nazi interrogators that he was hiding her, he arranged for her to hide at an acquaintance's house before authorities could inspect the cabin. The four family members survived the war and immigrated to the U.S. Yad Vashem offered the relatives the honor of being recognized as "Among the Righteous," but the family refused. Many could speculate that it was because of the association with Israel, as "Mervat Hassan said the family didn't want an award from Israel, but she quickly added: 'I respect Judaism as a religion and I respect Jews. Islam recognizes Judaism as a heavenly religion.'"[7]

Another example comes from the reactions to a new documentary, *Enemy of the Reich: The Noor Inayat Khan Story*, which shows how an Indian Muslim woman worked for British intelligence and assisted the French resistance, but was ultimately killed at Dachau concentration camp. Reactions to the film—the story of a courageous Muslim woman who acted against the Nazis—were polarized; an article in the March 18, 2014, *Islamic Monthly* by Iman Faridi, for example, covered her story as occupying a "dual and challenging role, as a dissenter of fascism and a woman with a colonized and radicalized heritage."[8]

In other words, there are many cases in which interreligious dialogue between Jews and Muslims about the Holocaust is derailed by the perception of one another as "oppositional" or "enemy." And yet interfaith dialogue in general can only be sustained as a religious dialogue about the commonalities and differences of faith and histories. In many of the events I have attended or been part of, when the Holocaust is mentioned there has been a failure to recognize the deep suffering of the Jewish people. Understanding Jews as people who suffered and endured persecutions, exiles and annihilation has become difficult for many Muslims; all too often, the conversation turns to debates about Israel's power, myths about Jews, and a relativizing of the Holocaust. And yet the particular success of interreligious dialogue has to begin with the acknowledgment of the suffering of each other as religions in the present.

There are points of shared suffering and concern, outlined at the beginning of this article, that could be part of these conversations. Especially in the wake of 9/11, Muslims feel that they have been targeted and their faith smeared as inherently ruthless and violent. Throughout the world, Muslims, too, suffer from the fear and violence of terrorism; today, in my own native country of Pakistan, we are suffering terrorist attacks. Spurred by Samuel Huntington's theory of a "clash of civilizations" and Bernard Lewis's *What Went Wrong? Western Impact and Middle Eastern Response,* post-9/11 conversations were polarized and many Americans were faced with the growth of a religion in their country about which they had no education. Dozens of books on Islam began to appear, some of them portraying Islam as a religion intent on destroying the U.S. It was a tough time for all Muslim-Americans and there was very little room for dialogue; most discussions were polemical or defensive. In this situation interreligious conversations became more important than ever:

> As public attention focused on Muslims in America after 9/11, many American Muslims asked themselves how their identities as Muslim individuals and communities living and participating in a western democracy fit into the American religious landscape. Muslim leaders and communities across the nation realized a need to educate their non-Muslim neighbors about Islam. Many Muslim communities opened their doors to the public, inviting non-Muslims to introductory lectures on Islam, and encouraging questions from non-Muslims. Even so, immediately post-9/11 many American Muslim women who had been veiling decided no longer to do so in order to look 'less Muslim.' The hijab has seen resurgence in popularity more recently, as these women seek to reassert themselves as American Muslim women... The years following 9/11 have also seen Muslim communities become more active in interfaith dialogue, co-hosting events with Christian, Jewish, or Hindu groups, and creating comfortable environments in which to converse and 'break bread' together.[9]

The wound of 9/11 brought with it a sense of urgency for interreligious dialogue, a feeling that perhaps Jews and Muslims have to live in the United States and need to understand one another. More and more interfaith projects grew around the country and people expressed interest in understanding one another in the face of 9/11 and as citizens in a pluralistic country. "There are so many interfaith councils and projects now, we can't even keep track," said Bettina Gray, chairwoman of the North American Interfaith Network. "From the Muslim side, there's more incentive to work with the broader community, and there's more receptiveness from the Christian and Jewish side."[10]

Such attempts at interreligious understanding continue to face many barriers and misunderstandings. The different periods of suffering on the part of both Jewish and Muslim communities, for different reasons and in different historical epochs, tend to reinforce memories of fear, isolation, and victimhood that make conversation—especially conversations about the Holocaust—difficult. In November 2013, I was part of a panel at a Holocaust Educators Conference on "Anti-Semitism and Islam" at the Jewish Heritage Museum, where I was the last speaker. The presentations by the other speakers were scholarly and factual but very frightening in their portrayal of Muslims and anti-Semitism. They demonstrated how Nazis had taken Qur'anic scripture and used it to propagate hatred towards Jews, how Iran is publicly anti-Semitic and about the dangerous phenomenon of new and radical anti-Semitism. The talks were disheartening for me on two levels. One was that the other speakers had very little background in Islam; the second was that, as a Muslim, I felt an overwhelming sense of how this non-contextual scholarship could lead to more polarization. My own talk contextualized the many factual representations of Muslims and anti-Semitism. I allowed the facts to speak for themselves about the deeply problematic issues of anti-Semitism, but added some context: for example, about how the Arabs were fed Nazi propaganda during the era of the Holocaust in the context of their tensions with the Allied Forces. In my remarks I chose to focus on the stories of cooperation and rescue, emphasizing how the mutual understanding of Muslim experiences under colonialism and the Jewish experience during the Holocaust might lead to a healthier dialogue.

The lessons of the Holocaust have taught me to rethink the historical memories of my own community and reflect on how interreligious dialogue has to be about listening to the concerns of the different religious communities and understanding how their histories impact the conversation. The memory of who we are and what we are can be the source of disconnect with "others" if we forget that the "others" are also caught in their own memory of suffering.

Notes

1. Omer Bartov and Phyllis Mack, eds. *In God's Name: Genocide and Religion in the Twentieth Century.* (New York: Berghahn Books, 2001), 3.

2. Zain, Abdullah. "A Muslim's Search for Meaning." *Harvard Divinity Bulletin* (Winter/Spring 2014), 23-4.

3. Robert Satloff, *Among the Righteous: Lost Stories from the Holocaust's Long Reach into Arab Lands.* (Washington D.C.: Public Affairs, 2006).

4. As quoted in the movie *Besa.* See also Norman Gershman, *Besa: Muslims Who Saved Jews During World War II* (New York: Syracuse University Press, 2008).

6. Cited in Meir Litvak and EstherWebman. *From Empathy to Denial: Arab Responses to the Holocaust* (New York: Columbia University Press, 2009), 1-2.

7. http://www.jewishpress.com/news/breaking-news/relatives-of-egyptian-righteous-gentile-refusing-yad-vashem-award/2013/10/20/ Retrieved March 20, 2014.

8. http://www.theislamicmonthly.com/the-noor-inayat-khan-story-a-double-edged-sword/ retrieved March 20, 2014

9. http://www.pluralism.org/religion/islam/issues/post-911 Retrieved March 21, 2014; the Pluralism Project has encouraged interreligious dialogue and is a valuable resource.

10. http://www.patheos.com/blogs/deaconsbench/2011/09/leaps-of-faith-christians-and-jews-reaching-out-to-muslims-after-911/ Retrieved March 21, 2014.

CHAPTER 15

Holocaust Education for Future Generations: The Role of a Catholic University

HARRIET SEPINWALL

During almost 25 years of work in Holocaust education at the College of Saint Elizabeth, models have been developed that can be replicated at other Catholic colleges/universities as well as other institutions of higher learning, whether religiously affiliated or secular. These models, incorporating Holocaust education into the curriculum as well as in campus and community education and commemorative programs, demonstrate ways in which people of diverse backgrounds can/will be involved. These programs are open to everyone on campus and to the community, and offered free of charge to all. Attendance at these programs continues to grow.

There is a special obligation of Catholic institutions to teach with integrity about Jews and Judaism, and to remember the Holocaust. Vatican teachings have supported this mission beginning with Vatican Council II's *Nostra Aetate* (Vatican, 1965), and continuing with the *Guidelines and Suggestions for Implementing the Conciliar Declaration Nostra Aetate* (Vatican, 1974), the *Notes* (Vatican, 1985), and *We Remember: A Reflection on the Shoah* (Vatican, 1998). Popes, from John XXIII, Paul VI, John Paul II, Benedict XVI, and now Francis, have committed the Church to engage with the Holocaust and work to ensure 'never again.' In the United States, publications of the National Conference of Catholic Bishops, based on Vatican teachings, have provided the rationale and guidelines for ensuring that these teachings are carried out (National Conference, 1998; National Conference, 2001).

Both academic accuracy and morality must guide education,

remembrance, and reflection. In his letter accompanying the text of *We Remember* (Vatican, 1998), Pope John Paul II noted:

> The inhumanity with which Jews were persecuted and massacred...is beyond the capacity of words to convey. All this was done to them for the sole reason that they were Jews. Historians, sociologists, political philosophers, psychologists, and theologians are all trying to learn more about the reality of the Shoah and its causes. Much scholarly study remains to be done. But such an event cannot be fully measured by the ordinary criteria of historical research alone. It calls for a 'moral and religious memory' and, particularly, a very serious reflection on what gave rise to it.

Highlighting the reasons for the Church's support for education and remembrance of the Holocaust, Archbishop Alexander J. Brunett (National Conference, 1998, p. 2) stated that:

1. There exists a close spiritual bond of faith which links Christians and Jews.
2. Many Christians were involved in the events of this catastrophe, some as fellow victims, some as rescuers, but too many others sadly as bystanders or perpetrators. As Christians, we are all linked together in the Church, not only with the goodness of saints, but also with the failure of saints.
3. One cannot overstate the abiding need to preserve the memory of the event itself as a warning for future generations.

The College of Saint Elizabeth, a small Catholic university in the liberal arts tradition, has been committed to teaching about the Holocaust through the academic and professional disciplines, and about Jews and Judaism in accordance with contemporary teachings of the Catholic Church. Interest in both education and commemoration of the Holocaust has continued to grow at the College. This is reflected in continual increases in attendance at on-campus programs, and participation by diverse groups, at all ages and stages, including students, teachers, survivors, clergy and members of many religious groups, civic leaders, and members of the community. The College has made a commitment to continue to offer Holocaust commemorations and educational programs, including film screenings, art exhibits, concerts, study travel, and on-campus conferences for students, teachers, and the diverse ethnic, religious, and civic community. Collaborations and partnerships with the Catholic, Protestant, Jewish, Muslim, and secular communities enhance outreach and engage wide and diverse participation in programs. Holocaust education conferences and workshops also are offered to teachers. Educational and commemorative programs are offered free of charge, with dedication to academic honesty and also to carrying out Pope John Paul II's commitment to "ensuring moral and religious memory." (Vatican, 1998).

In 1990, Campus Ministry offered a daytime commemoration of Kristallnacht as a way to teach and think about how the world's lack of response to Kristallnacht led to the Holocaust. Incorporating readings relating what took place on Kristallnacht in Germany and Austria as the world stood by, this first commemoration concluded with an interfaith service, including the reciting of the *Kaddish* prayer in Hebrew.

In 1991, the College extended the Kristallnacht Commemoration to a week-long commemoration for the campus as well as for the local community. This was planned to be consistent with the College Mission to teach in accordance with high academic standards as well as contemporary, post-Vatican II teachings of the Church. That first "College of Saint Elizabeth Week of Holocaust Remembrance" began with an evening Kristallnacht Commemoration with the testimony of a survivor of Kristallnacht, an interfaith service of remembrance, and candlelighting by Holocaust survivors. The MetroWest Jewish Federation's Holocaust Center began co-sponsoring what became an annual interfaith, community-wide Kristallnacht commemoration. In recent years, this Kristallnacht program has concluded with a dessert reception to honor the survivors. Attendees include CSE students as well as Holocaust survivors and members of the community. The week continues with what has become known as the College of Saint Elizabeth In-Class Faculty Sessions. In the first year, two faculty offered Holocaust-related sessions in their classes;[1] since that time, faculty involvement has increased greatly, offering sessions in their classes (open to their students and well as to the community) in disciplines such as history, theology, English, economics, biology, nursing, mathematics, world languages, journalism, music, art, justice studies, physical education, chemistry, philosophy, ethics, sociology, and psychology. These sessions provide important opportunities for faculty and students as well as for those in the community who come to campus to visit such classes and to learn with the students.

After the first year of the week-long commemoration, it was decided to offer an additional evening program following the Kristallnacht Commemoration in that same week. This provides opportunities to demonstrate the significance of interfaith dialogue after the Holocaust. Speakers have included highly respected Catholic, Jewish, Protestant, and Muslim theologians and religious leaders, including Fr. John Pawlikowski, Michael Berenbaum, Sr. Carol Rittner, Peter Ochs, Henry Knight, Sr. Rose Thering, Rabbi Irving Greenberg, Sr. Gemma Del Duca, Dr. Mohammed Chaudry, Fr. Ed Cuiba, Rabbi Alan Silverstein, Fr. Anthony Randazzo, Rev. Jeff Markay, Pastor Murdoch Macpherson, and Harun Alacadag. These sessions continue to serve as models for our community as well as for our undergraduate and lay ministry students. The sessions identify the progress being made in interfaith dialogue as well as the challenges.

By 1994, the College accepted the invitation of the New Jersey Commission on Holocaust Education to extend programming to include teacher training in order to help the state meet the New Jersey mandate for K–12 Holocaust and genocide education that had just been adopted. A Center was established in that year as the umbrella for all the programs that would be offered. The Center gained a designated physical space in 2007, inside the College's new building for the arts, culture, and theology. From the beginning, these training programs have provided important opportunities for teachers to develop goals and objectives as well as strategies and resources, based on what they learn at these sessions. Such programs attract not only public school teachers, but also those from Catholic, Jewish, and independent schools as well as school administrators, librarians, school nurses, and guidance counselors. While Catholic and other non-public schools are not bound by the New Jersey mandate, many teachers from these schools attend the College's programs and choose to apply what they learn in their curricula.

Teacher training conferences and workshops for teachers have focused on many topics. For example, we have provided programs for bilingual and ESL teachers and examined the roles of rescuers, hidden children, perpetrators, survivors, bystanders, and "upstanders." Programs have demonstrated how primary sources can be used to document what took place, and made teachers aware of the great variety of resources available for them. Outreach to Spanish-speakers has included a conference on finding Refuge, focusing on Latin America and the Holocaust; this program included a Spanish-language film and opportunities to learn from survivors who found refuge in Latin America. Another conference enabled educators to learning from the nation's Holocaust and genocide curriculum experts from the major Holocaust centers in the United States. Some programs also have focused on contemporary genocide. All programs for teacher training provide opportunities for educators to engage in personal contacts with survivors, both at formal sessions and at the networking lunch. These include survivors of the Holocaust and also of other genocides. In addition, films about contemporary genocide have been screened and discussed, showing that the "lessons" of the Holocaust remain to be learned.

Judith Miller (1990) has stated, "Abstraction is memory's most ardent enemy. It kills because it encourages distance and often indifference. We must remind ourselves that the Holocaust was not six million. It was one, plus one, plus one...." Knowing the survivors individually makes this possible. At CSE, we are committed to including opportunities to meet and learn from survivors at all the programs we offer, for as long as this will be possible. We also are extremely grateful to the survivors who have come, one by one, to trust us and to share their stories.

We aim to provide educators who attend our programs with something for their "head, heart, and hand," so that they leave with new knowledge, a personal commitment to this work, and meaningful ways to teach when they return to their schools. A new Certificate Program in Holocaust and Genocide Education for educators is planned, with graduate course credit. This program will extend opportunities for teachers, supervisors, librarians, and museum educators to enhance their ability to provide meaningful *Shoah* education.

Teachers also come to the College with their students for programs in which they learn together. At such programs, they meet and learn from survivors and view and discuss Holocaust and/or genocide-related films.

In addition, they have the opportunity to engage in dialogue about the significance of remembering what took place and about how to apply the "lessons" of what they are learning to make this a better world, where all people are respected and valued. In 2013, a USC Shoah Foundation program on our campus (2013) demonstrated how technology may be utilized to enable students to continue to experience survivor testimony even after the survivors are gone.

For our 18th ("Chai") anniversary in 2007, a conference was planned to consider the meaning of the work we are doing. "Memory and Memorialization: What, Why, and How Do We Remember? Lessons from the Holocaust" brought together students, teachers, Holocaust survivors, and members of the community to learn from outstanding Holocaust scholars. These included Michael Berenbaum, John K. Roth, and James A. Young, museum professionals such as Alice Greenwald, and representatives of area museums that had offered curated exhibits about the Holocaust and/or 9/11. Educators shared why/how they were teaching about such tragedies in history even years after such tragedies, and a panel composed of theologians from the Catholic, Protestant, Jewish, and Muslim faiths spoke about the importance and nature of interfaith dialogue after the Holocaust.

With the opening of a new art gallery at the College, the arts have become integral to Holocaust programming. The curator of the gallery works with the CSE Holocaust center to offer special, curated, Holocaust-related art exhibits of high quality and meaning. Among the works exhibited have been those of Michael Wolf (installation), Aileen Bassis (sculptures), and Muriel Nezhanie (Shoah tapestries); themes have included "Held Against Their Will" and "The Art of Healing." The chairperson of the Music Program has worked collaboratively with the Holocaust center to plan and offer special musical and dance programs, including a master class in klezmer music, music from Terezin, and the Carolyn Dorfman Dance Company's Shoah choreography.

Film programs have provided an additional dimension to learning about the Holocaust and other genocides. These programs have included speakers and screenings of Shoah and genocide films such as: "The Last Survivor," "The Trial of Adolf Eichmann," "Nicholas Winton: The Power of Good," "The Last Klezmer," "The Grey Zone," (New Jersey premiere),

"The Rape of Europa," and "Rosenstrasse." Some film programs have been planned as partnerships, including with the New Jersey Jewish Film Festival.

Travel/study programs for students have included the international March of Remembrance and Hope missions to Poland. CSE has offered guided tours at the United States Holocaust Memorial Museum and Museum of Jewish Heritage as well as at the local Jewish federation exhibit on local survivors. Internship programs have provided students with special opportunities at the Museum of Jewish Heritage (Lipper Internships), Auschwitz Jewish Center, United States Holocaust Memorial Museum, and the ADL Campus Leaders Mission to Israel.

Faculty development has also been encouraged, and faculty who are involved in offering the In-Class Faculty Sessions have begun to engage in seminars, graduate programs and travel to further their own knowledge of the Holocaust.

The Mission of the College of Saint Elizabeth (College, 2014) fully supports this work as contributing to Vatican teachings for "a community of learning, committed to scholarship and inquiry; just and ethical relationships; quality teaching; development of leadership in a spirit of service and social responsibility...." *Nostra Aetate* and subsequent Vatican teachings have influenced the scope, range, and nature of what is offered at CSE. The administration, faculty, students, community and alumnae are proud of what we offer, and determined to find ways to continue this work in perpetuity until the "lessons" have been learned.

Notes

1. The world cultures course offered "The Holocaust: From Statistics to People" and the theology class offered "The Christian Roots of Antisemitism."

References

College of Saint Elizabeth. Mission and values. (Morristown, NJ, accessed June 15 2012). www.cse.edu/about-cse/mission-and-values/

Miller, Judith. One by one by one: The landmark exploration of the Holocaust and the uses of memory [New York: Simon & Schuster, 1990].

National Conference of Catholic Bishops. Secretariat for Ecumenical and Interreligious Affairs. Catholic teaching on the Shoah: Implementing the Holy See's We Remember [Washington, DC, United States Catholic Conference, 2001].

National Conference of Catholic Bishops. Secretariat for Ecumenical and Interreligious Affairs. Catholics remember the Holocaust [United States Catholic Conference, 1998].

Vatican. Commission for religious relations with the Jews. Guidelines and suggestions for implementing the conciliar declaration *"Nostra Aetate"* (n. 4) [Vatican: October 22, 1974]. www.vatican.va/roman_curia/pontifical_councils/chrstuni/relations-jews-docs/rc_pc_chrstuni_doc_19741201_nostra-aetate.

Vatican. Commission for religious relations with the Jews. Notes on the correct way to present Jews and Judaism in preaching and catechesis in the Roman Catholic Church [Vatican: March 6, 1982]. www.vatican.va/roman_curia/pontifical_councils/chrstuni/relations-jews-docs/rc_pc_chrstuni_doc_19820306_jews-judaism.

Vatican. Commission for religious relations with the Jews. We remember: A reflection on the Shoah [Vatican: March 16, 1998]. www.vatican.va/roman-curia/pontifical_councils/chrstuni/documents/rc_pc_chrstuni_doc_16031998_shoah_en.html.

Vatican. *Nostra Aetate.* Declaration on the relation of the Church to non-Christian religions. *Nostra Aetate* proclaimed by his holiness Pope Paul VI [Vatican, October 28, 1965]. www.vatican.va/archive/hist_councils/ii_vatican_council/documents/vat-ii_decl_19651028_nostra-aetate_en.html.

CHAPTER 16

The Emergence of Holocaust Memoirs and the Future of Holocaust Education in Brazil

SARAH DA ROCHA VALENTE

Prefatory Note: Unless otherwise noted, all Portuguese translations are my own.

Brazilian literature has experienced the growth of a new genre in the last decade, with the significantly increasing number of published memoirs by Eastern European Holocaust survivors who immigrated to Brazil after World War II, With this phenomenon, there has also appeared an increasing interest by the public in general and by the educational institutions in particular, supported by local, state and federal government, to develop, implement and provide Holocaust studies for students in primary and secondary schools, new research university institutions, and in the public spheres through cultural centers and museums. This paper will provide an introduction to these new happenings in Brazil, as a way to acquaint the American reader on recent developments.

Before diving into the emergence of the memoirs in the last decade, it is important to briefly touch upon the historical and political scene of Brazil during the war years. Though Brazil participated in the allied effort to fight against the Nazis in World War II, this historical event does not have a predominantly felt presence within the country's literature, whether fiction or nonfiction.[1] Hence, the Holocaust has remained quite marginal in Brazilian cultural discourse and literature. Prior to 1942, the Vargas administration sided with Nazi Germany, and the political atmosphere in Brazil has been described as a combination of nativism, xenophobia, and anti-Semitism, which led to the creation of very restrictive immigration policies towards Jews. Scholars such as Jeff Lesser[2] and Maria Luiza Tucci Carneiro[3] have shown that the political and bureaucratic system remained anti-Semitic and racist even after Brazil joined the allied side in August 1942, with systematic secret political circulars that denied visas to Jews.

The number of Jews who were able to immigrate during the years was quite small, though not insignificant. The Jewish and General Immigration to Brazil, 1881-1942, was as follows:

Years	Overall Immigration to Brazil	Jewish Immigration to Brazil	%	As % of World Jewish Migration
1881-1900	1,654,101	1,000	0.06	0.1
1901-1914	1,252,678	8,750	0.07	0.5
1915-1920	189,417	2,000	1.0	2.2
1921-1925	386,631	7,139	1.8	1.7
1926-1930	453,584	22,296	4.9	12.9
1931-1935	180,652	13,075	7.2	5.5
1936-1942	120,318	14,576	12.1	3.6

Source: Lesser, Jeffrey H. Welcoming the Undesirables: Brazil and the Jewish Question *(Berkeley: University of California Press, 1995), 180.*

Specific years of immigration to Brazil, 1933-1942, was as follows:

Year	General immigration	Jewish immigration
1933	46,081	3,317
1934	46,027	3,794
1935	29,585	1,758
1936	12,773	3,418
1937	34,677	2,003
1938	19,388	530
1939	22,668	4,601
1940	18,449	2,416
1941	9,938	1,500
1942	2,425	108

Source: Lesser, Jeffrey H. Welcoming the Undesirables: Brazil and the Jewish Question *(Berkeley: University of California Press, 1995), 18.*

Though restrictive, quite frequently, policies changed from one extreme to the other and almost twenty-five thousand European Jews immigrated to Brazil between Hitler's rise to power in Germany in 1933, until the end of World War II in 1945. Most Brazilian states saw an increase in their Jewish population. The Jewish population of Brazil from 1940 to 1950 was as follows:

States with Largest Jewish Populations	**1940**	**1950**
São Paulo	20,379	26,443
Rio de Janeiro	1,920	2,209
Federal District	19,473	25,222
Rio Grande do Sul	6,619	8,048
Bahia	955	1,076
Paraná	1,033	1,340
Minas Gerais	1,431	1,528
Total Jewish Population of Brazil	**55,666**	**69,957**

Source: Lesser, Jeffrey H. Welcoming the Undesirables: Brazil and the Jewish Question *(Berkeley: University of California Press, 1995), 179.*

Despite the ever-occurring shifts in political policies and perceptions, the Jewish population increased by about fifteen thousand from 1940 to 1950 in major states. Soon thereafter, the twenty-one-year military dictatorship (1964-1985) posed new challenges for the small Jewish population in Brazil, creating fear of possible persecution or worse, especially among survivors. The authoritarian regime never provided the expected protection for minority groups, and political violence against dissenters led many Jews to relocate to Israel. From 1948 to 1977 about sixty-three hundred Brazilian Jews emigrated. For many who had found refuge in Brazil, this period proved to be one of horror and uncertainty.

With the number of Displaced Persons (DP) arriving in Brazil soon after liberation, from 1946-1949, a Jewish literature and Holocaust fiction began to appear.

Year	Total DP	São Paulo
1947	3,726	2,540
1948	6,004	3,726
1949	13,117	4,813
Total	**22,847**	**11,079**

Source: Tucci Caneiro, Maria Luiza. Cidadão do Mundo. *São Paulo: FAPESP, Editora Perspectiva, 2010), 404.*

I. Emergence of Holocaust Memoirs

The Emergence of Brazilian Jewish Literature can be divided into three categories: that of the (1) immigrant novel which includes books such as Frida Alexandr's *Filipson,* that chronicle the stories of immigrants who settled in the colonies and their experiences in their new Brazilian home. A small list of immigrant novels includes: Marcos Iolovitch's *Numa clara manhã de abril,*[4] Samuel Rawlet's *Contos do imigrante,*[5] Frida Alexandr's *Filipson: memórias da primeira colônia judaica no Rio Grande do Sul,*[6] Adão Voloch's *Um gaúcho a pé,*[7] Elisa Lispector's *No exílio,*[8] Alberto Dines's *Posso?,*[9] Moacyr Scliar's *A guerra no Bom Fim,*[10] and *Centauro no Jardim,*[11] and Sara Riwnka Erlich, *No tempo das acácias.*[12] The horrors of World War II and stories of the Holocaust sparked the literary curiosity of Jewish writers, usually first-generation Brazilian born, to write (2) Holocaust fiction. This category usually written by non-survivors includes books such as: Jacó Guinsburg's *O Retrato,*[13] Bóris Fausto's *Negócios e ócios: histórias da imigração,*[14] Esther Largman's *Jovens polacas,*[15] Roney Cytrynowicz's *A vida secreta dos relógios e outras histórias,*[16] Bernardo Ajzenberg's *Goldstein & Camargo,*[17] Samuel Reibscheid's *Breve Fantasia,*[18] and Cintia Moscovich's *Duas iguais: manual de amores e equívocos assemelhados.*[19]

The most recent emerging category is (3) Holocaust memoirs, written by survivors as early as the1950s, though these are mostly manuscripts that have been kept in private collections[20] by the survivors such as, Käte Kaphan's *Das kleine Judenmädchen*, Hertha Spier's *Das Leben in Auschwitz und Bergen-Belsen*, Eva Hirschberg's *Als die Männer im Lager waren,* Ilza Czapska's *Unser Weg von Obra nach Brasilien*, Trudi Landau, *My Life Story* (1990), Alice Brill Czapski, *Memories from 1939-1945*

(1991), Annelise Strauss, *A Story of My Life* (1991), and Renée-Marie Croose Parry, *Escape, Hope, and Disillusionment* (1992). Holocaust memoirs that have been published since 2000, include: Aleksander Laks' *O sobrevivente: Memórias de um brasileiro que escapou de Auschwitz* (The survivor: Memories of a Brazilian who escaped from Auschwitz),[21] Michel Kleinsinger's *Nas asas da esperança* (On the wings of hope),[22] Samuel Rozenberg's *Codinome, Paul Allain: memórias de um sobrevivente do Holocausto* (Codename: Paul Allain: Memories of a Holocaust survivor),[23] Arie Yaari's *O leão da montanha: dos campos da morte aos Campos do Jordão* (The mountain lion: from the death camps to Campos do Jordão),[24] Henry Katina's *Passagem para a liberdade: relato de um sobrevivente do Holocausto* (The pathway to freedom: an account by a Holocaust survivor),[25] and Sabina Kustin's *A vida e a luta de uma sobrevivente do Holocausto* (The life and struggles of a Holocaust survivor).[26]

The most recently published memoirs share three key striking characteristics, whereby survivors confront the Brazilian population's lack of knowledge about the Shoah directly. First, the survivors provide a basic history lesson about World War II, the Holocaust, either as a chronological table of events, or in the introduction, in order to teach the reader about the Shoah, as well as Jewish customs and traditions; Second, the survivor proceeds to tell his/her story, the family life in years prior to war, the war years and the experiences either in hiding or concentration camps, and life afterwards; Thirdly, in a concluding chapter or epilogue, the survivor explains why it matters that he/she survived to tell this story, and what the reader should proceed to do (remember it, act to change the world). A few examples will illustrate these features: Laks tells the reader the historical facts, dates, alongside his personal narrative; he includes close analysis of the Nazi regime, circumstances he faced and his miserable life in concentration and extermination camps; a very clear and loud criticism towards intolerance can be found throughout. Kleinsinger sets the Holocaust as the climax of historical persecution of the Jewish people. He provides the historical context of Polish anti-Semitism and explanations of Jewish customs and traditions. Rozenberg provides a detailed history of the rise and fall of Nazism and an historical account of anti-Semitism in Belgium. Yaari not only provides the historical context of the Holocaust, but also the history of the Jewish people since Ancient Rome; he decries existing intolerance and its acceptance by the general public. He strongly states that readers must speak out against injustice and violence of any kind. Katina's memoir contains chapters devoted to the historical context of Auschwitz, Bergen-Belsen, and other camps. He also gives detailed explanations about Judaism and his family traditions. Lastly, Kustin writes a historical context of Jewish life in Poland and the rise of Nazism. She states that her goal of writing her memoir is to protest against current political degradation, social injustice, and genocide.

In a majority of the memoirs, one can find underlying themes of fear and premonition of a possible repetition of the Holocaust, especially because these survivors not only experienced the Vargas Era and later the Military Dictatorship (1964–1985), but have also faced the daily increase of violence and crime in the urban cities of the country. Hence these survivors share their testimonies with an intense responsibility to share the past, as a strong effort to connect their narratives of memory to the present acts of violence in Brazil, and the rise of Holocaust denial around the world.

According to a scholar at the renowned University of Campinas, Dr. Marcio Seligmann-Silva, survivors' motives for writing iinclude 1) affirmation of the need to narrate this Event; the justification for this gesture is expressed in the need to ease the memory of a horrific past; 2) a debt in memory to those murdered; 3) an act of denunciation about the current world situation; 4) a legacy for future generations; and 5) a humanitarian act, the testimony serving as a warning.[27]

The burden which befalls these survivors is more than one of *having to tell the story*, as is commonly expressed by survivors in other memoirs who immigrated elsewhere, but rather as a responsibility they must fulfill to educate a population that barely knows about the Event; hence their testimony is presented as a source of history and memory at the same time. For example, after accomplishing his goal of setting his memories on paper, Henry Katina begins the last chapter of his memoir with the following words, "More than sixty years have passed since the war ended, yet not a day goes by without me remembering the tragic past. [...] What torments me the most is to remember my three brothers who perished so young, and naturally, to remember the tragic end that met my parents.

[...] I always ask: Where was Divine Justice? Where was God? Where were men?"[28]

Sabina Kustin takes these questions posed by Henry Katina a step further: "Has the world forgotten the biggest catastrophe Humanity every experienced? [...] Are we born to see such violent massacres? [...] Why has the world not woken up to stop the destruction of Humanity?"[29] As a protest against degradation of political rhetoric, injustice, and genocide, Kustin begins her narrative stating, "I was born an adult. I didn't have a childhood and I don't think I was ever a child."[30] Born in 1928, in Lodz, she was hidden by a Polish priest in the basement of a Catholic church along with other Jewish children for two years, while her entire family was first confined to the Lodz Ghetto and later taken to Auschwitz and Treblinka, where all of them were murdered. She was discovered, imprisoned and taken to Bergen-Belsen, from where she was liberated in 1945. Towards the end of her narrative, the memoir carries a conversational tone where Kustin confronts the reader in direct questions, which in turn makes the reader accountable for future actions and treatment of others,

> I know that the youth and majority of the Brazilian population don't understand the significance of the Holocaust. [...] It is difficult [for them] to imagine people, some still alive, being burned in crematorium, men, women, elderly, children killed in gas chambers [...] I write not only to remember facts but also to cry out to stop other horrors from happening [...] I hope that whoever reads this book understands the fight of the human being and becomes conscious of the value of life. I propose a path for the right to live and for people to learn how to become a human being.[31]

Similarly, Arie Yaari also uses a direct voice and instructs the reader to treat others with respect and kindness, from the very introduction of his memoir, where he states that the principal message of this book it to, "alert humanity of the existing intolerance and its acceptance by the general population."[32] Yaari, born in 1922 in Katowice, tells the reader that, just as one ducks before a threatening gesture because s/he once felt the pain of the blow, the human soul also ducks after having suffered so much. Having survived four concentration camps, forced death marches, and living in hiding, Yaari expresses his frustration in the afterword of his memoir, "I would like to express my revolt against the world's governments who have learned nothing with the Holocaust. We must not keep silence; we must protest with the resources available to us. My scream is like a drop of water."[33] By this he alludes to a popular Brazilian children's book, *Fiz o que pude* (I did what I could),[34] which tells the tale of a burning forest and of the little bird who, when the forest was catching on fire, filled his tiny beak with water and flying over the burning forest dropped drops of water. The other animals, who were standing afar, seeing this, scorned him saying, 'You fool, do you think your few drops of water will extinguish the fire?' and the small bird answered, 'I may not be able to extinguish the fire, but I did what I could. What about you, what did you do?' The same way, Yaari compels the reader to always do his/her part, to speak about the Holocaust to others, and to bring it to the forefront of conversation. Michel Kleinsinger also states that the purpose for his writing is to testify to the world, as a promise to bring people together, to show them that they must love rather than hate one another, despite their different nationalities and beliefs: "Love builds. Hatred destroys."[35]

Alexander Laks' memoir uses poetic language as a medium to re-create his memory. The fear and premonition of the reoccurrence of the Holocaust appears from the beginning, when he states that that which he experienced in his blood, bones, skin, nerves, and in each breath of life could have happened and could still happen to anyone. Writing from a premise of promise, Laks' testimonial account arises out of a promise he made to his father: "If you survive," his father Yaakov commanded him, "tell everything that happened to us. Always tell, even if people don't believe you."[36] The promise he made to his father, to be a living testimony unto others, is what he believes kept him alive. A promise to tell what happened is expressed in the other aforementioned Brazilian memoirs as well. However, Laks' memoir is quite peculiar in its unique, poetic nature. He begins the memoir with a Table of Contents, where he carefully arranged the chapter titles in a sequence that reads as a spine-chilling 12-line poem:[37]

In this way, he packages the whole book within a poetic vessel. Laks uses poetry as the means through which one can aim to restore the distance between word and meaning, as a way of restoring memory. Not only the structural layout but also the words that make up the titles, teach the reader how to approach the chapters and they give a preview of how to read the narrative. It is important to note that even though the message of the Table of Contents is one of no escape (implying that the only way out from the Lager was through the chimney), the eleventh chapter, gives a possibility of escape with the clear commands that the survivor must go west. The twelfth chapter gives the final and most important commandment, "Go to the West. Perhaps you will find more Jews." The need to find more Jews is imperative to the survivor's survival. This sentiment is shared by the others who immigrated to Brazil and who were able to build a new life surrounded by the Jewish communities in São Paulo, Rio de Janeiro, Paraná, and Rio Grande do Sul.

II. Recent past, current situation:

Following World War II, Brazil saw many new developments. In 1951, the *Confederação Israelita do Brasil* (CONIB), (Israeli Confederation of Brazil) was founded as the central body to represent 12 states of Brazil.

Still today CONIB serves as an umbrella organization for more than two hundred associations that promote Jewish education, culture, charity, and Zionist activity. When major Jewish immigration to Brazil happened in 1956, as a result of the Suez Crisis and the Russian invasion in Hungary, the Jewish populations in Brazil had already moved into middle-class status, many becoming members of national organizations and political offices. Cultural centers such as the *Centro da Cultura Judaica* in São Paulo, founded in 1964 by Leon Feffer, offer free events including music, theater, cinema, literature, art, photography, dance, and education. The last few decades have marked many firsts for the small, but thriving Brazilian Jewish community. In 1994, Jaime Lerner was elected head of the state of Paraná, becoming Brazil's first Jewish governor. In 1998, Dr. Eva Alterman Bay, a distinguished professor, became the first Jewish woman to serve in Brazil's Senate. Many Jews have also served in the country's Cabinet. In 2001, the Safra family, founders of the banking and investment empire Safra Group, reopened the old Kahal Zur Israel synagogue, closed since 1657, as a historical museum, and it now stands as the oldest synagogue in the Americas. In 2002, began the Interdisciplinary Journey to Teach the History of the Holocaust *Jornadas Interdisciplinar sobre o Ensino da História do Holocausto,* organized by B'nai B'rith do Brasil, LEER, Memorial da América Latina, and Municipal and State Secretaries of Education. These journeys take place in various states, with large numbers of teachers in attendance, to provide didactical material for them. New cultural centers have appeared as well, the *Midrash Centro Cultural* was inaugurated in August 2009, in Rio. This cultural center has been remarkable in providing courses, lectures, on history, philosophy, arts, literature, etc.

Jewish immigration has been recognized as of fundamental significance to Brazil and its culture. On 16 December 2009, the Brazilian Congress passed a law instituting March 18 as the official Jewish Immigration Day to "commemorate the contribution of the Jewish people in the foundation of Brazilian culture."[38] Aside from this recognition, a new desire to teach about the Holocaust enabled an unprecedented law to come about and in October of 2010, the city of Porto Alegre passed a law, the first of its kind, to mandate Holocaust education in all public schools' curricula. The measure affects an estimated 60,000 students in 96 schools. This measure comes as a reaction to recent neo-Nazi incidents, and as an attempt to build a more peaceful society that combats violence and intolerance. Also importantly, the first Holocaust Museum of Brazil was inaugurated in the city of Curitiba, Paraná in February 2012. To date it has been visited by more than 30,000 students, offered open free classes of 14-weeks, and has many initiatives in place to further education about the Holocaust in Brazil.

In 2012, through the partnership between the *Laboratório de Estudos sobre Etnicidade, Racismo e Discrimação (LEER)* at the University of São Paulo (USP) and B'nai B'rith do Brasil a brand new university research institute called the *Instituto Shoah de Direitos Humanos* opened, housing archives of over 12,000 documents, which were gathered by researches at LEER in the last few years from survivors. There are many projects, including the current "From Stateless to Brazilian Citizen: the Trajectories of the Lives of Jewish Refugees of Nazifascism, 1933-1945" (*De Apátriada à Cidadão Brasileiro: Trajetórias de Vida dos Judeus Refugiados do Nazifascismo, 1933-1960)* to identify the survivors who are still alive in Brazil. There are also plans in place for building a Holocaust museum in São Paulo.

Lastly, a new book was released in January called *Ensinando Sobre o Holocausto na Escola* (Teaching about the Holocaust in school)[39] to be used by the new programs of Holocaust education throughout the country. The book came about due to the need to create a guideline with instructions on how to tackle the theme of Holocaust and the weight that it holds in history. As one of the authors stated, "Teaching history is not only to teach about content. It is much more than that. Teachers must teach concepts, attitudes, and behaviors. Specifically in the case of the Holocaust, one must teach students about the effects of intolerance." He continues, "The rationality that created and made the existence of the Holocaust possible has not disappeared. It still exists in our modern time. The practice of hatred towards others has not disappeared, it has only changed forms."[40] Much like the urgency manifested in the most recently published memoirs, this new book aims to bring the topic of the Holocaust to the forefront in Brazilian schools with the hope of not only educating a new generation and the population at large, but also to bring awareness of the very nature of hatred that still afflicts and threatens the peace of our world today.

With the many new developments in the last decade, there is a strong indication that memoirs such as the ones introduced in this paper might take center stage in cultural and literary discourse within Brazilian schools, with memoirs such as the ones that urge action on the part of the reader. The increasing surge of Holocaust memoirs with strong messages of responsibility to the younger generation will become part of this new genre of writing, which is quickly developing. This is extremely significant and innovative in a country that is growing in terms of holding a strong body of literary works that reflects the most horrific, significant event of the 20th century. The presence of the Holocaust may have been extremely marginal in Brazilian cultural discourse and literature up to now, but the moment is ripe for this new phenomenon. The future of 21st century Holocaust studies seems promising for the continuation of education about the event, its integration into the larger context of Brazilian literature, and for the overall enhancement of Jewish culture in Brazil.

Notes

1. Marcio Seligmann-Silva, "Literatura da Shoah no Brasil," *Arquivo Maaravi: Revista Digital de Estudos Judaicos da UFMG*, v.1, n.1 (2007.)

2. Jeff Lesser, *Welcoming the Undesirables: Brazil and the Jewish Question (*Berkeley: University of California Press, 1995).

3. Maria Luiza Tucci Carneiro, *Cidadão do mundo: o Brasil diante do holocaust e dos judeus refugiados do nazifascismo (1933-1945)* (São Paulo: FAPESP, Perspectiva, 2010).

4. Marcos Iolovitch, *Numa clara manhã de abril* (Porto Alegre: Livraria do Globo, 1940).

5. Samuel Rawlet, *Contos do Imigrante* (Rio de Janeiro: Livraria José Olympio, 1956).

6. Frida Alexandr, *Filipson: memórias da primeira colônia judaica no Rio Grande do Sul* (São Paulo: Fulgor, 1967).

7. Adão Voloch, *Um gaúcho a pé* (Rio de Janeiro: Editora Novos Rumos, 1967).

8. Elisa Lispector, *No Exílio* (Brasília: Editora de Brasília, 1971).

9. Alberto Dines, *Posso?* (Rio de Janeiro: Sabiá, 1972).

10. Moacyr Scliar, *A Guerra no Bom Fim* (Rio de Janeiro: Editora Expressão e Cultura, 1972) and Centauro no Jardim (Rio de Janeiro: Editora Nova Fronteira, 1980).

11. Moacyr Scliar, *Centauro no Jardim* (Rio de Janeiro: Editora Nova Fronteira, 1980).

12. Sara Riwnka Erlich, *No tempo das acácias* (Rio de Janeiro: Civilização Brasileira, 1978).

13. Jacó Guinsburg, *O Retrato* (São Paulo: Ateliê Editorial, 1948).

14. Bóris Fausto, *Negócios e ócio: histórias da imigração* (São Paulo: Companhia das Letras, 1997).

15. Esther Largman, *Jovens polacas* (Rio de Janeiro: Editora Rosa dos Tempos, 1993.)

16. Roney Cytrynowicz, *A vida secreta dos relógios e outras histórias* (São Paulo: Scritta, 1994).

17. Bernardo Ajzenberg, *Goldstein & Camargo* (Rio de Janeiro: Imago, 1994).

18. Samuel Reibscheid, *Breve fantasia* (São Paulo: Scritta, 1995).

19. Cintia Moscovich, *Duas iguais: manual de amores e equívocos assemelhados* (Porto Alegre, L&PM Editores, 1998).

20. Many of these unpublished works later appeared, in part or whole, in Katherine Morris's *Odyssey of exile: Jewish women flee the Nazis for Brazil* (Detroit: Wayne State University Press, 1996).

21. Aleksander Laks, Tova Sender, *O Sobrevivente: Memórias de um brasileiro que escapou de Auschwitz.* (Rio de Janeiro: Editora Record, 2000).

22. Michel Kleinsinger, *Nas Asas da Esperança.* (São Paulo: Editora Vida & Consciencia, 2000).

23. Samuel Rozenberg, *Codinome, Paul Allain: memórias de um sobrevivente do Holocausto* (Rio de Janeiro: Garamond, 2004).

24. Yaari, Arie. *O Leão da Montanha: Dos Campos de Concentração as Campos do Jordão.* São Paulo: Editora ProLíbera, 2009.

25. Katina, Henry. *Passagem Para a Liberdade: Relato de um Sobrevivente do Holocausto.* São Paulo: Geração Editorial, 2009.

26. Kustin, Sabina. *A vida e a luta de Uma Sobrevivente do Holocausto*. São Paulo: Editora Humanitas, 2012.

27. Marcio Seligmann-Silva, "Literatura da Shoah no Brasil," *Arquivo Maaravi: Revista Digital de Estudos Judaicos da UFMG*, v.1, n.1 (2007).

28. Katina, Henry. *Passagem para a liberdade: relato de um sobrevivente do Holocausto* (São Paulo: Geração Editorial, 2009) 193. "Passaram-se mais de sessenta anos desde que a guerra acabou, mas não há nenhum dia que eu não me lembre do trágico passado. [...] O que mais me atormenta é a lembrança dos meus três irmãos que

faleceram tão jovens e, naturalmente, a lembrança do trágico fim que meus pais tiveram. [...] Pergunto-me sempre: Onde estava a Justiça Divina? Onde estava Deus? Onde estavam os homens?"

29. Ibid., 112. "Será que o mundo se esqueceu da maior catástrofe que a Humanidade já presenciou? [...] Será que nascemos para presenciar massacres tão violentos? [...] Por que o mundo não acorda para evitar a destruição da Humanidade?"

30. Ibid., 19. "Nasci já adulta. Não tive infância e penso que nunca fui criança."

31. Ibid., 112, 114. "Eu sei que a juventude e a maioria do povo brasileiro não entendem o significado do Holocausto [...]É difícil imaginar pessoas queimadas, algumas delas vivas, nos crematórios, mortas em câmaras de gás, homens, mulheres, idosos, crianças [...] Escrevo não só para relembrar fatos [...] Espero que quem ler este livro compreenda a luta do ser humano e se concientize do valor da vida. Proponho uma frente única pelo direito de viver e aprender a se tornar um ser humano."

32. Yaari, Arie. *O leão da montanha: dos campos de concentração as Campos do Jordão.* (São Paulo: Editora ProLíbera, 2009), 30. "alertar a humanidade para a intolerância existente e a sua aceitação pela população em geral."

33. Ibid., 319. "Quero expressar minha revolta contra os governos mundiais que, a meu ver, nada aprenderam com o Holocausto. Não devemos nos calar; devemos protestar com os meios que temos à nossa disposição. Meu grito é como uma gota d'água."

34. Lucília Junqueira de Almeida Prado, *Fiz o que pude* (São Paulo, Editora Moderna: 1992).

35. Michel Kleinsinger. *Nas asas da esperança* (São Paulo: Editora Vida & Consciencia, 2000), 9. "O amor constrói. O ódio destrói."

36. Aleksander Laks, Tova Sender. *O Sobrevivente: Memórias de um brasileiro que escapou de Auschwitz* (Rio de Janeiro: Editora Record, 2000), 126. "Se você sobreviver, conte tudo o que aconteceu conosco. Conte sempre, ainda que não acreditem."

37. Ibid., 9. "You.../ You are.../ You are in.../ You are in Auschwitz.../ You are in Auschwitz. From here.../ You are in Auschwitz. From here you.../ You are in Auschwitz. From here you only.../ You are in Auschwitz. From here you only leave.../ You are in Auschwitz. From here you only leave through.../ You are in Auschwitz. From here you only leave through the chimney./ Go to the West./ Go to the West. Perhaps you will find more Jews."

38. Planalto. Lei Nº 12.124, de 16 de Dezembro de 2009 (Presidência da República, Casa Civil: Subchefia para Assuntos Jurídicos: Brasília, 2009).

39. Milton Mullet Pereira, Ilton Gitz. *Ensinando sobre o Holocausto na escola* (Porto Alegre: Penso, 2014).

40. Milton Mullet Pereira, Ilton Gitz. *Ensinando sobre o Holocausto na escola* (Porto Alegre: Penso, 2014).

CHAPTER 17

A Course on "The Holocaust and Music" at Boston University: Ideas, Goals, Course Outline, and Student Response

LUDMILLA LEIBMAN

Boston University students perform the final chorus from Brundibar as part of the course, "The Holocaust and Music"

At a certain point in my doctoral study at Boston University I faced the necessity of choosing a topic for my dissertation. My advisor, Dr. Mary-Ann Norton, suggested writing about Soviet women musicologists, but I had another idea which Dr. Norton accepted after she heard my reasons.

I wanted to write about musical compositions which reflected on the tragedy of the Holocaust and to explore the reasons why the composers of such compositions were drawn to the theme. It was important for me personally that the subject of my dissertation written in America was connected to my being a Jew, having been subjected to anti-Semitism in Russia and subsequently electing to emigrate from my native land.

In the life of many emigrants, I am sure, as in my life, one reaches a point after which there is no turning back and the decision to leave your country becomes final. After that, everything else pales in importance, including leaving the city which you love, the educational institution where you have studied, friends whom you might never see again, and the cemetery where your grandparents were buried. I recall events which happened at the end of the 1980s and the beginning of the 90s when, in Leningrad's Ruminatsevsky Park, near the Art Academy, weekly meetings of the nationalistic neo-fascist society "Pamyat" ("Memory") frightened me with the zeal of its participants with their swastikas on their arm-bands, and the obvious inertia and indifference of the Soviet militia. Later we learned in the Leningard (St. Petersburg) State Rimsky-Korsakov Conservatory, where I studied as an undergraduate and graduate student and later taught, one of the members of the administration (the equal of a Vice-President in American higher educational administration) was, indeed, a member of the "Pamyat" Society. I was shocked but not surprised to see displayed, right above the Conservatory's Entrance No. 5, a poster the exact text of which I don't recall but its meaning I will never forget: "Russian students deserve to have Russian teachers (not Jewish ones)."

For me, therefore, choosing the topic for my dissertation was a means of coming to terms with my decision to emigrate and to pay tribute to those members of my family—on both my Father's and Mother's side—who were killed by the German invaders in 1941 in Belorussian shtetls (villages). The subject of my dissertation, "Teaching the Holocaust Through Music," was intended to address a theoretical analysis of educational strategies as well as to develop practical pedagogical methods. Shortly after I defended my dissertation (in 1999), I developed a course based on the dissertation and began teaching it at Boston University, in addition to teaching music theory. As far as I can determine, when I started teaching the course in 2001, it was the first such course offered in American higher education. I have to thank many people at Boston University for supporting this course, among whom were Dr. Mary-Ann Norton, Dr. Steven Katz, Dr. Jeremy Yudkin, Rabbi Joseph Polak, and Dr. John Silber.

In 2001 the course listed under the title "The Holocaust and Music CFA MU 425/CAS RN 338" was offered in both the College of Fine Arts and the College of Arts and Sciences, and it proved fascinating to teach for several reasons. First of all, unlike any of the music theory courses that I had taught in the past, both in the St. Petersburg State Rimsky-Korsakov Conservatory and at Boston University, this course was listed as an elective course, which meant that my teaching of the course depended on how many students enrolled in it. I was pleasantly surprised that it turned out that I did not have to worry because every semester the number of students taking the class was well over the administration's minimum requirement.

A student's choosing of a "non-required" course depends largely on the whim of student interest, and there is very little a teacher can do to influence it. Students usually talk among themselves and advise each other to take or not to take this or that course. This was 2001 when the internet and texting was only beginning to gain ground on word of mouth over coffee in the cafeteria. My music theory students did manage to post some warning comments that "Professor Leibman is very strict and her students have to study hard to get good grades"—but this didn't hinder those who were interested in the subject.

Teaching a new course of this kind offered by two different university colleges meant that it was open to students of any major to enroll—those who were majoring in music already having taken music theory classes with me and those who hadn't taken any music classes, did not play a musical instrument, and had no idea what an F sharp is. In 2001 I came into the classroom where, for the first time in my pedagogical practice, I faced future professional musicians as well as future engineers, medical doctors, lawyers—you name it—and I needed to find ways to create a methodology which would accommodate assignments equally engaging and challenging for many different perspectives.

A team presentation

The course consisted of three sections: 1. History of the *Kulturbund* in Germany, 1933-1941; 2. Musical events which took place in the ghettos and concentration camps in Europe during WWII, 1939-1945; and 3. Compositions written after the Holocaust as musical memorials to the tragedy, 1947-1988.

My goal as teacher was to maximally promote active involvement of my students and not allow them to be passive listeners and mindlessly taking notes; I tried to create assignments which would inspire their creativity. Music major students participated in presenting musical compositions of serious genres. They learned and performed classical compositions to illustrate their presentations about the *Judischer Kulturbund* (an extraordinary arts organization made up of Jewish singers, dancers, musicians and actors who had been fired from their places of work in 1933 when Hitler came to power and existed in Nazi Germany until 1941). Because during the years of *Kulturbund*'s existence this organization grew substantially and at one point had about 50 branches in different German cities, my students could choose from hundreds of compositions which were, at one point or another, in the repertoire of the *Kulturbund*'s concerts. Years later, in 2009, during the Educational Bridge Project's 15th Russian-American festival, "Days of American Culture in Russia," my former student Venus Loung (who was majoring in business administration) presented a program, "*Kulturbund* as a means of cultural survival in Nazi Germany," in St. Petersburg. Next year I invited another speaker on the same subject to come with us to Russia as part of the Educational Bridge Project's 17th festival. This was Martin Goldsmith from Washington, DC, a famous radio personality and author of the book about his mother, a violist, and father, a flutist, who were connected with that organization, "*The Inextinguishable Symphony: A True Story of Music and Love in Nazi Germany.*" In the spring of 2010, in one of the famous Russian palaces in the historical center of St. Petersburg, Martin Goldsmith gave a pre-concert talk based on his book which was followed by the Russian musicians' performances of musical compositions which had been played by his parents during their *Kulturbund* years.

Martin Goldsmith speaks about Kulturbund at the Russian Institute of Art History in St. Petersburg, May 20, 2010

Students from other Boston University colleges who did not have musical training (or music education, or a musical background), learned and performed songs from Polish and Belorussian ghettos, as well as fragments from Westerbork and Terezin cabaret. I will never forget the Korean student who sang a song from the Lodz cabaret in Yiddish.

The Holocaust in Music Course, Spring 2003
Guest—Edgar Krasa

Every year "The Holocaust and Music" students staged the children's opera "Brundibar" by Hans Krasa. Everyone participated, music majors or not; those who could read music helped those who could not, and I accompanied on the piano. Such performances would be preceded by a student's talk on the history of this opera and included the fascinating story of how I met one of "Brundibar's" original performers, Michael Gruenbaum, who as a child in Terezin sang in the chorus in 1941.

I related to my students having given a talk at Brandeis University on musical activities in Terezin during WWII. One of the photos which I included in the presentation showed the whole cast of children singing the final chorus. While I was giving my comments about the photo, one of the audience members, unknown to me, stood up, came to the screen, pointed to the boy in the picture on the left and said, "This is I." Can you imagine what effect this had on my audience and me? I felt goose bumps and could not believe what I was witnessing. That was the beginning of my friendship with Misha—Michael Gruenbaum—who in 2010 celebrated his 80th year and now lives in Boston.

A class rehearsal of "Brundibar"—the backdrop made by one of the students replicates the original one from Terezin

Those who wanted to try themselves as dramatic actors participated in the annual staging of the "Master-class," a play by the British playwright David Pownall. In this play the author simulates a conversation among four people one night at the Kremlin headquarters of the General Secretary Joseph Stalin. There, upon Stalin's order, one of the major figures of the Soviet government and an author of the concept of "social realism," Andrei Zhdanov, invites two leading Soviet composers, Sergei Prokofiev and Dmitri Shostakovich, for a "conversation." The four discuss matters of extreme importance: Which goals and objectives should be identified by the composers of a socialist country as most important? What is the main mission of a Soviet composers' work? Does a Soviet composer realize that he bears responsibility for each piece he writes? And if not, does he, a Soviet composer, understand the consequences of his irresponsibility? Even though Pownall's play is the product of artistic imagination and such a scene with Stalin, Zhdanov, Prokofiev, and Shostakovich never took place, the British playwright definitely knew about the infamous article, "Muddle Instead of Music" published in *Pravda* in 1936 which condemned both composers (and some others) with the deadly sin of "formalism." Twelve years later, in 1948, Shostakovich, along with many other composers, was again denounced for formalism in the Zhdanov decree.

"Master Class" by David Pownall: students as Zhdanov, Stalin (with pipe) Prokofiev (played by a female student) and Shostakovich; I (on the right) was directing the play

The main reason for introducing my students to Shostakovich and involving them in acting the scenes from Pownall's "Master Class" was to help them to understand the concept of the good fortune of artistic freedom which was—in my view—important for their appreciation and understanding of why Dmitri Shostakovich, a non-Jewish composer, wrote music on Jewish themes and in particular, on the theme of the Holocaust. The famous Shostakovich's symphony, "Babi Yar," written in 1962 and based on a poem by Yevgeny Yevtushenko, was one of the central compositions in the third and last segment of the course when we studied music written after the Holocaust and dedicated to the memorialization of the tragedy.

Among the many compositions written as musical memorials to the Shoah, I selected three as the most distinguished: "A Survivor from Warsaw" by Arnold Schoenberg (1947), "Babi Yar" by Dmitri Shostakovich (1962), and "Different Trains" by Steve Reich (1988). I was showing the students how these compositions, written at different times by composers of different nationalities and backgrounds, represent three important kinds of connections existing between the creative author and the subject of his composition: 1) direct connection: a Jewish composer writing about the tragedy of Jewish people (Schoenberg);

2) connection by association: a non-Jewish composer identifying himself with Holocaust victims (Shostakovich); and 3) imagined connection: a Jewish composer contemplating the Holocaust from the "what if I had been there" point of view (Reich).

With the students we examined the impact these three compositions made on listeners in the concert halls, and I shared with them my personal experiences as a Professor in the departments of Music Theory and Judaic Studies at Boston University. I contrasted my students' initial reactions to these three musical compositions with their reactions after the works were put into historic context and analyzed theoretically. In addition, we discussed several cases in which students felt compelled to turn to their own personal family histories only to discover, to their amazement, tragic episodes in their grandparents' past which had never before been related to them.

The last piece in the course was "Different Trains," written in 1988 by the living American composer Steve Reich. Reich was born in 1936 in America and spent lots of time during his childhood traveling by train from one of his divorced parents in New York to another in Los Angeles. "Different Trains" is about the trains Steve Reich did not take but he might have, had he, a Jew, been born in Europe. As a source of musical material for the "Different Trains" the composer used electronically transformed melodic lines of the voices of people telling stories about their experiences during WWII in occupied Europe. When my students studied "Different Trains," the main pedagogical strategy was to present this composition in historical context and to demonstrate how the 1988 composition corresponded with the compositions of the Terezin composers who traveled on one of those "different trains"—in fact, on a very particular train "Er" which left Terezin on October 16, 1944, and had among its 1,500 travelers the composers, Pavel Haas, Gideon Klein, Hans Krasa, and Viktor Ullmann, who spent their last years in Terezin, the infamous model concentration camp situated near Prague during WWII. While prisoners in Terezin were treated better than in other camps, the true picture of the camp's eerie existence is revealed upon studying the schedule of incoming and outgoing trains which were routinely bringing new prisoners to the camp from the West and taking others to the labor camps and extermination camps further to the East. According to this schedule, the four composers, Haas, Klein, Krasa, and Ullmann, along with 1,496 other prisoners were ordered to board the train identified by two letters, "Er," on October 16, 1944. Of 1,500 people on the "Er" train only 110 survived the war; the four composers were not among them. Three were gassed the next day in Auschwitz, and Gideon Klein, the youngest of the four, lived for a few months longer.

In his Terezin diary, "The Strange Passenger," which miraculously survived, Viktor Ullmann wrote, "... *by no means did we sit weeping on the banks of the waters of Babylon.*" The composer emphasized the importance of being active in the times of no hope and no future. My students came to understand that well.

Conclusion: From the Syllabus (Spring 2004)

During the course, which involves a lot of research and project work, students will listen to music, analyze it, give class presentations, participate in group discussions of the related readings, and perform the camp and ghetto songs. With the powerful theme of the Holocaust as the unifying factor, students will be drawn to appreciate a complex and widely varying language of the music of twentieth-century composers who represent different countries of origin, different musical styles and aesthetics, different life circumstances, and different degrees of involvement in Jewish politics.

Twenty Five Most Important Sources for the Students (Spring 2004)

Art, Music, and Education as Strategies for Survival: Theresienstadt 1941-45. Ed. With an introduction by A. Dutlinger.

Blokker, Roy and Dearling, Robert. *The Music of Dmitri Shostakovich: The Symphonies.* Cranbury: Associated University Press, 1979, pp. 133-137.

Crittenden, Camille. "Texts and Contexts of *A Survivor from Warsaw*, op. 46." Cross, Charlotte M. and Berman, Russell A. (eds.) *Political and Religious Ideas in the Works of Arnold Schoenberg.* New York: Garland, 2000. Chapter 9, pp. 231-258.

Fenelon, Faina. *Playing for Time.* New York: Atheneum, 1977.

Flam, Gila. *Singing for Survival. Songs of the Lodz Ghetto, 1940-45.* Urbana, IL: University of Illinois Press, 1992.

Goldsmith, Martin. *The Inextinguishable Symphony: The True Story of Love and Music in Nazi Germany.* New York: John Wiley & Sons, c2000.

Kalish, Shoshana with Meister, Barbara. *Yes, We Sang! Songs of the Ghettos and Concentration Camps.* New York: Harper & Row, 1985.

Karas, Joza. *Music in Terezin 1941-1945.* New York: Beaufort Books, 1985.

Kater, Michael H. *The Twisted Muse: Musicians and Their Music in the Third Reich.* New York: Oxford University Press, 1997.

Krizkova. Marie R. *We Are Children Just the Same.* "Vedem," the Secret Magazine by the Boys of Terezin. Aventinum, 1994.

Laks, Szymon. *Music of Another World.* Evanston: Northwestern University Press, 1989, pp. 36-42.

Levi, Erik. *Music in the Third Reich.* NY: St. Martin's Press, 1994.

Lieberman, David I. "Schoenberg Rewrites his Will: *A Survivor from Warsaw*, op. 46." Cross, Charlotte M. and Berman, Russell A. (eds.) *Political and Religious Ideas in Work of Arnold Schoenberg.* New York: Garland, 2000. Chapter 8, pp. 193-220.

Music and Nazism: Art Under Tyranny, 1933-1945. M. Kater and A. Riethmuller, ed. Laaber-Verlag, Laaber, 2003.

Newman, Richard and Kirtley, Karen. *Alma Rose. Vienna to Auschwitz.* Portland: Amadeus Press 2000.

Powitz, Stephen. "Musical Life in the Warsaw Ghetto." *Journal of Jewish Music and Liturgy,* vol. IV, 1981-1982/5741-5742, pp. 2-10.

Pownall, David. *Master Class.* (A Play) London: Faber & Faber, 1983.

Reich, Steve. *Writings About Music.* New York: New York University Press, 1974.

Ringer, Alexander R. *Arnold Schoenberg: The Composer as Jew.* Oxford: Clarendon Press, 1990.

Schoenberg, Arnold. "A Four-Point Program for Jewry." *Journal of the Arnold Schoenberg Institute* (March 1979) vol. III, no. 1, pp. 49-67.

Schwertfeger, Ruth. *Women of Theresienstad: Voices form a Concentration Camp.* New York, NY: Berg, 1989.

Stein, Leonard. "Schoenberg's Jewish Identity (A Chronology of Source Material)." *Journal of the Arnold Schoenberg Institute* (March 1979), vol. III, no. 1, pp. 3-10.

Strasser, Michael. "'A Survivor from Warsaw' as Personal Parable." *Music and Letters* (February 1995) 76, no. 1, pp. 52-64.

Szpilman, Wladyslaw. *The Pianist. The Extraordinary True Story of One Man's Survival in Warsaw, 1939-1945.* Translated by Anthea Bell. New York: Picador USA c1999.

We Are Here. Songs of the Holocaust. Compiled by Eleanor Mlotek and Malke Gottlieb. Foreword by Elie Wiesel. New York: Educational Department of the Workmen's Circle and Hippocrene Books, Inc. 1983.

Contributors

Mehnaz M. Afridi

Mehnaz Afridi is Assistant Professor of Religious Studies and Director of Holocaust, Genocide, and Interfaith Education Center at Manhattan College teaching a variety of courses on Islam, Judaism, world religions, genocide studies, women and religion, and Arab and Israeli Literature. She has written extensively on both Islam and the Holocaust; her forthcoming book is *Shoah through Muslim Eyes* (Academic Studies Press).

Michael Berenbaum

Michael Berenbaum is the Director of the Sigi Ziering Institute: Exploring the Ethical and Religious Implications of the Holocaust and a Professor of Jewish Studies at the American Jewish University. The author and editor of 20 books, he was Project Director overseeing the creation of the United States Holocaust Memorial Museum and the first Director of its Research Institute and later served as President and CEO of the Survivors of the Shoah Visual History Foundation, which took the testimony of 52,000 Holocaust survivors in 32 languages and 57 countries.

Richard Dekmejian

Richard Dekmejian is Professor of Political Science and Director of the USC Institute of Armenian Studies at the University of Southern California. His research interests include International/Comparative Politics, Comparative Genocides and Terrorism. He has authored five books and many articles on the subjects.

Karen Spiegal Franklin

Karen Spiegel Franklin is an exhibit researcher at the Museum of Jewish Heritage and director of the Lehman Family Rescue Activities Project. She is a vice-chair of the Memorial Museums Committee of the International Council of Museums and serves on the Advisory Board of the European Shoah Legacy Institute as a member of the Judaic and Jewish Cultural Property Working Group.

Sona Haroutyunian

Sona Haroutyunian is a professor of Armenian language and literature at the University of Venice, Italy and the Kazan Visiting Professor in Armenian Studies at California State University, Fresno. Author of four books and many scholarly papers, her current project is an encyclopedic compendium of Armenian Genocide memoirs and fiction published in the USA and the countries of the European Union.

Yitzchak Kerem

Yitzchak Kerem is an Historian and Researcher on Greek and Sephardic Jewry at Aristotle University, Thessaloniki, Greece, and The Hebrew University of Jerusalem. He is Founder and Director of the Institute of Hellenic-Jewish Relations, University of Denver, Denver, Colorado, and Editor of the monthly academic e-mail publication "Sefarad, the Sephardic Newsletter."

Richard Libowitz

Richard Libowitz is Associate Professor in the Intellectual Heritage Program at Temple University. He is the author/editor of a dozen books, primarily on Holocaust-related subjects. His most recent book, *Crowns, Crosses and Stars,* was published by Purdue University Press in 2013.

Ludmilla Liebman

Ludmilla Leibman is a pianist, musicologist, and lecturer. Prior to immigrating to the United States in 1991, she taught music theory at her alma mater, the Rimsky-Korsakov Conservatory (Saint Petersburg). She is a faculty member of the School of Music at Boston University. Dr. Leibman continues to lecture and publish in the United States and internationally on a wide variety of topics.

Marcia Sachs Littell

Marcia Sachs Littell is Emeritus Professor of Holocaust & Genocide Studies at Stockton University where she founded the Master of Arts Program in Holocaust & Genocide Studies. She serves on the Editorial Board of *PRISM,* a journal sponsored by the Azrieli Graduate School of Yeshiva University and on the Editorial Board of the *Journal of Ecumenical*

Studies. Among her books are, *Holocaust Education: A Resource Book for Educators & Professional Leaders and Women in the Holocaust: Responses, Insights and Perspectives.*

Harold Marcuse

Harold Marcuse is a professor of German history at the University of California, Santa Barbara. His monograph, *Legacies of Dachau: The Uses and Abuses of a Concentration Camp, 1933-2001,* was published by Cambridge University Press in 2001 and won the Hans Rosenberg Prize of the Conference Group for Central European History in 2003. He has published numerous articles on memorials and museums dedicated to the remembrance of events during the Nazi era.

David Patterson

David Patterson holds the Hillel Feinberg Chair in Holocaust Studies in the Ackerman Center for Holocaust Studies at the University of Texas at Dallas. A winner of the National Jewish Book Award and the Koret Jewish Book Award, he has published more than 30 books and 150 articles and book chapters. His most recent books include the forthcoming *Anti-Semitism and Its Metaphysical Origins* and *Genocide in Jewish Thought* (2012).

Rubina Peroomian

Rubina Peroomian is a Research Associate at UCLA. She has written extensively in the field of genocide studies, in both English and Armenian. Her most recent work is *The Armenian Genocide in Literature, Perceptions of Those Who Lived through the Years of Calamity* (2012).

Joan Peterson

Joan Peterson is a Professor of Education at Saint Mary's College of California where she teaches in the graduate Education Department and offers courses on the Holocaust to undergraduates. Recent publications include *Iterations of Babi Yar*, in the Journal of Ecumenical Studies and *Thoughts on the Teaching of the Holocaust.*

Diane Plotkin

Diane Plotkin a member of the faculty of Brookhaven College and also offers courses at the Dallas Memorial Center for Holocaust Studies and the University of North Texas. Her published works include *Sisters in Sorrow: Voices of Care in the Holocaust*, co-authored with Roger Ritvo, and many papers on a variety of aspects of the Holocaust.

Richard Rubenstein

Richard Rubenstein is President Emeritus, Distinguished Research Professor of Religion, University of Bridgeport; Lawton Distinguished Professor of Religion Emeritus, Florida State University. Author of many volumes, his text *After Auschwitz* remains a classic study in post-Shoah theology.

Shimon Samuels

Shimon Samuels is Director for International Relations, Simon Wiesenthal Center, Paris, France, and Honorary President of the Europe-Israel Forum. A voluminous writer, he travels and speaks throughout the world in defense of Jews and Judaism.

Harriet Sepinwall

Dr. Harriet Lipman Sepinwall is Professor of Holocaust Studies at the College of Saint Elizabeth (Morristown, New Jersey) and founding co-director of the College of Saint Elizabeth Holocaust Education Resource Center. She has focused on education to end prejudice, discrimination, bullying, anti-immigrant bias, and anti-Semitism, and to encourage interfaith dialogue and respect for diversity.

Sharon Steeley

Sharon Steeley, Executive Director of the Annual Scholars Conference, has been with the Conference since 2001. She earned her MBA degree from Saint Joseph's University and has been responsible for all financial, community relations, and operational matters.

Harriet Tamen

Harriet Tamen is a lawyer in private practice specializing in structuring and negotiating complex commercial, financial and trade transactions, including business deals with domestic start-up companies, domestic companies doing business abroad, and foreign companies entering the U.S. market. She was co-lead counsel in suits brought against French banks for their actions in freezing the accounts of Jews during World War II, and is lead counsel in Freund v. SNCF—the suit against the French railroad for deporting 75,000 Jews to the camps

Frances Titcombe

Frances Titcombe is the Conference Coordinator of the Annual Scholars' Conference. A Temple University graduate with a major in economics, she has been an invaluable asset to our conference team with her multi-tasking expertise and maintaining close contact with the participants.

Sarah Valente

Sarah Valente is pursuing a Ph.D. degree in Humanities at The University of Texas at Dallas under the supervision of Dr. Zsuzsanna Ozsvath, Leah and Paul Lewis Chair in Holocaust Studies. She is a recipient of the Belofsky Fellowship from the Ackerman Center for Holocaust Studies at UT Dallas. Her research focus includes Holocaust literature, the emergence of Holocaust Studies in 21st century Brazil, the history of Portuguese Jews expelled from Portugal and found in Brazil at its inception in 1500, and their descendants.

Special Mention

In keeping with our commitment to nurture and encourage "a succeeding generation," we regret that page limitations in this volume did not permit us to include papers from all the graduate students and rising young scholars who attended the 44th Annual Conference and delivered papers. We have listed them, with their institutional affiliations and the titles of their presentations:

Diane Bannon, Stockton University & Thomas Jefferson Hospital
Linking the Generations: Holocaust Education & Obligations Perspectives of 2nd and 3rd Generations

Lillian Hussong, Stockton University
The Ethics of Armenian Genocide Denial in Academia

Jeffrey Levine, Stockton University
Served as Conference Assistant and Session Chair

Ida Malloy, Stockton University & Rescue Mission of Trenton
Genocide and Trauma: How Young Adult Literature Examines the Memories of Survivors

Arda Melkonian, University of California, Los Angeles
Armenian Evangelical Clergy Responses to the Genocide

Doris Melkonian, University of California, Los Angeles
Crisis Within: Faith and the Armenian Genocide

Mary Catherine Mueller, University of Texas, Dallas
The Significance of the Four Prophet Figures in Elie Wiesel's Holocaust Memoir, "Night"

Elyse Rast, Lesley University—Cambridge, MA
Using Empathy to Teach Genocide

Kathy Tabasso, Stockton University
The Power of Story in Remembering for the Future

Charles Weisbecker, Stockton University
An Analysis of Bystander Behavior in Erich Hackl's Farewell, "Sidonia"

Index

C

D

O

P

Y

Z